Bureaucracy and
the Labor Process

Bureaucracy and the Labor Process

The Transformation
of U.S. Industry,
1860–1920

Dan Clawson

Monthly Review Press
New York and London

Copyright © 1980 by Dan Clawson

Library of Congress Cataloging in Publication Data

Clawson, Dan.
   Bureaucracy and the labor process.
   Bibliography: p.
   1. Factory system—United States—History.
2. Industrial management—United States—History.
3. Labor and laboring classes—United States—History.
4. Bureaucracy—United States—History.   I. Title.
HD2356.U5C55   658'.00973   79-3885
ISBN 0-85345-542-2
ISBN 0-85345-543-0 (pbk.)

Monthly Review Press
62 West 14th Street, New York, N.Y. 10011
47 Red Lion Street, London WC1R 4PF

Manufactured in the United States of America

10 9 8 7 6 5 4 3 2 1

DEDICATED TO
the Cultural Revolution in China
May 1968 in France
wildcat strikes and the new left in the United States
which put these issues on the agenda for our time

Contents

Acknowledgments

Five people have been especially important in making this book what it is:

George Rawick introduced me to Marx, and along with that an appreciation of history. No one outside my family has had an equivalent impact on my political and intellectual orientations; in important ways there is nothing in this work which was not implicit in what George taught me.

Michael Schwartz defended me throughout my time in graduate school, providing the space in which I could do what I thought was important, rather than worry about mainstream academic sociology. He provided a model of what a Marxist academic should be.

Despite his initial reservations, Charles Perrow not only offered the support I needed to make the project possible, he was the person on whom I tested many of these ideas and formulations, and his critiques forced me to clarify (and modify) my ideas.

I have learned much from Patrick Clawson, who has done and is doing work on similar sorts of issues. Conversations with him, and his comments on various drafts, have been important not only in formulating my views but in keeping me aware of issues and orientations, both political and intellectual, which I would otherwise have neglected.

Unquestionably, Mary Ann Clawson is the person who has had the largest impact on both my general intellectual-political thought and on this book in particular. To limit the acknowledgments to her role in this manuscript: these ideas took shape in discussions with her and her impact was crucial in the process of developing these positions; she is the only person who has read every draft of the manuscript, and for essentially every version of every chapter her comments have been the most insightful and important.

The following helped make this a better book, by reading and commenting on the manuscript or by helping with child care: Ron Aminzade, Maggie Bimbane, Michael Burawoy, Linda Ellman, Rick Fantasia, Peter Freitag, Howard Gospel, Sandra Graham, Dick Howard, Nonotuck Child Care, Donnie Rotkin, Bob Sherry, Frank Sirianni, Mary Sirianni, Cindy Stillinger, the Stony Brook *Capital* study group, Gerry Zeitz.

1
Introduction:
Class Struggle and the Origins of
Industrial Bureaucracy

In the past hundred-odd years, many attacks have been made on Marx and Marxism. One, led by economists, has focused on the technical aspects of Marxian economics, arguing that the labor theory of value, the transformation problem, the falling rate of profit, and so on, and so on, are logically or empirically inadequate. A second major attack holds, essentially, that life—at least in the United States—is so much better now than it was in Marx's time that people do not want a revolutionary change: virtuous, talented workers will move up in the world; the class structure is changing in such a way that there are no longer many blue-collar workers; and in any case, most workers' incomes are now high enough that people should be satisfied with the material wealth they possess. Both these arguments have been important, forcing the international Marxist movement to develop new theoretical and empirical materials to meet these challenges, and neither should be dismissed lightly, although it is tempting to laugh at the notion that the bourgeois economics which has led the economy into stagflation is theoretically or practically superior to Marxian economics, and the ideologues who explain that working people are now rich and happy would not for the world agree to live as ordinary workers. Marxism has not ignored either of these attacks, and a growing body of literature refutes these positions and develops a more accurate view of the world around us.

It seems to me, however, that in political terms a third attack has been perhaps the most powerful: the belief that a meaningful revolution is no longer possible. According to this view, it is impossible to have both material wealth and interesting, creative work. Since most people want the affluence of today, work must "inevitably" (we are told) be hierarchical, mindless, and repetitive.

In order to have the material wealth of advanced industrial societies, we must follow the dictates of modern technology and modern bureaucratic organizational forms, which means that we must give up any hope of pleasant, creative, or democratic work settings. Revolution is therefore impossible; socialism in Marx's sense is a chimera; the most socialism could mean is a more egalitarian, less militarist, better planned version of contemporary society, with "good people" in power (the Democratic Socialist Organizing Committee vision). Socialism in the sense of a nonhierarchical organization of work, where work time does not dominate life time but is rather a way for the great mass of people to express and develop their creativity and human potential—socialism in this sense is impossible. Sometimes it is added that if we wish work to be this way we must return to early handicraft production, and accept the relative poverty associated with that. While this limited bureaucratic socialism might be preferable to what we now have, it is unlikely that many people would want to commit their lives to a struggle for such a vision.*

This third criticism of Marxism—the impossibility of meaningful revolution—is probably the most widely held of the three. Most people do not believe their lives are so wonderful they cannot be improved, nor do they retain much commitment to the capitalist ideology of "free market competition," which is widely recognized as a fiction.† However, workers generally do accept the contention that a fundamental transformation of the labor process and the social relations of production is impossible. In their day-to-day struggles at the workplace, workers often reject this criticism, struggling for a transformation of the organization of the work process. But they rarely formulate this as a conscious position: the more abstractly the question is posed, the more likely are workers to respond with

---

*In recent years the women's movement has brought to the fore another critique of Marxism: socialist struggles have generally ignored women and have not led even potentially to the liberation of women. I think this is a fair criticism of Marxist theory and practice, which requires fundamental modifications and changes in Marxism. However, the three critiques discussed in the text are attacks on Marxism which if true make Marxism in any form impossible. Feminism poses a real challenge to Marxism, but I would argue that feminism and Marxism are basically compatible, and the interaction of the two must enrich and modify them both.

†Recent poll results, for example, show that a majority of Americans believe the oil crisis is a fraud.

ideological answers about the impossibility of change. The same workers who recognize that much of what their supervisor does hinders rather than helps production nonetheless insist on the necessity of a hierarchical and bureaucratic organization; the same people who see that their jobs could be done differently believe that technological demands make it impossible to fundamentally change work. The acceptance of these beliefs mean that even workers who are very dissatisfied with their situation are unlikely to fight for socialism, since they lack a clear vision of what it is possible to create.

I would argue that we can have a meaningful revolution, that work can be satisfying, creative, and stimulating at the same time as it is materially productive: we can have material abundance along with interesting work.

There are various ways in which this argument could be made. Perhaps the most obvious is to consider situations where workers do have control of production (at least to some significant degree): these cases generally show that productivity actually improves (not just fails to go down) when workers take control of production (see Hunnius et al., 1973; Blumberg, 1973). Another approach is to consider the so-called socialist or communist countries and show that their "failure" to achieve the kind of society Marx envisioned resulted not from the inability to overcome technical or organizational problems, but rather from the fact that they never really attempted to systematically revolutionize social relations and introduce socialism. Various authors have argued that China and the Soviet Union can in no sense be considered socialist (see Bettelheim, 1976, 1978; Sweezy, 1974, 1975, 1976).*

I have adopted a third approach: a historical analysis of some aspects of the creation of modern technology and bureaucracy in industrial corporations. The attack on Marxism, the argument that once we opt for material abundance degraded work is necessary and inevitable, required by the dictates of technology and bureaucracy, rests on the unstated assumption that present-day technology

---

*In this book, when I use the terms "socialism" or "communism" I do not refer to any existing society—not Sweden, Cuba, the USSR, or China—but rather to a possible future society, the society I believe Marx envisioned when he used the term "communism." In my opinion, by this criterion no existing society can be characterized as communist.

and bureaucracy are neutral in their origins and effects. In order for this critique of Marxism to be valid, the bureaucracy and technology that now exist must have developed outside of the class struggle, simply because they were "the best" or "the most efficient" in some "objective" sense. If they did not develop in this way, if technology and bureaucracy have been to a significant degree developed and introduced by capitalists in order to better control workers and maximize profits, then it would at least be possible to develop other technologies and other forms of organization. This might well be a difficult and protracted task requiring many years, but it would at least be on the historical agenda as a focus of struggle.

In no sense will this book "prove" that it is possible to have communism of the sort that Marx envisioned (creative, interesting, varied work freely performed by people when and as they want, leading to the development of people's full capacities, in a world of material abundance). I intend to show, however, that the degraded work which we have today is neither inevitable nor necessary: it has instead been developed and introduced for specifically capitalist purposes.

As Herbert Marcuse wrote in his second preface to *Reason and Revolution:*

> This book was written in the hope that it would make a small contribution to the revival, not of Hegel, but of a mental faculty which is in danger of being obliterated: the power of negative thinking. As Hegel defines it: "Thinking is, indeed, essentially the negation of that which is immediately before us. . . ."
> For to comprehend reality means to comprehend what things really are, and this in turn means rejecting their mere factuality. . . . [The function of dialectical thought] is to break down the self-assurance and self-contentment of common sense, to undermine the sinister confidence in the power and language of facts . . . to express and define that-which-is on its own terms is to distort and falsify reality. (1960: vii, x)

The focus here is exclusively on industrial production, and especially on the development of bureaucracy in industry. When most people hear the term "bureaucracy" they think of the state, and the tremendous increase in the relative size of the state sector. This has been an important change in capitalist society, but there already exists a large body of Marxist work that attempts to grapple with the problem of the state. The rise of the state bureaucracy cannot be separated from the larger question of the capitalist state, and that would be a separate study. Moreover, since my ultimate political purpose is to argue for the possibility of creating a society where there is both material abundance and interesting democratically controlled work, the key question is what happens in the production of goods. In a socialist society the state would wither away, but even in a communist one there would continue to be a need to produce material goods. Marxists must therefore be primarily concerned with whether or not this kind of work requires hierarchy, mindlessness, and monotony in order to produce sufficient quantities of goods to ensure a nonscarcity society. The problem of bureaucracy in industry is thus absolutely fundamental to the task of socialist construction.

The Inevitability Argument

To the extent that there is a coherent articulation of the view that the rationalization of work is necessary to efficient production, and hence work must be degraded if we are to have material abundance, it is found in academic sociology, and especially among the specialists in the study of bureaucracy. Charles Perrow maintains: "If we want our material civilization to continue as it is, we will have to have large-scale bureaucratic enterprises in the economic, social, and governmental areas. This is the most efficient way to get the routine work of a society done" (1972: 58). And for Peter Blau, bureaucracies not only are the "most efficient" way to organize production, they are the *only* efficient way to do so: "Factories are bureaucratically organized, as are government agencies, and if this were not the case they could not operate efficiently on a large scale" (1956: 19). According to Blau:

> Modern machines could not be utilized without the complex administrative machinery needed for running factories employing thousands of workers. . . . Rationalization in administration is a prerequisite for the full exploitation of technological knowledge in mass production, and thus for a higher standard of living. (Ibid.: 16)

This position is not confined to academic sociology. In one variant or another it is widely accepted. For example, a fundamentally similar position holds that modern technology requires degraded work, since mass production requires machinery, with interchangeable parts: the introduction by Eli Whitney of interchangeable parts not only produced "hundreds of exactly alike triggers attached to hundreds of exactly alike barrels. In the process Whitney transformed workers from skilled artisans into unskilled machine tenders repetitively performing simple tasks" (*New York Times,* July 28, 1976).*

The arguments about the inevitable nature of bureaucracy generally refer back to the work of Max Weber, an enormously influential German sociologist of the early twentieth century, who believed that bureaucracy would come increasingly to dominate society. According to Weber, a bureaucracy is an organization with a fixed division of labor where the regular activities are official duties, some people have the authority to give commands to others, there are rules governing this and requiring that the duties be performed, and only qualified people are employed. Moreover, "the pure type of bureaucratic official is *appointed* by a superior authority. An official elected by the governed is not a purely bureaucratic figure" (1958: 200; emphasis in original).

Weber's view of a bureaucratic division of labor is almost diametrically opposed to Marx's vision of work in communist society:

> in communist society, where nobody has one exclusive sphere of activity but each can become accomplished in any branch he wishes, society regulates the general production and thus makes it possible for me to do one thing to-day and another tomorrow, to hunt in the morning, fish in the afternoon, rear cattle in the evening, criticize after dinner, just as I have a mind, without ever becoming hunter, fisherman, shepherd or critic. (Marx, 1846: 22)

A bureaucracy necessarily involves hierarchy, with some people giving orders to others, and with officials being appointed, not elected. In contrast, communism involves total democracy, the election of anyone above the level of an ordinary worker, with no fixed hierarchy and no one having the right to give commands (except insofar as this right is temporarily delegated, with the commands

---

ee Chapters Three and Four for the historical evidence demonstrating the falsity
claim.

always subject to review by the group as a whole). Moreover, instead of a plethora of rules and an illusory focus on bureaucratically defined expertise, in communism regulations are reduced to a minimum, freedom is maximized, and everyone becomes technically competent to do the work.

Weber also argued that because of its technical advantages, increasing bureaucratization is inevitable.

> The decisive reason for the advance of bureaucratic organization has always been its purely technical superiority over any other form of organization. The fully developed bureaucratic mechanism compares with other organizations exactly as does the machine with the non-mechanical modes of production.
>
> Precision, speed, unambiguity, knowledge of the files, continuity, discretion, unity, strict subordination, reduction of friction and of material and personal costs—these are raised to the optimum point in the strictly bureaucratic administration. (1958: 214)

Not only does bureaucracy increase for these reasons, but once it is established in any area it is essentially impossible to uproot it, both because it is an instrument of power for those who control it, and because "the ruled for their part cannot dispense with or replace the bureaucratic apparatus of authority once it exists," since if they did so chaos would result (ibid.: 229).

Though Weber is offered as the source and grounding for arguments of bureaucratic inevitability, Weber himself does no more than state this position, never examining it or offering evidence to support his assertions. What makes Weber's argument so powerful is that it is essentially classless: bureaucracy advances not so much because people fight for it, as because it is the only way. In important ways, bureaucracy is to everyone's advantage, since it is technically superior and allows the work to be done better with the use of fewer resources. At the same time, bureaucracy has deadening and chilling effects, which also seem to apply to everyone equally. If bureaucracy is as Weber sees it—a purely technical advance over other forms of organization, which neither benefits nor harms one class at the expense of another—then bureaucracy is not a sensible issue for class analysis or class politics. In that case, bureaucracy is, or should be, outside the sphere of class struggle.

If Weber is wrong—if bureaucracy is something that some people are for and others against because of their particular class interests—then the advance of bureaucracy can be an issue on the political agenda, an important focus for class struggle. Weber and academic sociologists want us to believe that bureaucracy just happens: none of us want it, but none of us can escape it. Marx, on the other hand, offers an analysis which sees bureaucracy as part of the class struggle. Marx's position, heretofore largely ignored in these debates, is the major challenge to technological or bureaucratic arguments about the inevitability of bureaucracy and degraded work.

Marx's Analysis

Marx begins Volume I of *Capital* with an analysis of the twofold nature of a commodity, as use value and as exchange value. This duality characterizes not just the commodity, the finished object, but also the labor process itself. If the labor, the process of producing the commodity, did not have this twofold nature, the commodity could not have it either. Marx considered this point absolutely crucial: "I was the first to point out and to examine critically this two-fold nature of the labour contained in commodities. *As this point is the pivot on which a clear comprehension of Political Economy turns,* we must go more into detail" (1867: 49; emphasis added). Unless one understands the twofold nature of the labor involved in producing commodities, one cannot understand capitalism.

The labor process, on the one hand, "is human action with a view to the production of use-values, appropriation of natural substances to human requirements; it is the necessary condition for effecting exchange of matter between man and Nature; it is the ever-lasting Nature-imposed condition of human existence, and therefore is independent of every social phase of that existence, or rather, is common to every such phase" (ibid.: 179). This is the labor necessary to produce use value, something which every society must do.

Capitalism, however, not only produces use value, it must also ~roduce exchange value. Labor done under capitalism has special ditions. While Marx devoted only a few pages to the considera- f labor as the production of use values, he devoted hundreds of pages to an analysis of labor as the production of surplus value.* Two facts about capitalist production are crucial to this analysis: "The labour-process, turned into the process by which the capitalist consumes labour-power, exhibits two characteristic phenomena. First, the labourer works under the control of the capitalist to whom his labour belongs. . . . Secondly, the product is the property of the capitalist and not that of the labourer, its immediate producer" (ibid.: 180).

At first capital simply converts independent commodity producers into wage laborers, without changing the social organization or technical conditions of the labor process. Soon, however, the capitalist institutes changes, beginning with the introduction of cooperative labor.† Cooperation adds a new productive force, the power of social labor, but this force did not develop because of the decision of the laborers. Not their own act, but the act of capital, brought large numbers of workers together; it is under the capitalist's direction and control that cooperation takes place. Since the cooperation does not take place until work for the capitalist has begun, and since once this has happened the workers (having sold their ability to work) no longer have any rights to the products of their labor, the extra production due to cooperation belongs to the capitalist, even though it comes from the increased social productive power of labor. "Because this power costs capital nothing, and because, on the other hand, the labourer himself does not develop it before his labour belongs to capital, it appears as a power with which capital is endowed by Nature—a productive power that is immanent in capital" (ibid.: 315). The capitalist, who at first was an unnecessary part of the process of production, a purely formal and external agent whose only connection to the labor process was his ownership of the means of production, now becomes a requisite for the carrying on of social production.

In the cooperation of numerous wage laborers, as in any other

---

*Use value is discussed in Volume I, chapter 7, section 1, of *Capital* while surplus value is discussed throughout the rest of the volume, at least until Part 8 on primitive accumulation.

†Cooperation under capitalism differs from prehistorical forms of cooperation in that it is no longer based on common ownership and is separated from the community itself.

form of capitalist production, one must distinguish between the labor of producing use values and the labor of producing exchange value. Marx is perfectly clear in saying that any cooperative form of labor would require some sort of direction and coordination, but the capitalistic production of exchange value and surplus value requires something more.

> All combined labour on a large scale requires, more or less, a directing authority, in order to secure the harmonious working of the individual in the action of the combined organism, as distinguished from the action of its separate organs. A single violin player is his own conductor; an orchestra requires a separate one. The work of directing, superintending, and adjusting, becomes one of the functions of capital, from the moment that the labour under the control of capital becomes co-operative. Once a function of capital, it acquires special characteristics. (Ibid.: 313)

Under capitalism, it is necessary to have not only the kind of supervision and coordination needed in order to produce the goods, it is also necessary to have supervision to make sure that workers work. Once workers have sold their ability to labor, their labor power, they do not work for themselves, but for the capitalist, who has sole and exclusive rights to whatever is produced. The capitalist has the rights to the worker's ability to labor for one day (or one hour, or whatever) and wishes to be sure that the worker will do as much as possible during that time. The workers, on the other hand, wish to do no more than is necessary, since they will not get the benefit of the extra production, and since they are not doing what they choose to do, but what the capitalist directs them to do. As Marx notes, "the less [the laborer] is attracted by the nature of the work, and the mode in which it is carried on, and the less, therefore, he enjoys it as something which gives play to his bodily and mental powers, the more close his attention is forced to be" (ibid.: 174). The workers struggle to control their own working time, to do what they want to do. But the workers have sold their labor power; therefore, "if the labourer consumes his disposable time for himself, he robs the capitalist" (ibid.: 224).

To ensure that capitalist goals are met, supervision of a special is necessary. Workers must be kept to their work, and the enterprise must be oriented toward the capitalist's goal of producing the greatest possible amount of surplus value. Marx says that this leads to something which we can plainly recognize as the beginnings of industrial bureaucracy:

> If, then, the control of the capitalist is in substance two-fold by reason of the two-fold nature of the process of production itself—which, on the one hand, is a social process for producing use-values, on the other, a process for creating surplus-value—in form that control is despotic. As co-operation extends its scale, this despotism takes forms peculiar to itself. Just as at first the capitalist is relieved from actual labour so soon as his capital has reached that minimum amount with which capitalist production, as such, begins, so now, he hands over the work of direct and constant supervision of the individual workmen, and groups of workmen, to a special kind of wage-labourer. An industrial army of workmen, under the command of a capitalist, requires, like a real army, officers (managers), and sergeants (foremen, overlookers), who, while the work is being done, command in the name of the capitalist. The work of supervision becomes their established and exclusive function. When comparing the mode of production of isolated peasants and artisans with production by slave-labour, the political economist counts this labour of superintendence among the *faux frais* of production. But, when considering the capitalist mode of production, he, on the contrary, treats the work of control made necessary by the co-operative character of the labour-process as identical with the different work of control, necessitated by the capitalist character of that process and the antagonism of interests between capitalist and labourer. (Ibid.: 314)

Certain kinds of coordination are obviously necessary simply to get the job done, even if cost were no object—as Marx notes, an orchestra needs a conductor. Many of the things supervisors do under capitalism would have to be done in some way for there to be social production. For example, workers who need help, advice, or training sometimes get this from their supervisor, and workers who receive contradictory or inadequate instructions generally go to the supervisor to have the situation clarified.* However, supervisors and bureaucrats also exercise control of a kind which is only necessary

---

*Though it is probably more common for workers to receive their training from other workers, and even when there are contradictory orders workers may resolve the situation without resort to a supervisor (see Houbolt and Kusterer, 1977).

because of the capitalistic nature of the work process: the inherent antagonism between workers and capitalists, and the need for the capitalist to make a profit. This is the case when supervisors keep track of workers in order to force them to produce more. If workers arrived later, left earlier, socialized on the job, and took more rest periods, this would not keep the goods from being produced, though of course it would lower profits. In a communist society workers would be attracted to the work, so there would be much less need for coercion. Moreover, work discipline would probably be enforced by the social pressure of the work group as a whole, rather than being the job of a special functionary. In capitalism this is of course impossible, because the interests of workers are in contradiction to the interests of capital.

The distinction between the two kinds of supervision is analytic: most acts of supervision contain elements of both. To a large extent it is impossible to say this act was only necessary for profits, that act was needed to produce use values. The distinction is largely irrelevant to capital, which is generally unaware of it.* Capital wants to make a profit, and it matters little to this end whether it does so by improving the way of producing the goods or by increasing the exploitation of workers. Insofar as capitalists are aware of the distinction, it is in their interests to blend the two kinds of supervision as thoroughly as possible, thus making it more difficult for workers to press for the elimination of the specifically capitalist control features.

If a company had two different sets of supervisors, one group which helped produce the goods and had *no* control functions, another which did nothing to help with production and *only* had control functions, then both the reality of the situation and the possible solutions would be clear, and many unions would presumably fight on this issue. The actual situation, where essentially all supervisors and officials do both duties in varying proportions, makes it harder to end the system, and means that the work of almost every official contains some control functions. The need to control and exploit workers thus shapes the entire character of capitalist produc-

_____

*e distinction is fundamental, however, to those who are interested in building a
 society. A widespread awareness of this difference has to be one foundation
 rs' struggles to control and reshape the production process.

tion, and is not simply an appendage that can be removed through the abolition of a limited number of officials who do nothing but exploit workers.

Marx notes that "when comparing the mode of production of isolated peasants and artisans with production by slave-labour, the political economist counts this labour of superintendence among the *faux frais* of production." An awareness of the inefficiencies of slave production caused by the resistance of slaves is fairly widespread. In *The Political Economy of Slavery* Eugene Genovese discusses the distorted methods of production which were necessary under slavery. Only the crudest hoes could be used; the better quality hoe used in the north was too frequently broken by slaves. Mules had to be used instead of horses, even though horses could do more work, because mules were better able to withstand abuse.

> The most obvious obstacle to the employment of better equipment was the slave himself. In 1843 a Southern editor sharply rebuked planters and overseers for complaining that Negroes could not handle tools. Such a complaint was, he said, merely a confession of poor management, for with proper supervision Negro slaves would provide proper care. The editor was unfair. Careful supervision of unwilling laborers would have entailed either more overseers than most planters could afford or a slave force too small to provide the advantages of large-scale operation. (Genovese, 1965: 54–55)

It is usual for people who study slave systems to be aware of these inefficiencies, of the extra cost of supervision which is necessary in order to produce with slaves that would not be necessary if production were done by free wage laborers. (The extra cost of supervision is presumably recouped by making the slaves work harder and for a lower cost.) People point to this necessary supervision and control as one of the key reasons why slavery was inefficient and was superseded by a more advanced form of production, capitalism. However, when considering the capitalist mode of production the assumption is usually made that all of the supervision and control is necessary simply because of the cooperative character of the labor process. No allowance is made for "the different work of control, necessitated by the capitalist character of that process and the antagonism of interests between capitalist and labourer." What is generally admitted for slavery (and always seen as open to argument) is rarely mentioned for capitalism—not only is the extra cost of supervision not granted, it is not even considered. In fact, of course, communism—where (in Marx's vision) people would work because they want to, and actively try to improve production through the use of their talents, initiative, and creativity—would be as far superior to capitalism (wage labor) as the latter is to slavery. The bureaucratic control apparatus necessitated by the opposition of capitalists and workers involves tremendous costs and inefficiencies.

It is important to stress two points about this Marxist analysis, both of which will be supported and more fully developed throughout the book. First, in considering the impact of these capitalist considerations in shaping the labor process, it would be totally inadequate to focus on how many bureaucrats and supervisors spend how many hours a day exclusively attempting to control and exploit workers. This is one factor to be considered, but it is only the tip of the iceberg. These specifically capitalist ends permeate and fundamentally shape every aspect of the labor process.

Second, this analysis does not see bureaucracy as something which capitalists want in and of itself. In a crucial way, it is not capitalists who force bureaucracy on us, it is the class struggle. This struggle is not primarily about the distribution of income; most fundamentally it is about the control of the labor process. If workers did not resist, if they were truly and fully socialized to be happy and obedient, capitalists would not need the enormous and complex apparatus that is bureaucracy, nor would they need to distort the entire labor process to ensure exploitation. If workers could be counted on always to do what they were told, even without the presence of an enforcement mechanism; if they worked as hard as possible willingly, simply because that was what the bargain was; if workers tried always to do what their masters wanted, then bureaucracy would be unnecessary. Bureaucracy itself is a cost to the capitalist, an extra that must be paid for out of surplus value. In a sense, bureaucracy would be unnecessary if either side could win a final and decisive victory. If workers could abolish hierarchy, domination, and exploitation and establish communism, then we could dispense with bureaucracy; if capitalists could achieve a final solution, with workers so deadened and spirited that they really adopted their employers' goals as their own, then deal of the present bureaucracy would be superfluous.

The Rise of Bureaucracy: An Overview

The Marxist analysis which I have just presented as to the specifically capitalist reasons for bureaucracy should not be conceived in static terms. The development of bureaucracy (or the shaping of capitalist technology) is a *process,* not a one-time creation. The need to accumulate capital leads to a theoretical necessity, a law of the dynamics of capitalism, for capital to (attempt to) take more and more control over the labor process.* This is a structural necessity, a determined development. At the same time, it is essential to emphasize that this process is not something which takes place in an inevitable, ahistorical manner, beyond the will or consciousness of the actors involved.† It is a process, not a static structure; it is shaped and determined by class struggle, not by some technical necessity beyond human will. Neither, however, should this struggle be seen as a pure contest of wills where anything can happen, with the consciousness of the participants the only determinant of the outcome.‡

In *The Eighteenth Brumaire of Louis Bonaparte* Marx begins with a very clear and simple statement of his approach to history:

> Men make their own history, but they do not make it just as they please; they do not make it under circumstances chosen by themselves, but under circumstances directly encountered, given and transmitted from the past. The tradition of all the dead generations weighs like a nightmare on the brain of the living. (1852: 96)

Since Marx, however, Marxists have had great difficulty in simultaneously holding to both sides of this statement: determination, but a historically conditioned social determination, not something external to any human will or action. Raymond Williams has noted that "a Marxism without some concept of determination is in effect worthless. A Marxism with many of the concepts of determination it now has is quite radically disabled" (1977: 83). Determination must be understood as the setting of limits and exerting of pressures, not

---

*There are obviously counteracting tendencies to this, as to any other law of capitalist development.

†This is the view explicitly expressed by structuralists such as Louis Althusser and Nicos Poulantzas. For critiques and alternative approaches, see Thompson (1979) and Williams (1977).

‡Jeremy Brecher's book *Strike!* (1972) suffers to some degree from such an approach.

as some structural (timeless) necessity which unfolds in absolutely objective conditions. Again to quote Raymond Williams:

> The key question is the degree to which the "objective" conditions are seen as *external*. Since, by definition, within Marxism, the objective conditions are and can only be the result of human actions in the material world, the real distinction can be only between *historical* objectivity—the conditions into which, at any particular point in time, men find themselves born, thus the "accessible" conditions into which they "enter"—and *abstract* objectivity, in which the "determining" process is "independent of their will" not in the historical sense that they have inherited it but in the absolute sense that they cannot control it; they can seek only to understand it and guide their actions accordingly.
>
> This abstract objectivity is the basis of what became widely known, in Marxism, as "economism." (Ibid.: 85)

The economism which Williams refers to has been the dominant Marxist position on the labor process and the problem of transforming the relations of production, a position which has been given coherence as the theory of productive forces. According to this theory, the development of technology and productivity are the motor forces of history; new machinery and equipment revolutionize production and transform society. Coupled with this is a view of technology as neutral in the class struggle, and determinant of the relations of production. The development of the productive forces is accepted a priori as preparing a basis for socialism and thus to be encouraged. In essence, capitalism needs to be replaced because it has become a barrier to the development of productivity: capitalism is characterized by anarchy in production, which must be replaced with conscious control through the state. Since production relations themselves are not problematic, "the state is viewed as a technocratic tool for the control of the economy; this lends itself nicely to a 'substitutionist' analysis (in which the question of who controls the state is overlooked; control by the party is identified with control by the state, control by the Central Committee with control by the party, etc.)" (P. Clawson, 1975a: 5). Socialism will simply take over productive forces developed under capitalism, and will change the relations of production as narrowly conceived, meaning the abstract sorts of juridical property forms (state ownership, etc.) and exchange relations (the market). No thought is given to transforming relations of production on the shop floor or in the offices. Class struggle in this view is effectively limited to abstract electoral or insurrectionary activity, with little or no attempt to transform the means of production, the process of production, or the immediately encountered day to day relations of production.*

This book undertakes to refute this economistic theory of productive forces, as well as the bourgeois view of the technological and bureaucratic necessity for degraded work. It does so through a historical analysis of the process of capitalist development, as well as reference to Marx's own work. I attempt to show not only that Marx utterly opposed these views, that they are theoretically suspect, and that an alternative theoretical conception can be presented, but more fundamentally that historically these views do not correspond with the actual development of capitalism. If there is value to this work it is because the theoretical statements are grounded in and emerge from the historical materials. It is not a question of what one or another theorist has written, but of what has actually happened. Moreover, it is not simply a matter of the unfolding of some externally determined process. Capitalist development is shaped above all by class struggle, and I hope to show that human will and intentionality on the part of both parties in the struggle have shaped all aspects of production, creating the world in which we live. Capitalists have not unknowingly or unintentionally degraded work, nor has workers' resistance been instinctive or irrational. It matters not only what happened, but why it happened. Neither abstract theory nor mindless empiricism can resolve these questions.

Obviously, in no sense does this pretend to be a complete or definitive study of capitalist development. Even where my own research has been the most extensive (for example, on inside contracting) I am aware of a host of sources and materials which I did not have the time or resources to investigate, and undoubtedly further research would uncover many sources of which I am not now aware. Moreover, my research has been concentrated in particular geographic areas, industries, and time periods.

It is an inherent tendency of capitalist development for capital to take more and more control over the work process. One of the main

---

*For excellent critiques of these economic views see Charles Bettelheim (1976), especially the preface, and Patrick Clawson (1975a).

purposes throughout the book is to document and argue for this proposition. My main focus is the United States from 1860 to 1920, a period I consider crucial, since it introduces a major transformation in the control of the labor process. However, were the analysis to begin in 1860 it would be necessary to take as given some of the most essential and problematic aspects of capitalism. It would be possible to begin this analysis with the reasons for, and effect of, the putting out system, which transformed independent commodity producers into wage laborers—but wage laborers who continued to work in their own homes, had control over how many hours they worked, were subject to no work discipline, and could adopt whatever schedule, pace, or methods they chose. Instead, I begin with the creation of the factory, which forced workers to labor in a location determined by capital, for the length of time determined by capital, at a schedule set by capital, and under the supervision and work discipline of capital.

Even well after the creation of the factory, capital left the discipline and control of the workforce, the task of extracting surplus value, to a semi-independent third party. In the 1860s and 1870s, inside contracting (which is considered in Chapter Three) was one of the most important ways of organizing and controlling production. Inside contractors were similar to independent subcontractors, in that they sold a product to the company and made a profit on it, hired and fired their own employees, set their wages, disciplined them, determined the methods of production, often introduced technological changes, and so on. Inside contractors, however, were employees of the company, worked inside the company's building, sold their entire output to the company, and used the company's machinery, raw materials, and equipment. Inside contracting persisted in many places into the twentieth century, but after the 1870s it rarely was introduced in new factories, and as time passed capitalists modified the system in ways that increased their control over the production process. However, even in factories with foremen rather than inside contractors, the foremen of the late nineteenth century had powers ilar to those of inside contractors, except that foremen received day wage and not a profit on each piece produced.

portant ways the foreman's (or the inside contractor's) powers gated to workers, especially skilled workers, who made many of the decisions about the details of the work process. Rather than being given detailed orders, specifications, and directives they were usually on their own to a considerable degree in deciding how to do the work, and their initiative and cooperation were necessary to get the goods produced.

Capital was in a sense forced to attack this method of organizing production, because workers generally established a social as well as a technical control of the workplace. Workers self-consciously and collectively enforced output quotas that seemed to them reasonable, and which kept the work experience from becoming too miserable. Capitalists did not push for more control over the work process because they were instinctively vicious and mean. The imperatives of the accumulation process forced them to do so or themselves be swept aside.

The power inequalities in capitalism favored the capitalists in this struggle, but they did not win the fight either quickly or easily. In the 1870s and 1880s the main capitalist strategy to increase surplus value was the introduction of piecework, which made wages dependent on output and thus gave each individual worker an incentive to exceed the collectively established output quotas. If a significant number of workers did increase output, capitalists would simply cut the price per piece. The work group as a whole would suffer, since everyone would have to work harder for approximately the same wage, but the rate buster would benefit because in the interim period he or she would earn a substantial premium. As a capitalist strategy this was only a very limited success, because workers learned their lessons quickly and thoroughly, and responded by strengthening their enforcement of output quotas. Capitalists attempted to add various features to the basics of piecework so as to increase control and exploitation. Piecework both made it more possible for capitalists to gain knowledge and control over the production process, and (given worker resistance) made it more necessary to do so if they were to benefit from the new ways. Therefore, capitalists introduced more extensive record keeping, and attempted to learn about the production process so they could reorganize, increase the division of labor, or change technology in such a way that output levels could be ratcheted up to a new level. Although these strategies were generally frustrated by worker resistance, they provided the groundwork for a solution (Taylorism) by both permitting and impelling capitalists to study and attempt to control the production process.

These capitalist offensives were partially successful, but it is necessary to understand the underlying characteristic of all these strategies: basic decisions about the way in which the work was to be done remained in the hands of the people who did the work. A distinction can be made between craft and bureaucratic organizations of production: in craft production most or all of the basic decisions about how to produce a product are made by persons who are themselves directly involved in physically producing it; in bureaucratic production these decisions are made by people not on the work crew. In the 1880s capitalists tried to take more control of the labor process, but they accepted it as given that basic decisions about how to do the work would have to be made by production workers. Therefore, production depended on the voluntary cooperation and active initiative of workers. Capitalists could not really conceive (much less implement) an alternative organization of production: they took it for granted that workers would know more than anyone else about how to do the work and they would therefore retain control of the details of the labor process. This was the basic problem capitalists faced throughout this period. While workers had such control capitalists could win individual battles but could not really win the war, since each victory tended to leave workers in a position of strength from which to continue the contest.

Frederick Taylor was the capitalist genius who not only recognized the problem and devised a solution, but himself led the struggle to introduce the new way. Taylor insisted that it was both possible and necessary to create a new category, management, which would learn what workers already knew—how to plan and direct the details of the work process—and would use this knowledge to issue detailed specific orders to each individual worker. This required a great increase in bureaucracy (which Taylor referred to as "unproductive" labor), but in this way workers could be forced to obey capitalist directives and increase output. Capital did not want bureaucracy, did
' introduce it lightly, unthinkingly, or for transient reasons. Twenty
' of struggle convinced capitalists that it was impossible to have
' control in the workplace: one side or the other must rule.
'nvention of management and bureaucracy made it possible

for capitalists to control the production process. Despite the grave problems involved in this step, Taylor insisted it was the only way for capital to take control of the speed of production. Capital cannot simply do whatever it wants: what it does (and what it does not do) is fundamentally shaped by workers' class struggle.

Readers of Harry Braverman's *Labor and Monopoly Capital* (1974) will recognize that my argument is completely compatible with (though not identical to) the position contained in that book. Three serious and persistent criticisms of Braverman's analysis have become widespread among people on the left. The formulation here is from Richard Edwards, since he makes all three criticisms clearly and forcefully, but many other sources could be cited:

> The book accepts or seems to accept writings on management theory as evidence for actual developments on the shop or office floor. The most important example is Braverman's reading of Frederick Taylor's writings as though they described real processes rather than simply Taylor's thinking and theories. The book has therefore taken what are clearly ideological sources of information and treated them as though the processes they describe were real. (1978: 109)

> [Braverman's] view overestimates scientific management's impact. . . . Taylorism failed to solve the crisis of control because most big corporations failed even to give it a try. The extent and incidence of scientific management has always been something of a mystery, but the available evidence suggests that Taylorism was largely confined to smaller, usually nonunionized, enterprises. In any event, the new industrial giants—U.S. Steel, International Harvester, and the others—showed little interest in it. (Ibid.: 98, 101)*

> The book fails to take account of labor responses to the new forms of "degraded" work that employers have developed. In Braverman's

---

*Critical reactions are not limited to these of course: the book also provoked an economic analysis of the kind already mentioned. Al Szymanski, a member of the *Insurgent Sociologist* editorial collective, rejected Braverman's arguments and favored instead a theory of productive forces in a recent article, which was summarized by the collective in its winter 1978 issue:

Szymanski questions, first of all, the priority which Braverman gives to class struggle at the point of production as the dynamic force which underlies capitalist social and economic development, insisting that struggles over control of the labor process are essentially peripheral and ultimately subordinate to the inexorable tendencies which grow out of the logic of profit maximization

story, new, fragmented, de-skilled methods of work are developed and implemented by capitalists, with drastic effects on workers but with little apparent resistance. No impact results from what resistance does occur. Unions play no role, and there is no class struggle. (Ibid.: 109)

These are serious criticisms, which in one form or another, have become widely debated (if not fully accepted) on the left. My work provides extensive material and analysis to deal with each of these points.

The first criticism, the claim that Braverman based his analysis on "what are clearly ideological sources of information and treated them as though the processes they describe were real," potentially undercuts Braverman's entire consideration of Taylorism. It is correct that Braverman based essentially his entire analysis of Taylorism on Taylor's own writings. This is a potentially important criticism, but my considerably more extensive research demonstrates that Braverman's analysis of Taylorism *did* describe "real processes" and *not* simply "Taylor's thinking and theories." The criticism turns out to be relatively unimportant because Braverman was particularly insightful in his ability to recognize what parts of Taylor's work were of real importance and what parts were simply ideology; on the whole the critics have done little independent investigation, but have simply opposed their assertions to Braverman's limited but solid and insightful research and analysis.

Second, the claim that Braverman overestimates the impact of Taylorism is based on two errors. On the one hand, the critics have once again made hasty judgments based on inadequate investigation. My research shows that even by the strictest criteria Taylorism had a giant impact. On the other hand, this criticism is based on a failure to understand what was involved in Taylorism. Braverman was con-

---

and the dictates of technical efficiency. This includes a rejection of Braverman's view that existing technologies and forms of industrial organization reflect the logic of capitalist domination as well as the requirements of technical efficiency. Szymanski retains the notion of modern technology as a socially neutral and essentially progressive force which poses few problems for integration within a socialist context. Second, Szymanski challenges the priority which Braverman grants to "qualitative" struggles of workers for control over the immediate conditions of their labor activity. Such struggles are characterized by Szymanski as a backward-looking defense of the individual privileges of a small minority of "craft" workers which inhibits the more effective struggle of labor for collective control of the economy through political means. (1978: 35)

cerned not with the surface appearance of Taylorism, with the specific mechanics of his system, but rather with the way in which Taylorism marked a fundamental change in the control of the labor process. I would have thought Braverman made this very clear.* However, perhaps I can make the point more comprehensible through my analysis of pre-Taylor methods of organizing work and pre-Taylor offensives by capital.

The third criticism of Braverman—that he does not analyze workers' activities—is correct, and the only one of the criticisms which I accept as true and important. Again, however, Braverman himself recognized this, and on the whole the critics have done no more than Braverman himself: they have pointed to the problem, but not helped to resolve it. I hope that my account, which is heavily focused on class struggle by workers, can begin to address the problem. I stress that workers' struggles should not be viewed as simply as "response" to Taylorism (it is more nearly the other way around), nor as "resistance" to capital's offensive. Workers' activities were not derivative from what capital did: they fundamentally shaped what happened. Indeed, what capital did (specifically including Taylorism and the rise of bureaucracy) is hardly comprehensible except as a response to workers' success in resisting previous capitalist attempts at control.

It is unquestionably difficult to find information on workers' activities and struggles. Data of any kind on the actual work process is hard to find, but materials that allow us to see and understand what workers were doing and thinking are especially so. Often this information must be gleaned from other sources. For example, in the 1880s and 1890s a number of journals were founded to tell managers how to run their shops and control their workers. From these articles it is often possible to understand not only what management wanted to do, but what it was that workers were doing that posed a problem. Similarly, reports by outside management experts called in to reorganize factories often contain plainly biased, but nonetheless useful, accounts of what workers were doing. In addi-

---

*An example of the confusion and misunderstanding is the fact that Richard Edwards downplays Taylorism and finds it of comparatively little importance. Later in his book, however, Edwards describes what he considers the really crucial control mechanism in modern industry, what he calls "bureaucratic control," and this turns out to be essentially identical to Taylorism as Braverman or I understand it.

tion to the obvious bias, reports by outside experts or articles in management journals generally did not appear until the previously existing craft system was under attack, and by this time there had often been substantial changes in the way the system worked.

Material from the viewpoint of those within the craft system is harder to come by. There are several sources of such information: (1) autobiographical accounts left by workers, or by sympathetic observers who worked for a time, (2) union work rules, providing we remember that the very existence of a rule indicates that workers' ability to control the given practice was under challenge, or there would have been no need to formulate the rule, (3) government (or even management) reports that gave workers a chance to state their case, and (4) government hearings. I have made heavy use of the hearings of a special committee of the U.S. House of Representatives that was created in the wake of a strike at the Watertown Arsenal and charged with examining Taylor's and other systems of management and their introduction into government arsenals. These hearings took testimony not just from experts and high officials (though they did that too: Taylor himself gave a couple of hundred pages of testimony); they allowed workers to testify as well. The workers who testified were not representative of the workforce as a whole—almost all the testimony came from skilled workers or foremen—but their testimony does give us a view of the nature of day-to-day production in the shop, which is not available in most other sources. The congressmen's questions generally—though by no means always—were repetitive, uninteresting, and limited to "official" sorts of concerns. However, union officials, workers at the armories, and the officers in charge were also allowed to question the witnesses, and this produced a mass of very interesting material.*

---

*Since I have made heavy use of the congressional hearings to investigate Taylorism and other management systems at the arsenals, let me note and briefly respond to two objections that could be raised to this data: (1) government arsenals are not representative of private industry. However, the arsenals competed directly with private industry, the officers often became managers at private companies when they left the service, and the workers had worked at (and often discussed) profit-making companies. (2) The arsenals, especially the Watertown Arsenal, produced small quantities of large items such as gun carriages rather than engaging in mass production. This is true of the Watertown Arsenal but not true of some of the other arsenals (for example, Rock Island). I would prefer more testimony from mass production industries. On the other hand, this testimony was taken very late (1911): other evidence

One final note: it could be believed that whatever the reasons why capitalists wanted to introduce bureaucracy or technologies of control, these would not have persisted—much less become dominant—unless they were more efficient than the old ways of doing things. I will not take this up at this point except to note that, as I will argue, this is incorrect, unless the term "efficiency" is given a very special class biased meaning.

---

indicates that this way of organizing production was found to a considerable degree even in mass production at an earlier period, but in 1911 it was becoming increasingly rare, and tended to hold on more in small batch sorts of industry (which nonetheless were often very large units of capital).

2
The Rise of the Factory: Technology as a Social Control Device

The bulk of this book focuses on changes in the labor process within capitalist factories in the United States from 1860 to 1920. But by 1860 many basic changes had been made; some of the key problems in capitalist control of the labor process had been solved. Were the analysis to begin with 1860, it would be necessary to take as given many of the key elements of capitalist social relations.

Precapitalist Work Patterns

In order to understand some of the special characteristics of capitalist work, it is useful to begin by considering the reasons for the creation of the earliest factories. Factories first emerged in the textile industry in Britain, so that will be my main focus in this chapter. The creation of factories is comprehensible only with reference to some background on precapitalist work patterns. Unthinkingly, we tend to accept the present organization of work as "natural," to assume for example that people will work a fixed number of hours per week. It is easy to forget how recently capitalism emerged: four hundred years ago there was essentially no capitalism. For the first million years of human existence, people lived in hunting and gathering societies, in which work was directed almost exclusively toward subsistence. Since such societies usually had no way to preserve or store food, bands moved camp frequently to follow food supplies. Animals were always moving, and plant foods quickly used up, meaning that in most cases it took a large area to support even a small number of people. In general, therefore, gathering was done each day, for that day only, and when hunting provided a large catch, further hunting stopped until the meat was gone—"simply because there is nothing to be done with a large surplus" (Service, 1966: 13).

Today, societies that subsist by hunting and gathering occupy marginal territories, continually encroached on by agricultural settlements. Since their members live so close to the margins of existence, anthropologists generally assumed they had to work long and hard, "compelled to spend most of their working hours in the search for food and other necessities of life" (Lenski, 1966: 121). Recent field studies, however, indicate that large amounts of leisure time are the norm even in present-day hunting and gathering societies. One quantitative study revealed that "despite their harsh environment, [people] devote from twelve to nineteen hours a week to getting food." Women spent additional time on food preparation, but even this was substantially less than women today on the average devote to housework (Lee, 1968: 31; see also Sahlins, 1968).

To emphasize simply the amount of work done would be to miss the most important part of the difference. Work for hunters and gatherers does not have the same kind of compulsive quality as it does for us. As one anthropologist quipped, "Hadza men are much more preoccupied with games of chance than with chances of game" (Sahlins, 1968: 89). It is not that each individual (or nuclear family unit) works hard for a few days to build up a hoard, then rests until that is eaten and returns to hard work. Essentially all food (and other possessions) is shared within the band, which changes the nature of work for any individual. Men may not hunt for days, if they feel the time is not right (Lee, 1968: 37), while women's gathering activities are combined with other activities, so they are not obliged to forego time spent with friends or children.

> It is not unusual for a man to hunt avidly for a week and then do no hunting at all for two or three weeks. Since hunting is an unpredictable business and subject to magical control, hunters sometimes experience a run of bad luck and stop hunting for a month or longer. During these periods, visiting, entertaining, and especially dancing are the primary activities of men. (Ibid.: 37)

Almost ten thousand years ago people began to cultivate plants and animals, thus beginning one of the most profound changes in human history. It was no longer necessary to move frequently, since agriculture can produce larger food supplies in a given area; it was not really possible to move, since the crops required tending and harvesting. Thus gradually semipermanent and permanent settlements developed, and with them larger populations. At the same time increased food production meant that larger populations could be supported in the same area. In most areas agricultural societies not only can, but must, accumulate a sizeable store, both as seed to plant the next round of crops, and as food to live on until the next harvest.

The change in labor patterns was also fundamental. Work patterns now followed the rhythm of the agricultural year: intense labor for weeks on end at planting or harvest time, alternated with periods of comparative leisure in between. Agricultural societies varied greatly in the total amount of work done, but, without irrigation, it was usually impossible to work all year long in agriculture alone. Even today in most cases it would be worse than useless to plant immediately after the crops are harvested. Farmers must pattern their work on the seasons and labor demands "are generally phased fairly uniformly for the population of an entire region" (Adams, 1966: 41). All who work on the land have their periods of intense labor—planting, harvesting, or whatever—at more or less the same time, and all also enjoy periods of leisure and social activity at the same time. The community is tied together by these common rhythms and activities.

The rhythms of agricultural work generally are shaped around the work year, reflected in a yearly cycle of holidays and religious activities, in contrast to the labor patterns of modern industrial society, which are shaped around the work week. In medieval Europe there were perhaps a hundred days a year dedicated to some saint or other, and kept as festivals (Hill, 1967: 148). These saints' days were distributed throughout the year, more or less following the rhythms of the agricultural year—in slack periods when there was in any case little to do there would be many saints' days, and in busy periods there would be fewer.

Capitalist Work Patterns

About four hundred years ago, handicraft commodity production began to become an important part of Western European (especially

British) society. Until this time work patterns had involved a task orientation: animals hunted, nuts gathered, cows milked, or seeds planted. As E. P. Thompson has noted, there is a sense in which task orientation "is more humanly comprehensible than timed labour. The peasant or labourer appears to attend upon what is an observed necessity" (1967: 60). The emerging capitalist time orientation involved working by the clock, day in and day out, not because of any natural necessity, but simply because there was always a job to be done. It is important to note how recent this capitalistic work pattern is. We are not dealing with human nature, not even with a practice that has characterized most "civilized" societies. Historically speaking, a capitalist work pattern and a time orientation to work have only emerged in the recent past. Both were practically nonexistent before 1600, and did not become dominant anywhere until the late eighteenth or early nineteenth centuries.

The technical possibility of continuous labor certainly did not mean that it was necessary, or quickly became dominant. In many ways, the early manufacturing work rhythm was more similar to the labor patterns of agricultural society than to those of modern capitalism. As in agricultural societies, the pattern was one of intense labor followed by rests; but as in industrial society, this took place more or less within the context of a work week, not a work year. For example, the Puritans insisted on working on saints' days, which were legal rest days, and were therefore punished in court for these infractions (Hill, 1967: 155, 157). Most people (including for example, Queen Elizabeth's ministers) worked on Sundays, but the Puritans insisted on total abstinence from labor on the Sabbath (Sunday) at the same time that they were fighting for the right to work on holy days. England was becoming a commercial and manufacturing society, and Puritans felt the need for a "*regular* day of rest and meditation suited to the regular and continuous rhythms of modern industrial society" (ibid.: 146). Just as important as the regular day of rest, and just as much of a break with the past, was the insistence that the other six days a week should be devoted to labor, week after week, all year long.

An eighteenth-century weaver offers a typical example of such a work situation. The weaver and family might live in a cottage with a bit of land for a garden. The cottage was not only where they ate and slept, but also their workplace. The man did the weaving, the woman and children the spinning, cleaning, and so on. The family owned their looms, their raw material, and the other tools needed. It was almost completely up to them how much to work, how hard to work, and when to work. Once each week, on Saturday, weavers would take however much cloth they had woven in the previous week and go to market to sell it:

> In Halifax, "the clothiers who work in the surrounding villages come to town every Saturday, each bringing with him the cloth he has made. . . . The cloth merchant goes to the Hall, and buys from the clothiers the white cloth, which he gets dyed or dressed according to his requirements." (Quoted in Mantoux, 1928: 59)

Thousands of small producers would come to market each Saturday: " 'The clothiers come early in the morning with their cloth . . . *few clothiers bring more than one piece,* ' " since that is all that one person would weave in a week (quoted in ibid.: 59; emphasis in original).

Workers who controlled their own work did not work eight hours a day, five days a week. "The weavers were used to 'play frequently all day on Monday, and the greater part of Tuesday, and work very late on Thursday night, and frequently all night on Friday' " so as to have their cloth ready for the market on Saturday (Pollard, 1963: 256). Moreover, weavers usually continued to help with agricultural work, especially during the peak harvest period. An act of Parliament of 1662 begins with a preamble stating " 'The custome hath been retained time out of mind and found expedient that there should be a cessation of weaving every yeare, in the time of harvest, in regard the spinners of yarn, which the said weavers doe use, at that time chiefly employed in harvest worke. . .' " (Mantoux, 1928: 63). As late as 1827, the Manchester *Chronicle* predicted that " 'as the hay and harvest seasons will of course take off a great number of hands from their usual occupation at the loom, the quantity of cloth produced from the handloom will decrease weekly until the end of August or beginning of September' " (Bythell, 1969: 59; see also Mantoux, 1928: 215).

This brief description has focused on the "pure" case of independent commodity production. But even before the rise of the factory the development of capitalism had begun to destroy workers' independence and control over production. In particular, by the 1770s and 1780s, when textile factories emerged, most textile workers had already been converted from independent commodity producers to wage workers under a putting out system. Under this system, workers continued to own their own looms or spinning wheels, continued to work at home when and as they pleased, but no longer owned the raw material or sold the product in the market. Instead, the raw material was supplied to, and the product taken from, the worker by a merchant putter out. The putter out might take the wool to one worker to be spun, pay the spinner and take the thread to another worker to be woven into cloth, pay the weaver and take the cloth to another worker to be dyed, and so on. Under this system, which was more or less prevalent by the middle of the eighteenth century, workers continued to have considerable independence over when and how to work, but the power relationship had shifted significantly, and workers were employees on a wage subject to much more coercion, even though on an hour by hour (or day by day) basis their time was under their own control.

The Rise of the Factory

Between the middle of the eighteenth century and the end of the nineteenth century independent commodity production and the putting out system gave way to factory production. During this period also technology changed drastically, from hand production to power machinery. It does not follow, however, that the change in technology caused the change in work organization. It is just as logical to assume that the change in the organization of work led to a change in the technology, or that the two changes were unrelated, or that both changes were caused by some third factor (for example, the rise of capitalism). This chapter examines in turn three theories which attempt to explain the rise of the factory. The first, technological determinism, is briefly stated. The second, a simple social control theory, requires more elaboration since it is less commonly accepted and more subject to challenge. The third attempts to move beyond either of the others into an analysis which incorporates and transcends them both.

The Technological Determinist Argument

The *first,* and by far the most common, explanation for the rise of the factory holds that factories were established when a new technology, specifically power-driven machinery, required the use of a central power source. The necessity of a central power source to operate the machinery meant that people could no longer work in their own homes, scattered all over the countryside, but had to be concentrated into a few central locations, so that a large number of machines could be operated off of one power source. The workers in these new factories had to give up their old work patterns so that work could be coordinated and the machinery kept going. This conventional wisdom is almost never elaborated or argued—presumably the assumption is that this view is so obviously correct that no argument need be presented.

Such a position is a variant of technological determinism: technology is seen as an unmoved mover, an independent force without class bias. Technology develops not because of its relation to society, but as part of some general superhistorical movement—growing rationality, the progress of science, or the like. Technology is not the creation *of* any particular group, nor is it developed and applied *for* any particular interest.* Because it is an objective, inexorable force, there are only two ways to relate to it: to identify with the march of progress and accept whatever technological changes take place, or to oppose technology and progress. According to the technological determinist view, accepting technological change necessarily involves accepting certain other social changes and consequences. For example, power driven machinery necessarily involves central workshops, factory production, repetitive work, central supervision

---

*David Noble has pointed out:

When we trace a certain happening back to a particular piece of legislation, for example, rarely do we stop there but instead go on to explore how that legislation came into existence. Yet, when our inquiry takes us back, say, to a new machine, rarely do we likewise push on to discover where that machine came from. Instead we simply accept it as a given, seconding the often self-serving explanations of those who have designed or deployed it (something we certainly would *not* do in the case of a politician's explanation for his or her products). (1978: 4)

and control. The technological determinist may agree that some of the consequences of factories (or other technological changes) are unfortunate, perhaps even deplorable. He or she might even agree that the consequences are serious enough that we should oppose the use of the new technology. But the technological determinist will never agree to consider for whom and in what way the technology itself is shaped, will not question whether it is necessary for power-driven machinery to involve central workshops under the discipline and control of a capitalist or supervisor.* In this view, the new organization of work was not something that particular interests wanted or fought to impose; it was the necessary but unintended consequence of the new technology. We know that this new organization of work was necessary, because that is what people at the time adopted. The political implications are clear—technological necessity decides the character of society. While minor adjustments are possible, it is utopian or irrational to want or expect a fundamentally different society: utopian because we cannot have the benefits of technology without loss of control over the work process; irrational because we would be foolish to sacrifice material progress to an outdated social ideal.

The Social Control Argument

Only recently has the technological determinist explanation for the rise of the factory been seriously challenged. The person most responsible for raising the issue and demonstrating its political importance is Stephen Marglin, whose provocative article, "What Do Bosses Do? The Origins and Functions of Hierarchy in Capitalist Production," proposes the view that factories were devised by capitalists as a means of social control. Though many of his arguments have been made earlier—in particular by Karl Marx—Marglin's article has sparked renewed debate. It has, moreover, presented the

---

*This is a quintessentially liberal position. Begin by accepting the "facts" imposed by current social organization. Then, without questioning or changing any of these facts, allow free play to morality and attempts to moderate or counteract that which this social organization requires.

issues both clearly and forcefully. My presentation of this position thus relies heavily on Marglin.*

Marglin maintains that the rise of the factory had "little or nothing" to do with the need for a central power source to operate machinery; instead, he argues, factories were created so that capitalists could better discipline and control their workers. Factories or central workshops with large numbers of workers concentrated in a limited area under the supervision and control of a capitalist or overseer have substantial advantages (from the capitalist's point of view) over the putting out system, even if there is no difference in the technology employed. In the putting out system, workers could decide for themselves how many hours a day and how many days a week to work. The result was that workers chose to have a lot of leisure; nevertheless, they were able to earn a subsistence wage.

Precapitalist laborers worked irregularly. As one employer complained:

> "When the framework knitters or makers of silk stockings had a great price for their work, they have been observed seldom to work on Mondays and Tuesdays but to spend most of their time at the ale-house or nine-pins. . . . The weavers, 'tis common with them to be drunk on Mondays, have their head-ache on Tuesday, and their tools out of order on Wednesday. As for the shoemakers, they'll rather be hanged than not remember St. Crispin on Monday . . . and it commonly holds as long as they have a penny of money or pennyworth of credit." (Quoted in Thompson, 1967: 72)

One commonly recommended solution was a wage reduction, since "the poor in the manufacturing countries will never work any more time in general than is necessary just to live and support their weekly debauches" (quoted in Mantoux, 1928: 69), but such wage reductions were found to be either impossible to introduce or ineffective in eliciting extra work. Employers' complaints about the idleness of workers were a constant refrain in the late eighteenth century, but the complaints themselves show that employers were not yet in firm command. Josiah Wedgewood, noted as a discipli-

---

*Marglin noted that his research was still in progress, and the paper was published "in its present form to stimulate discussion and comment" (1974: 33). While critical of his position, I am very much indebted to Marglin for my own analysis.

narian, complained in 1772: "Our men will go to the Wakes, if they were sure to go to the D——l the next. I have not spared them in threats and I would have thrash'd them right heartily if I could" (quoted in Pollard, 1965: 214).

Employers also tried to enforce work discipline and speed-up on their scattered outworkers by means of the law. "In the eighteenth century, Parliament twice enacted laws requiring domestic woolen workers to complete and return work within specified periods of time. In 1749 the period was fixed at twenty-one days, and in 1777 the period was reduced to eight days" (Marglin, 1974: 50). The law was also used in an attempt to control another serious problem of the putting out system: embezzlement of materials by workers.

The problem of embezzlement must be understood in the context of workers' traditional rights to a part of the product of their labor, a right which was still accepted by many in the eighteenth century. The alienation of workers from their product was of course one of the four types of alienation which Marx attributed to capitalism. Historically, it is clearly related to the development of the money wage on the one hand and the modern concept of private property on the other, concepts which were still not completely accepted in the eighteenth century, even within the ruling classes.

In precapitalist societies the notion of "private" property does not exist; at all levels "ownership" is infused with and constrained by traditional rights and duties. For example, under feudalism, who "owned" a piece of land farmed by a serf? In one sense the lord did, since the serf could not sell the land and had to give half the product to the lord. On the other hand, the serf did because he could not be displaced, and he could bequeath the land to his children. The church had certain rights to the crop as well. If the peasant wished to sell his land, even if he had his lord's permission, the land had first to be offered to the peasant's family, since a sale negotiated without the express permission of the extended family could be reversed if any relative later complained. As one final complication, the community also had rights over the land: at a certain date after the grain had been harvested cattle were turned loose in the fields, with all the cattle entitled to graze on anyone's land. This meant that if the serf tried to grow a different crop or use a later harvest date, the cattle could destroy his crop (Bloch, 1961).

Before capitalism was established, instead of a wage, workers took a part of their product, or a part of the raw materials, which they either sold on their own or made into a product which they sold. Though this system had prevailed for centuries, in the last half of the eighteenth century the emerging capitalist class began to attack or criticize it, since capitalists as a class were attempting to create a moral and legal redefinition of the concepts of property and the wage. Increasingly "severe and explicit" legislation of 1749, 1774, and 1777 tried to stop embezzlement (Pollard, 1965: 46). Despite the fact that this legislation allowed workers' homes to be searched on mere suspicion, and if suspicious goods were found workers were legally guilty unless they could prove their innocence, the laws proved ineffective (Marglin, 1974: 51). The very severity of the laws is a testament to their ineffectiveness, and the difficulties in controlling embezzlement through the law. Cases were too hard to prove and too expensive to prosecute; each worker would have to be prosecuted individually, and evidence was hard to come by, even with the right of search. As long as workers controlled their materials and the work process, they had considerable power and many options.

The problem of embezzlement was not so serious as control over the hours worked, but it was much more serious than people today usually assume. Weavers who received a certain quantity of yarn were supposed to return a stated quantity of cloth, but this was never easy to enforce. The natural variation in the materials made it difficult to predict how much cloth would result, and weavers could resort to many tricks (wetting or stretching the cloth, substituting cheap material for expensive, etc.). As late as 1824, by which time the practice was much reduced, a correspondent to the *Blackburn Mail* estimated that one-sixth of the cotton goods produced were the product of embezzled materials (Bythell, 1969: 72, 124–25). At the Deptford Docks, shipyard workers were allowed to take "chips" or scrap wood. The navy accepted this as a traditional right, a part of the wage, and only tried to restrict workers to one load a day, the amount that could be carried out under one arm. Workers fought for the right to use both arms and their shoulders (and even for the right to have their wives and children help them carry out scrap). "Rightful chips" were worth one-third to one-half as much as the money earnings, but workers did not restrict themselves to what the navy considered "rightful." Workers were accused of taking the best wood for themselves to sell, and leaving the green, warped, and unseasoned wood for the navy. Scrap pieces had to be short enough to fit between two posts at the exit; the size of this "scrap" determined the construction of doors, windows, and stairways of many houses in the area. Estimates by naval officials indicated that less than half the timber coming into the yard was used in ships; more than half left the yard as chips. The navy tried to forcibly impose a higher wage in place of the right to chips; several times they failed to do so. The higher wage was to be a 40 or 50 percent increase over the existing wage, and still the workers refused it (Linebaugh, 1975).*

The social control view emphasizes capitalists' inability, under a putting out system, to control workers' hours and their embezzlement as key reasons for the rise of the factory. Where the law, wage reductions, and moral exhortations failed, factories succeeded. As soon as capitalists established factories, embezzlement could be easily controlled: workers could be searched when they entered and when they left, and not allowed to take anything out of the workplace. Such a simple check could be much more effective than a great deal of costly litigation. There is no technological change involved if workers are prevented from directly appropriating the product, with the product going instead to capitalists, merely a redistribution of income from workers to capitalists. Nonetheless, this factor was important enough "for some contemporaries to advocate the use of

---

*Reinhard Bendix is one of the few sociologists to deal with the history of management attempts to control the workforce. Unfortunately, despite its title, *Work and Authority in Industry,* his work deals neither with work nor authority, but rather with ideologies of management. Moreover, he often writes the kind of history that comes from believing in the smooth operation of a free market, and all the ideological paraphernalia which goes with that, and projecting back as fact the way history must have been, given that there was a free market. For example, here is Bendix' analysis—unsupported by any citation—of domestic work and early factories:

In the household industry, for example, the merchant employer furnished the raw materials to each of a number of domestic workers in separate households, and their performance could be supervised with accuracy when the finished product was delivered and the piece rate paid. Under these conditions, there was no "need" for an ethic of work performance, because this organization of production imposed the whole burden of substandard work performance upon the worker himself, and, hence, did not present a managerial problem. (1956: 203)

the powerloom largely as a means of reducing the manufacturer's losses by embezzlement" (Bythell, 1969: 124).

Much more important, however, the creation of the factory meant that capitalists could decide the hours of labor. Workers were given the "choice" of not working at all (and presumably starving), or else working on the capitalist's terms, which required employees to work twelve or fourteen hours a day, six days a week. Workers could not choose to arrive late or leave early, to take a day off once in a while, or to work fewer days on a regular basis. These and other options either did not exist at all or were offenses, with heavy fines (Fitton and Wadsworth, 1958: 234–38). All such decisions were to be made by the capitalist.

The rise of factories meant that workers had to spend about twice as many hours a week actually working, but they still earned no more than a subsistence wage. As a result, according to Marglin, even if weekly wages were marginally higher, capitalists could make far greater profits.* A given amount of money bought about twice as many hours of labor (even though the same number of workers were employed), since each worker worked twice as many hours per week. The result was that twice as many goods would be produced for a given labor cost, even if there were no change in the technology employed. The only difference was that in the factory, workers expended far more effort, did more labor, and the benefit of this extra labor went to the capitalist. Factories benefit capitalists, at the expense of workers, even with no difference in technology. Therefore, the rise of factories can be explained because it benefited capitalists, and because capitalists had the power to impose this change on workers. Marglin's argument is that the success of the factory

> had little or nothing to do with the technological superiority of large-scale machinery. The key to the success of the factory, as well as its aspiration, was the substitution of capitalists' for workers' control of the production process; discipline and supervision could and did reduce costs *without* being technologically superior. (1974: 46; emphasis in original)

---

*All the social control position requires is that the extra output from factory work was higher than the extra cost for labor. Obviously, the greater the difference, the more incentive there was to start factories.

Marglin's theory is both politically radical and intellectually non-obvious; yet interestingly enough this was essentially the analysis of leading capitalists and their ideologues at the time factories were first being created. The leading capitalist apologist Andrew Ure offered such an explanation for the success of Richard Arkwright, the spinning industrialist who above all others was responsible for the creation of the factory. While Arkwright patented the water frame and claimed to be its inventor, this claim was proved to be false even within his lifetime. The machine had actually been developed thirty years earlier by Louis Paul or John Wyatt; several attempts to make a success of the innovation had failed. Andrew Ure, writing in 1835, at a time when spinning was still the only industry unequivocally dominated by factory production, explained why it was Arkwright and no other who deserved the credit for the creation of the factory:

> The main difficulty [in the automatic factory] . . . lay . . . above all in training human beings to renounce their desultory habits of work, and to identify themselves with the unvarying regularity of the complex automaton. To devise and administer a successful code of factory discipline, suited to the necessities of factory diligence, was the Herculean enterprise, the noble achievement of Arkwright! Even at the present day, when the system is perfectly organized and its labour lightened to the utmost, it is found nearly impossible to convert persons past the age of puberty, into useful factory hands. (Ure, cited in Marx, 1867: 399)

Lest there be any misunderstanding, Ure explicitly explained that Arkwright deserves the credit for the creation of the factory, even though his technical contribution was nil, since he was the person who was mean enough, greedy enough, and strong enough to smash the workers:

> If the factory Briareus could have been created by mechanical genius alone, it should have come into being thirty years sooner; for upwards of ninety years have now [1835] elapsed since John Wyatt, of Birmingham, not only invented the series of fluted rollers (the spinning fingers usually ascribed to Arkwright) but obtained a patent for the invention, and erected "a spinning engine without hands" in his native town. . . . Wyatt was a man of good education, in a respectable walk of life, much esteemed by his superiors, and therefore favourably placed, in a mechanical point of view, for maturing his admirable scheme. But he

was of a gentle and passive spirit, little qualified to cope with the hardships of a new manufacturing enterprise. It required, in fact, a man of a Napoleon nerve and ambition, to subdue the refractory tempers of work-people accustomed to irregular paroxysms of diligence, and to urge on his multifarious and intricate constructions in the face of prejudice, passion, and envy. Such was Arkwright. (Ure, 1835: 16)

Similarly, Matthew Boulton, later James Watt's partner in the manufacture of steam engines, switched from reliance on innumerable separate workshops to a single factory primarily for organizational rather than technical reasons (Pollard, 1965: 100). Arkwright started a majority of the early spinning factories; Boulton made a majority of the early steam engines. It is thus very significant that the success of these people's factories was seen, by themselves and by their contemporaries, as depending on organizational and control factors rather than on technical innovation.

A final argument for the social control view is the existence of central workshops that did not involve power-driven machinery. If the technological argument were right, and factories were started because of the need to concentrate workers around a central power source, there would not have been any concentration of workers without an accompanying technical change to power-driven machinery. In fact, however, there were a great many cases when the organizational change to large groups working under supervision preceded the technical change to power machinery. While a technological determinist argument cannot account for such instances, they are exactly what a social control argument would predict. Such central workshops were found in a number of industries (Bythell, 1969: 34), but by far the most important examples were in weaving, where handloom sheds

provided important precedents for the development of the cotton-and-worsted-spinning industries. . . . There was already a marked degree of concentration in workshops and factories by the time Arkwright and Hargreaves [originators of the new machinery] came to Nottingham. (Chapman, 1967: 34; see also 99)

Power looms were not introduced until many years after spinning was totally dominated by factories using power-driven machinery. It is difficult to establish exactly how important such handloom shops were, but they were far more than isolated instances. Based primarily on sale notices in the local press, Bythell has found evidence of handloom sheds in two dozen locations.

> Although [the handloom weaving shed] was never anything like the predominant form of organization in cotton weaving, it was not negligible, nor was it confined, as H. D. Fong suggested, to fancy goods only. According to the historian of Rossendale, in the period 1815–1830, when "the trade of cotton weaving on the handloom was at its briskest, there were at the lowest computation thirty weaving shops, apart from the looms in dwelling houses, in the forest of Rossendale." . . . Isolated cases have been found with as many as 150 or 200 handlooms, quite a few with between 50 and 100, and a considerable number with 20 or more. (1969: 33; see also Smelser, 1959: 143)

Social Control or Class Struggle?

Under the putting out system, capitalists tried in various ways to make workers do more work, but they were generally unable to undercut workers' control over their labor by means of threats, laws, price cuts, and so on. The successful attack on the existing balance of power was made through the details of the work process. Only by changing the organization of work through the introduction of the factory system was it possible to force workers to do more. In my opinion, this social control view is not wrong, merely incomplete.

This view conceptualizes the process of change as one in which one group, employers, were historically active and imposed their will on another group, workers, who remained essentially quiescent, without will, consciousness, or activity of their own. It is much more fruitful, and obviously the only Marxist approach, to understand the process as one of class struggle: capitalists tried to impose social control in the form of factories, while workers struggled to resist. In this struggle, technological innovations were crucial capitalist weapons to help change the balance of power.

It is easy to show that workers resisted the introduction of factories. One telling piece of evidence is the simple fact that employers were forced to offer higher wages for factory work. Women in Ireland refused to work in factories at eight pence a day though in their own homes they were satisfied with four or five pence. Even such tremendous wage differentials do not measure workers' resistance: as Sidney Pollard notes, "higher money wages by themselves . . . would have been utterly inadequate" to attract a labor force—only external compulsion, poverty, and enclosures provided workers for the early factories (1965: 191).

The enclosure movement is justly notorious in this regard, and enclosures often were instituted explicitly to create dependent wage laborers (Thompson, 1963: 217, 219; Lazonick, 1974). Beyond this, however, in order to recruit a sufficient number of workers it was necessary to resort to various kinds of forced and unfree labor.* As much as one-third of the labor force in early factories was unfree, even if we accept the normal capitalist definition of a wage laborer as a "free" worker (Pollard, 1965: 203).

> There were few areas of the country in which the modern industries, particularly the textiles, if carried on in large buildings, were not associated with prisons, workhouses, and orphanages. . . . The most widespread cause of the association of the new large-scale industry with unfree labour, however, was the massive employment of pauper apprentices in private industry. (Ibid.: 192, 194)

Though these children are called "apprentices," it would be a mistake to infer that they were taught a trade which could support them as adults. One study of 780 "apprentices" found that only two, or one-quarter of 1 percent, were recorded as having been employed as adults at the factory where they were apprentices. Over three-quarters of the apprentices were children of the poor, who had been supported out of the parish poor rates and were given over to employers, for whom they were legally required to work for up to eight years in order to save the parish the cost of supporting them. Less than one in ten of these apprentices was brought to the factory

---

*This is in addition to (1) the slave plantations of the West Indies, which were perhaps the earliest large-scale management enterprises to produce commodities almost exclusively for the (world) market, and (2) the fact that "till 1775, the workers in the coal mines and the salt pits of Scotland were serfs in the full legal sense of the word. Bound for life to the coal mines or salt pits, they could be sold along with them" (Mantoux, 1928: 74).

by parents, relatives, or private individuals.* So hated were the early factories that "in the beginning the pauper children represented the only type of labour which in many areas could be driven into" factories (ibid.: 195). It would be totally incorrect to see factories as a change with benefits obvious to all, which enticed somewhat reluctant workers through the promise of marginally higher wages. Nor would it be correct to view workers as totally helpless, easily driven to do whatever capitalists wanted. The struggle was a long and bitter one, since the conflict was "between two cultural modes or ways of life" (Thompson, 1963: 305).

Viewing the conflict after two hundred years of capitalism, it would be easy for us to forget that these workers were not "harking back to a mythical golden age, but [defending] *existing* social relationships" (Pollard, 1965: 192; emphasis in original). Wage labor, the factory system, and a lack of freedom while at work have become accepted as the norm, but it was not always so: "We look back after wage labour has won a respected position by two centuries of struggle. We forget the time when complete dependence on wages had for centuries been rejected by all who regarded themselves as free men" (Hill, 1964: 63).

As long as workers had any choice, they preferred the cottage to the factory (see Thompson, 1963: 269–314). In the early days, riots and destruction of factories were frequent occurrences (see for example Chapman, 1967; Thompson, 1963: 552–603). Working-class opposition to factories was a powerful force counteracting the capitalist wish for factories. In some cases this opposition even forced the abandonment of factories and the return to domestic outwork:

"I found the utmost distaste [one hosier reported] on the part of the men, to any regular hours or regular habits. . . . The men themselves

---

*Even these imprisoned children resisted the factory: one in six ran away, and one in eight were returned to their overseers or parents. Another one in twelve died during their "apprenticeships." Stanley Chapman, who collected this data, lumps all of these categories together and without apology or explanation complains about the "high degree of wastage," by which he means that "more than a third of the apprentices recruited died, absconded, or had to be returned to the overseers, parents, or the connections that sent them" (1967: 170). From a capitalist point of view, "wastage" is of course an appropriate term. Whether the children died from overwork and abuse, or escaped to freedom and a better life, in either case their lives were "wasted" since they did not continue to produce surplus value for capital.

were considerably dissatisfied, because they could not go in and out as they pleased, and have what holidays they pleased, and go on just as they had been used to do; and were subject, during after-hours, to the ill-natured observations of other workmen, to such an extent as completely to disgust them with the whole system, and I was obliged to break it up." (Quoted in Pollard, 1965: 191)

Resistance and active opposition by workers were sufficiently successful to greatly limit capital's ability to impose social control. Attempting to achieve control through the details of the work process was a great step forward for capital, but purely organizational and control changes were not enough to ensure a speedy capitalist victory. Something more was needed, and this something was technology. Stephen Marglin believes that "the agglomeration of workers into factories . . . had little or nothing to do with the technological superiority of large-scale machinery" (1974: 46). In contrast, I would argue that while capitalists instituted factory organization largely to impose control over the work process, they were unable to realize this goal without the aid of an accompanying technical change, the introduction of power-driven machinery.

If technology was basically irrelevant to the imposition of capitalist control, factories should have been as likely to appear and become dominant in those industries that did not undergo technological change (the spread of power-driven machinery), as they were in industries that did experience major technological change. A social control analysis therefore predicts a similar proportion of factory production in the closely linked industries of spinning and weaving in, say, 1810, despite the fact that the successful inventions for spinning were widely adopted two decades before those in weaving.*

The fact that there were a significant number of instances in which capitalists supervised large groups of handloom weavers working under one roof is evidence in favor of a social control as opposed to a technological determinist argument. The argument cuts both ways, however. The social control theory further predicts that there should

---

*The basic spinning inventions had been made by 1779, the powerloom not until 1787. More important, the spinning inventions were quickly adopted—there were four to five million spindles in mule spinning alone by 1812—but powerlooms spread very slowly—only a handful were in use in 1808, and they were not dominant until after 1830 (Mantoux, 1928: 242; Bythell, 1969: 5, 74; Pollard, 1965: 51).

have been as much concentrated production in weaving as in spinning even before the introduction of the powerloom. If anything, there should have been more incentive to start hand workshops for weaving, since wages were higher in weaving than they were in spinning. This was not at all what happened: concentrated production totally dominated spinning at a time when it was uncommon in weaving. Up until 1800 or later, the term "factory" was practically synonymous with the term "spinning mill," and there were perhaps one hundred such large mills, often employing many hundreds of workers (Chapman, 1967: 64). While there were handloom weaving sheds, and while these were not negligible, they were smaller than spinning factories and less common. By 1800 over half of the total amount of cotton was spun in factories, whereas it was not until after 1830 that a majority of the weaving took place in concentrated workshops, and even then this was only because the powerloom was at last coming into widespread use. There is no question that greater technological change was associated with more factories; it is hard to see how a social control argument can account for this.

A Marxist Analysis

In moving beyond the social control and technological determinist explanations for the rise of the factory, elements of both views can be used in transcending the two analyses. The technological determinist view is correct in its insistence on the importance of technology; the social control view is correct in arguing that factories were shaped by specifically capitalist ends. An initial step toward a Marxist argument is the recognition that the insights of the social control argument must be applied to technology as well as organization.

For the technological determinist view to be valid, technology would have to be independent of social forces, and thus in some way inevitable. This implies a lack of choice among available technologies, but plainly there is always some selection among technologies. If the technology is selected not because it is the best in some objective sense, but rather because it is the best for capitalists, then the needs of capitalism are more important than "objective" technological requirements in determining the organization of work. For example, suppose that two technologies existed that were exactly equal in terms of costs and benefits. One was best suited to domestic production, and benefited workers, in that they could do the same amount of work in less time or with less effort; the other was best used in factories and allowed employers to produce more without raising wages or hiring more workers. In a capitalist system, there is more incentive to seek out, develop, and use the latter kind of technology. It is capitalists who have the power to decide which technologies are used, and capitalists will obviously prefer technologies that benefit them rather than workers.*

The above example is hypothetical, for illustrative purposes. But it is not completely fanciful: Hargreaves' spinning jenny was suitable for use in domestic production; Arkwright's water frame required a factory. The only money to be made off the spinning jenny was by manufacturing it and selling it to domestic workers. But the jenny was an easy machine to copy, and thousands of scattered people could easily avoid paying royalties to the inventor. The initial benefit of the invention therefore went to thousands of workers. Arkwright's water frame could be used only in factories, and factories were large enough that it was possible to be sure there was no unauthorized use of the invention. The main benefit of the water frame therefore went to Arkwright (and his partners). Neither inventor started out especially poor or especially rich. At his death, Hargreaves left an estate worth 4,000 English pounds; Arkwright's estate was worth 500,000 pounds (Mantoux, 1928: 218, 232). The difference illustrates why capitalists would prefer to develop one kind of invention rather than the other.†

---

*"No capitalist ever voluntarily introduces a new method of production, no matter how much more productive it may be . . . so long as it reduces the rate of profit" (Marx, 1894: 264).

†I obviously do not mean to suggest that the only relevant difference was the nature of the inventions. Arkwright, by all accounts, was a much better businessman; in addition, he died later and so had more time to accumulate an estate.

To complete the story, it is worth noting that Crompton, whose mule was a better machine than either the jenny or the water frame, and soon became more widely used, decided his invention could not be patented. Rather than trying to keep it secret and work it for himself (as a good capitalist would do), Crompton offered the mule to the public as a gift. A public subscription to thank him for this gift brought only 67 pounds, and Crompton died poor.

An understanding of the way in which capital influences technology helps to supplement the correct but incomplete social control model. A complete analysis, however, needs to explain not only what capital did and why, but also the way in which workers' struggles influence the dynamic of the process. Such an analysis already exists: it was presented by Marx more than one hundred years ago in Volume I of *Capital*. One key contribution of Marx's account of the development of capitalism is that it distinguishes three stages of production—handicraft, manufacture, and modern industry—and analyzes the dynamic that leads from one stage to the next.

Handicraft production is typified by the medieval guilds, in which one person manufactures a complete commodity, performing all of the necessary tasks. For example, a person would be a shoemaker, a clockmaker, a gunsmith, or a pinmaker. The gunsmith would cast the barrel, drill out the bore, make the stock, trigger, lock, and firing pin, put on the sights, and assemble the whole into a working rifle. Similarly, a clockmaker would make all of the wheels, gears, weights, chimes, mechanism, and case for a clock, and a shoemaker would cut the leather, stitch the pieces, attach the heels, and complete the shoe. Obviously, to be able to make all of the various parts of a gun or clock required extensive training, practice, and skill. Becoming a gunsmith took years, and people devoted their lives to this handicraft. Each gun would be individually produced; parts were not interchangeable. Gunsmiths made their reputations on the quality of the guns they made.

Although Marglin does not say so, and evidently does not define the problem in this way, his analysis concerns what Marx described as the transition from handicraft to manufacture. In this transition, workers are gathered together into large groups under the discipline and control of a capitalist. Even though no new tools or machines are introduced, capitalists achieve all the benefits which are described by the social control theory (control over work hours, embezzlement, and work rhythms). The point of Marx's analysis is that this *organizational* change precedes, both historically and analytically, the technological revolution which is the foundation of modern industry. The transition to manufacture is a social, not a technical change. To understand why it took place we should look not to technology but to the material interest of the emerging capitalist class.

The social control aspects of this change represent very important gains for the capitalist, and Marx discusses them, but social control is not the only gain: there is a technical increase in productivity as well. In this central workshop the workers cooperate, each performing a detailed part of the whole. The work remains the same: the same processes are performed, with the same tools and equipment, in the same way, as before. But the tasks each worker performs change: no worker performs the whole operation, everyone does a more limited number of processes over and over. Initially there is no change in the tools and machinery employed: only the organization of work is different. Each worker becomes a detail laborer, performing over and over again one (or a few) of the steps necessary to produce the commodity. For example, one person casts rifle barrels, another drills out the bore, a third makes stocks, and so on. Instead of being a gunsmith, a person becomes a rifle stock maker. Only the shop as a whole produces the commodity: only due to the cooperation of the workers does the object get made.

Marx, following Adam Smith, argues that the cooperative character of the work leads to real improvements in production. Since the workers are all under one roof, less time is needed to transport the unfinished object from worker to worker (1867: 325). Workers become more expert at their jobs, and less time is lost in changing from one operation to another. The Babbage principle so brilliantly explained by Harry Braverman (1974) means that employers can reduce their wage bill by buying only the minimum skills necessary. Finally,

> the manufacturing period simplifies, improves, and multiplies the implements of labour, by adapting them to the exclusively special functions of each detail labourer. It thus creates at the same time one of the material conditions for the existence of machinery, which consists of a combination of simple instruments. (Marx, 1867: 323)

Capital benefits from the transition to manufactures both through increased social control and through an increase in the goods produced per hour of labor,* but these benefits are to a considerable extent brought about at the expense of workers. Workers are forced

---

*In technical Marxist terms, this leads to a decrease in necessary labor and therefore an increase in relative surplus value.

to work harder, and are subjected to the discipline and control of a capitalist. Their work time is no longer under their own control. Nor is this all: "In manufacture, in order to make the collective labourer, and through him capital, rich in social productive power, each labourer must be made poor in individual productive powers" (ibid.: 341). The perfection of the collective laborer, that is, the shop as a whole, requires that detail laborers become onesided and deficient, specialists in one narrow operation. Marx notes as one example the "abnormal development of some muscles,"* but by far the most important form this crippling of the laborer takes is in the separation of planning and execution:

> The knowledge, the judgment, and the will, which, though in ever so small a degree, are practised by the independent peasant or handi-craftsman . . . these faculties are now required only for the workshop as a whole. Intelligence in production expands in one direction, because it vanishes in many others. What is lost by the detail labourers, is concentrated in the capital that employs them. It is a result of the division of labour in manufactures, that the labourer is brought face to face with the intellectual potencies of the material process of produc-tion, as the property of another, and as a ruling power. This separation begins in simple co-operation, where the capitalist represents to the single workman, the oneness and the will of the associated labour. It is developed in manufacture which cuts down the labourer into a detail labourer. It is completed in modern industry, which makes science a productive force distinct from labour and presses it into the service of capital. (Ibid.: 341)†

Although Marx does not here use the term, this is plainly an analysis

---

*Today, on assembly lines, this abnormal development of some muscles is a requisite of production. This is one reason why workers on assembly lines turn down opportunities to switch jobs. Performing a particular job develops strength in certain muscles; a new job would take strength in muscles that are presently weak; therefore, switching jobs means several days of soreness until the new muscles strengthen and harden.

†Adam Smith admits these are the effects of the system he recommends. The worker's "'dexterity at his own particular trade seems in this manner to be acquired at the expense of his intellectual, social, and martial virtues. But in every improved and civilised society, this is the state into which the labouring poor, that is, the great body of the people, must necessarily fall.'" Quoting this, Marx notes, "For preventing the complete deterioration of the great mass of the people by division of labour, A. Smith recommends education of the people by the State, but prudently, and in homeopathic doses" (ibid.: 342).

of alienation; just as plainly, modern bureaucracy carries this tendency to new heights.

What Marx is trying to show in his analysis of the three stages of production is that the transition from handicrafts to manufacture is a social change, which precedes the technological change (to modern industry). The period of manufacture still relies on a technical foundation very similar to that of handicrafts: the skill, strength, and intelligence of the worker using hand tools.

> Whether complex or simple, each operation has to be done by hand, retains the character of a handicraft, and is therefore dependent on the strength, skill, quickness, and sureness, of the individual workman in handling his tools. The handicraft continues to be the basis. (Ibid.: 320)

It is the organization of work that has changed—now each worker does only one detail operation over and over, and the whole is controlled and coordinated by capital. There has been an organizational revolution, but no technical revolution. It is not the technological change which has forced industry to adopt a certain form of organization; not that machinery, independently developed following an inner technological imperative, has required organizational innovations in order to be successfully used; rather, capitalism has selected and developed a certain form of organization which fits its purposes. The new capitalist organization of work "creates the material conditions for the existence of machinery." Technological development takes place within the framework of a capitalist organization of production.

The stage of manufactures, however, was not a stable state. Neither the very real social control advantages nor the increased productivity of this stage were enough to overcome workers' resistance, so that manufactures never became the predominant form of organization for most industries. Only the technological change, the coming of machinery, made concentrated production in a central location the dominant form. According to Mantoux, "in spite of its obvious advantages from the point of view of organization and supervision, the bringing together of many workmen in large shops had never been in general use" (1928: 246).

Despite the very real benefits capital received from the transition to manufactures, there continued to be important limitations. Since each particular operation continued to have a handicraft basis, production "owed its existence to personal strength and personal skill, and depended on the muscular development, the keenness of sight, and the cunning of hand, with which the detail workmen in manufactures, and the manual labourers in handicrafts, wielded their dwarfish implements" (Marx, 1867: 361). The technical disadvantages of hand production are serious, but far more important is the strong position workers retain.

> Since handicraft skill is the foundation of manufacture, and since the mechanism of manufacture as a whole possesses no framework, apart from the labourers themselves, capital is constantly compelled to wrestle with the insubordination of the workmen. (Ibid.: 346)

Workers in capitalism usually try to resist and struggle; a key question is their ability to enforce their will: if the chances of success are small, workers are not likely to engage in continued losing battles. (Instead they will choose a different tactic, a new form of struggle.) In the period of manufactures, the fact that the workers' skill and strength were the foundations of production gave them a very powerful position. "'By the infirmity of human nature,' says friend Ure, 'it happens that the more skillful the workman, the more self-willed and intractable he is apt to become, and of course the less fit a component of a mechanical system in which . . . he may do great damage to the whole'" (ibid.: 346–47).

The solution to this problem, as Marx notes, is machines: "it is they that sweep away the handicraftsman's work as the regulating principle of social production" (ibid.: 347). Machinery provides a framework independent of the workers. Workers must adapt themselves to the machinery, while in the stage of manufactures workers' skill was crucial so that capitalists continually had to rely on, and reach an accommodation with, skilled workers. In manufacturing the organizational form had been revolutionized and was suited to capital's needs, but the technical basis was still dependent on workers' handicraft skill. In the stage of modern industry for the first time capital achieves a technology appropriate to its organizational form and capitalist social relations of production.

With the development of machinery and modern industry workers become, from the point of view of capital, little more than appendages to and servants of the machines. Their skill, knowledge, and ability are no longer as crucial to the production process. Cars used to be made and assembled by skilled machinists, but with the coming of the assembly line almost anyone can do most of the work. This fact greatly increases the capitalist's power vis à vis the worker. As Marx notes, in the production of surplus value, workers do not work for themselves, but for the capitalist. They do not do what they want to do, but what the capitalist directs them to do. Workers do not make use of the tools, machinery, raw materials, and supplies for their own purposes. The purpose of production, from the capitalist's point of view, is to produce surplus value. From this strange perspective (which, of course, dominates modern production), the worker's purposes are unimportant. Rather, the worker is to serve the capitalist's purpose by taking care of the instruments of labor and the raw material and ensuring that "their" goal (actually, the capitalist's goal) of acquiring and transmitting value is fulfilled. The purpose of production is not for workers to use the instruments of labor for their purposes; it is for the raw materials and the instruments of labor to absorb and pass on abstract labor. The worker's task is to serve these lifeless objects in "their" quest to embody value, so they can be sold as commodities at a profit. This is true of all capitalist production, but in the stage of manufacture it appears that workers are using the tools and raw materials which must do as the workers direct. In modern industry there is no such deception: workers quite literally must serve the machine and adapt themselves to the machine's movement (best seen on an assembly line). Capitalism at last has acquired a fitting technical form, with the technology itself embodying capitalist relations of production.

> Every kind of capitalist production, in so far as it is not only a labour-process, but also a process of creating surplus-value, has this in common, that it is not the workman that employs the instruments of labour, but the instruments of labour that employ the workman. But it is only in the factory system that this inversion for the first time acquires technical and palpable reality. (Ibid.: 399)

With machinery the nature of capitalist production becomes perfectly clear:

> In handicrafts and manufacture, the workman makes use of a tool, in the factory, the machine makes use of him. There the movements of

the instrument of labour proceed from him, here it is the movements of the machine that he must follow. In manufacture the workmen are parts of a living mechanism. In the factory we have a lifeless mechanism independent of the workman, who becomes its mere living appendage. (Ibid.: 398)

Machinery has both technical and social control advantages over the methods of manufacture. Marx strongly emphasized the technical advantages of machinery: it not only allows much greater output for a given expenditure of energy, it also allows certain things to be produced that would not be possible without machinery. For example, Marx noted that it was not until modern industry began using machines to construct machines "that it built up for itself a fitting technical foundation, and stood on its own feet" (ibid.: 363): "such machines as the modern hydraulic press, the modern power-loom, and modern carding engine, would never have been furnished by manufacture" (ibid.: 362). That is, machinery makes it possible to do things which would otherwise be impossible.

The technical advantages of machinery are thus crucial, but the social control advantages are no less important. In Marx's view, technology is not a neutral force, standing outside society and unaffected by it. Technology is a part of society, and reveals the character of social relations: "Technology discloses man's mode of dealing with Nature, the process of production by which he sustains his life, and thereby also lays bare the mode of formation of his social relations, and of the mental conceptions that flow from them" (ibid.: 352).

Under capitalism, every aspect of society is shaped by the class struggle. Nowhere is this more true than in the technology developed under capitalism, since technology is so intimately tied to the process of production:

> Machinery not only acts as a competitor who gets the better of the workman, and is constantly on the point of making him superfluous. It is also a power inimical to him, and as such capital proclaims it from the roof tops and as such makes use of it. *It is the most powerful weapon for repressing strikes,* those periodical revolts of the working-class against the autocracy of capital. . . . It would be possible to write quite a history of the inventions, made since 1830, for the sole purpose of supplying capital with weapons against the revolts of the working-class. (Ibid.: 410–11; emphasis added)

Since capitalists are the ruling class, they are the people who shape the technology (and ideology) of the society. Inventions are sought precisely because of their effect on the class struggle, because they allow capitalists to defeat workers. Whenever a group of workers achieves a powerful and (relatively) privileged position, capital will try to smash them. Machinery designed to do this is one of the capitalist's most powerful weapons. Marx quotes Ure on the self-acting mule: "'This invention confirms the great doctrine already propounded, that when capital enlists science into her service, the refractory hand of labour will always be taught docility'" (ibid.: 411). Those workers who cannot be beaten into submission can be replaced. Capitalists seek to develop machinery the purpose of which is to replace workers whose strength, skill, and/or organization makes it difficult to "teach" them "docility" (that is, to smash them). Capitalists know that this is one important purpose of machinery. Marx quotes a British Parliamentary report: "'The great advantage of the machinery employed in brickmaking consists in this, that the employer is made entirely independent of skilled labourers'" (ibid.: 407). Science and technology *are* in the service of capitalism, and to the extent that they are, one of their most important purposes is to repress the working class.

Marx himself is not entirely consistent in his view of technology and machinery. The material I have quoted reveals his basic insight that technology is shaped by the needs of capitalism. But at times he seems to accept machinery itself as neutral and to argue that we need only change the exploitative way machinery is used under capitalism. While Marx never argues for this position in the way that he grounds the concept of technology as an element in class struggle, at times he seems to adopt such a view.

For example, he writes: "It took both time and experience before the working-people learnt to distinguish between machinery and its employment by capital, and to direct their attacks, not against the material instruments of production, but against the mode in which they are used" (ibid.: 404).* This could be interpreted to mean that workers thought they could destroy exploitation by actually break-

---

*It should be noted that while it may have taken workers until, say, 1830 to learn to tell the difference, this is something that many social scientists have yet to learn. They all too often think that they defend capitalism by defending machinery.

ing the machines, whereas they had to learn that it was the system of production which needed to be destroyed. However, Marx seems to imply something else: that the machinery developed within a capitalist social system could be used in a nonexploitative manner if it were removed from capitalist profit maximizing control. Marx thus contradicts the implications of his analysis in *Capital* which insists that technology and machinery are shaped by specifically capitalist ends.

Marx's work may not have been completely consistent in its treatment of technology—sometimes insisting on the way in which technology was shaped by capitalist ends, other times seeming to accept technology as neutral—but this is far less of a problem than the total consistency of later Marxists, who have uniformly neglected—or explicitly denied—Marx's analysis of the capitalist character of science and technology. Thus there are painful passages in Lenin which praise Taylorism and call on the Soviet Union to adopt it as progressive. Stalin wrote in 1938 that "first the productive forces of society change and develop, and then, depending on these changes and in conformity with them, men's relations of production, their economic relations, change." Trotsky is even more extreme: "Marxism sets out from the development of technique as the fundamental spring of progress, and constructs the communist programme upon the dynamic of the productive forces" (quoted in Bettelheim, 1976: 23, 28). It is only recently that Marxists have begun to consider Marx's argument that both the organization of work and the technologies employed are shaped by specifically capitalist principles, and to question, for example, whether assembly lines have any place in a socialist society. As Marx's original analysis makes clear, there is machinery the entire design and purpose of which is exploitation, and which could hardly be used outside of an exploitative society.

One of the most common responses to an argument that technology is shaped to be specifically capitalist is the question: If so, can you name me a dozen examples of developed machines that were suppressed or destroyed despite the fact that they worked perfectly well? Why not? Why isn't the history of technology a perfectly obvious series of open battles between capitalists and workers over which machinery was to be used?

These questions are not so hard to answer if we begin by recognizing that they are based on a very inaccurate view of the way in which technology evolves (what Mantoux has called "the romantic theory of invention"). The entire history of the Industrial Revolution establishes the truth of Mantoux' characterization:

> An idea which flashes suddenly into the mind of a genius, and whose application produces no less suddenly an economic revolution, is what we might describe as the romantic theory of invention. Nowhere do we find evidence of such creations *a nihilo,* bursting forth like miracles, which only the mysterious power of individual inspiration could explain. The history of inventions is not only that of inventors but that of collective experience, which gradually solves the problems set by collective needs. (Mantoux, 1928: 206)

As soon as we understand the nature of invention it becomes possible to see why there is little evidence of conflict over technology. If the history of inventions is the history of collective experience, which gradually solves the problems set by collective needs, then it becomes crucial to know who defines the needs, what goals are being sought, what rewards are being offered for what kinds of solutions, what resources are being committed to the various available options, and so on. It becomes easy to understand how a minor improvement, not particularly significant in itself, but as a piece of a problem, would be adopted if it led to a technology beneficial to capitalists, but would not be adopted if it led to a technology more beneficial to workers than to capitalists. Similarly, in cases where the potential reward was great, people would be willing to meet with repeated failures and still (they or others would) keep trying.

Capitalists have the resources and the rewards. They decide what technology is to be developed and adopted. Therefore, they shape this technology in all kinds of subtle and not so subtle ways. This shaping takes place in the very process of development. A technology would never be developed if it ran directly counter to capitalism, if it allowed workers to dispense with capitalists and produce on their own, for example, or gave all the benefit of the improved process to workers and none to capitalists. From the capitalist point of view, such a development would be, at best, a waste of resources. Therefore, we can expect no more than ambiguous examples of some options being pursued despite difficulties, while other avenues were not pursued even though they were in some sense promising.*

For example, William Strutt was one of Arkwright's partners in the earliest factories; with Arkwright, he made a fortune on the basis of the water frame. Strutt was also one of the early experimenters with the mule, which later became the dominant way of spinning cotton, since it was capable of giving both strength and extreme fineness to the thread, while the water frame could produce only coarse thread (Mantoux, 1928: 234). The water frame was used exclusively in factories from the very beginning; initially the mule was used in domestic production, and only later adapted to the factory. Why did Strutt fail to experiment with and develop the mule, which was later shown to be technologically superior to the water frame? Stanley Chapman, a conservative historian, can see only one answer to this question:

> Why William Strutt failed to capitalize his experiments with the early mule remains a mystery, the only logical explanation being that the Strutts had so much capital tied up in factory production that they were less interested in an invention which, for the time being at any rate, was a domestic machine. Strutt turned instead to the further exploitation of the established techniques of factory production. (1967: 212)

Given the difference in productivity between factory and domestic production, Strutt may well have made a rational capitalist (profit-maximizing) decision.

A second example of a technological option not being pursued is the powerloom. The first powerloom factory, established in 1792 with four hundred powerlooms run by steam, was totally destroyed by a hostile crowd of weavers. For many years thereafter the powerloom was rarely used; sixteen years later there were only about thirty powerloom factories, and all of them were small. One of

---

*In today's energy crisis, for example, capitalists and the government are devoting comparatively few resources and little effort to certain options—conservation, solar energy, renewable resources such as wood—despite their evident promise; large sums and major commitments are made to other options—nuclear energy, oil shale, synthetic fuels—despite their high cost and environmental destruction. Perhaps the major explanation for this are the differences in who will benefit from, and who will control, the energy which is produced.

the largest employers of hand weavers at that time, with four thousand employees under the putting out system, testified before a Parliamentary committee that there would have been ten thousand powerlooms at work within ten years of their first use had it not been for fear of having the looms destroyed (Bythell, 1969: 30, 74–76). Early historians such as Mantoux and Halevy also attributed the failure to develop the powerloom to fear of worker activity (Mantoux, 1928: 242; Halevy, cited in Bythell, 1969: 6). Historians today generally disagree and explain the failure to adopt the power-loom as due to its technical limitations and imperfections. The problem with this explanation is that in their early phases most inventions have technical imperfections—it is only attempts to use the invention that help work out the bugs. To be convincing, modern scholars would have to show that there were persistent and widespread attempts to use the powerloom, which nevertheless were unable to solve the technical problems. In the absence of such evidence, it is more reasonable to explain the technical imperfections of the powerloom as a result of its lack of use, which was in turn caused by a fear of retaliation by workers.

The most interesting and important example of the shaping of organization and technology to fit capitalist needs is the creation of management and industrial discipline. Though it is hard for us to realize it today, "the concept of industrial discipline was new, and called for as much innovation as the technical innovations of the age" (Pollard, 1965: 217). Capitalism confronted a major technological and organizational difficulty: the creation of management.

In the eighteenth century it was generally believed that factories, workshops, or other business organizations could not be success-fully run by managers. "This was a powerful argument against the enlargement of firms beyond the point at which an intermediate stratum of managers became necessary" (ibid.: 35). Adam Smith, for example, argued that firms run by managers were almost certain to be failures.

> The wealth of evidence was overwhelmingly in favour of these views, quite apart from the list of fifty-five joint-stock trading companies, quoted by the Abbe Morellet in 1769, which had been set up in various parts of Europe since 1600, "and which, according to him, have all failed from mismanagement, notwithstanding they had exclu-

sive privileges." Indeed, looking at the actual history of joint-stock enterprises, particularly those in mining and manufacturing industry, even from the less dogmatic point of view of the twentieth century rather than the antimercantilism of the eighteenth, such a conclusion is inevitable. These companies, no matter how well favoured by royal concessions, by monopolies or by technical innovation, came to grief almost without exception. The wonder was that there should be a body of men willing to invest in them in each new generation, rather than that the public should distrust their managers. (Ibid.: 25)

As Pollard documents, people just didn't think management-run companies, or companies above a certain size, could work—*and the historical record up to that point showed these views to be correct.* If the bourgeoisie had been faint of heart, and had accepted repeated failures as evidence of impossibility, we would never have had capitalism. But the bourgeoisie used the Hegelian power of negative thinking, and liberated themselves, if not the proletariat, from the tyranny of facts; they proceeded to do the impossible, by establishing successful large-scale, management-run enterprises.

> After 1750 developments in marketing and in technology made it imperative, if progress was to continue, that businesses should grow beyond the size which a single proprietor or a small group of partners could directly overlook. Firms *had* to cope, and they learnt to do so. (Ibid.: 36; emphasis in original)

For "progress" substitute the word "capitalism." The point remains: if development was to continue in the same path, the problem of industrial management simply had to be solved. It was solved, but only after repeated failures. Had development ended up taking a totally different path—for example, if domestic industry had triumphed over the factory in some way—we would now confidently declare that management-run large-scale operations were "impossible," and had been proven to be such by a great wealth of historical experience. Today, analogous statements are frequently made to the effect that worker control of industry is impossible, that we must have managers, owners, and bureaucrats—and this despite the fact that the evidence indicates that worker control is at least as "efficient" and "productive" as normal capitalist methods, even in the distorted and limited conditions of today (see Blumberg, 1973; Hunnius et al., 1973).

This chapter began with precapitalist work patterns, people working irregularly, following rhythms that were more or less nature imposed, to a considerable degree controlling their own work patterns, consuming at least a large fraction of the goods they produced. It ends with an established factory system: large groups of people engaged in cooperative labor, a fairly highly developed division of labor, with work patterns determined by capital, work taking place under capitalist supervision, and the product appropriated by capital. There can be no question that the development of the factory was a momentous change, one of the most important in the history of capitalism. The creation of the factory system determined the framework within which later developments took place. It seemed to me important to begin with this, both because the change was crucial, and because to start the analysis after the creation of the factory would be to take as given some of the most crucial and problematic aspects of capitalism.

However, it would be mistaken to believe that the rise of the factory settled all the issues, marked the final and definitive triumph of capitalist control over the labor process. Stephen Marglin writes that "the factory effectively put an end both to 'dishonesty' and 'laziness'" (1974: 51). Such a statement is perfectly in keeping with a view of social control being *imposed,* but it is at odds with a Marxist perspective, which focuses on the *process* of class struggle. The factory was a giant step, but the process and the struggle continued within the factory, both then and now, an ever-present part of life in a capitalist society.

The book now shifts time period, location, and industry, to consider a particular instance of that struggle among American machinists in the period from 1860 to 1920. The analysis focuses on precisely the questions which Marglin apparently believes were settled by the creation of the factory: continuing class struggle over how much work people were to do, in what ways, under what conditions.

3
Inside Contracting, a Contradictory System

A striking illustration of the differences between the factory of 1860 and the factory of today is the existence of the system of inside contracting, an early (postfactory) capitalist way of trying to discipline workers and get the most out of them.

Inside contractors were in most respects similar to independent subcontractors. The inside contractor made an agreement with the general superintendent or owners of a company to make a part of their product and receive a certain price for each completed unit. For example, for gun barrels alone the Winchester Repeating Arms Company had separate contractors to do each of the following operations: forging, drilling, machining, filing, fitting with sights, and either blueing or browning. Other contractors worked on one operation or another to help produce the stocks and lock mechanisms. The company also had regular day wage employees who made other parts of the rifle, inspected completed pieces, and assembled the parts into rifles (Buttrick, 1952: 208).

Inside contractors had complete charge of production in their area, hiring their own employees and supervising the work process. These were not independent subcontractors, however. They did all of their business with the company, and the company relied on them for the entire production of that particular item. More important, as inside contractors they worked *inside* the factory buildings owned by the company, and used the company's machinery, equipment, and raw materials. Inside contractors were employees of the company, and in most cases they received a day wage from the company as well as a certain amount per completed piece.

A simple example helps illustrate how the system worked. At the Whitin Machine Works in Whitinsville, Massachusetts, one of the most important manufacturers of textile machinery, Cyrus F. Baker was an inside contractor who had three employees in the period from January to March 1874. Baker and his three employees each worked about twenty-five days a month, and each was paid at a rate of about $2.25 a day, a monthly wage of about $55. Total wages of $660 were paid in the quarter, including the wages paid to Baker himself. During these same three months, Baker and his three employees produced 370 loom lathes, at a price of $2.25 per loom lathe, for a total credit of $832. Since the credit was larger than the wages that had been charged to Baker's account ($660, including the wage Baker paid himself), Baker was paid the difference, which in this case was $172. During the three months, Baker, like his employees, had received about $165 ($55 a month for three months). But since Baker was an inside contractor whose production unit had done well, Cyrus Baker received an extra $172 for his "job work" as a contractor. His income was more than doubled, while his employees received no additional payment for their performance.

In most variations of the system, contractors represented the only level of supervision between the workers and the superintendent of the entire factory or other top officers of the company. Contractors had far greater powers than the foremen of today, as they hired their own employees, on whatever basis they chose. (Many contractors, perhaps a majority, had members of their own families working for them.) They also fired their employees, and determined how the work was shared when there was not enough work for everyone. They set employees' wages, and decided whether or not workers were trained, how they were trained, and what skills they learned. In addition to these powers over labor, contractors also ordered materials, expedited delivery, controlled the levels of inventory, had sole responsibility for deciding on the methods of production, and even made innovations and introduced technological change. Finally, they supervised the day-to-day work process as do foremen today.

Great as the powers of contractors were, it is important to remember that the top levels of the company retained considerable power. The price the contractor received was determined by negotiation between the contractor and the company, and this price obviously had a big impact on the contractor's earnings and the wages he could afford to pay his employees. The company had the sole power to determine how many parts it would buy, though this did not absolutely determine the day-to-day production level, since the contractor had control over inventory. The company always had a right to change the product a contractor made, though contractors themselves sometimes introduced improvements or changes. Finally, the company maintained control over certain general policies—whether there was to be an eight-hour day or a ten-hour day, what time work started, whether or not workers could be union members, and so on.

Issues and Preliminaries

It is important to stress that inside contracting is a nonbureaucratic way of organizing production. The contractor differed from a bureaucratic official in a number of ways: in most cases he himself did production work as well as supervision, there were no set qualifications, no levels of authority, essentially no written documents or files were kept, and there were no codified rules (or very few rules). Almost all the characteristics of a bureaucracy are missing, unless the term "bureaucracy" is extended to include all nonegalitarian organizations.* Thus the system of inside contracting—if it were sufficiently widespread, and found in advanced industries—could provide considerable evidence against the view of modern organizational sociologists presented in Chapter One, which holds that factories must be bureaucratically organized in order to operate efficiently on a large scale and to employ modern machinery.

Even the few "bureaucratic" rules and procedures which did exist usually were evaded. Consider the situation at the Whitin Machine Works:

> In 1886 the shop was still as loosely decentralized as in 1860. Theoretically, full control over operations reposed in the superintendency, but in actual practice the superintendent was more a coordinator than an administrator, for his principal duty was to keep individual departments working together smoothly and in harmony. Real authority in

---

*There is no question that inside contracting *was* hierarchical, as will be discussed later in the chapter.

the shop rested in the hands of department heads who brooked no
interference in the conduct of their departments' affairs. . . .

Theoretically, [each department head] was required by the shop's
building orders to comply with a number of restricting regulations, but
in actual fact he ran his department with independent autonomy. Although he was required by the building orders to requisition forgings
and castings "in such quantities as shall be determined by the Superintendent" and was expected to include a report of "all spare pieces of
Castings or Finished Work on hand," in actual practice he seldom did
either. So well was he acquainted with the parts needed for the machines
made in his department that he could place his foundry and forge orders
from memory without any reliance on the superintendent. Most department heads took pride in their ability to have hidden away in some
obscure bin a store of spare parts on which to rely in a pinch. To accumulate such a store they often took it upon themselves to turn out a
larger number of pieces than an order called for. (Navin, 1950: 139–40)

The system of inside contracting, or job work, raises a number of
questions. (1) Was the system widespread and important, or is it just
an unusual curiosity? (2) Are there any special characteristics of the
industries where the system was found? For example, was inside
contracting limited to the most backward and small-scale industries,
or did it also exist in technologically advanced industries? (3) Was
inside contracting capable of handling or generating technological
progress and improvements in productivity? (4) What was the scale
of inside contracting? How many employees did contractors have,
and how much money did they earn? (5) Within a plant or industry,
was there a difference between the kind of work contractors did and
the work done by other employees? Specifically, did contractors do
only skilled work while regular employees did unskilled or semiskilled work? (6) What were the class relations between contractors
and their employees, and between the owners (or other top officials)
and contractors? (7) How and why did the system end?

Extent and Nature of Inside Contracting

How extensive was the system of inside contracting? If it was
unusual or unique it might still be interesting as a test case showing

alternative possibilities, but it would not be that valuable in attempting to understand the organization of work at that time. In fact, however, the system was very widespread. It was one of the key systems, perhaps the most important such system, in the transition to the modern organization of production.

Inside contracting is not just an American phenomenon: Sidney Pollard found the system to be common in Britain. It was dominant in mining with large subcontractors employing a substantial number of workers. In the cotton industry a large number of skilled workers each employed a few assistants, usually children. A survey by the Factory Commission in 1833 showed "that almost exactly half of the 20,000 child workers investigated were still employed by other operatives, the other half being employed by the firm; among spinners alone, however, 8,136 operatives under the age of 18 were hired by other workers, and only 1,043 direct by the firm" (Pollard, 1965: 25–26; 56–58). Subcontracting was also important in iron works, pottery, building, civil engineering, and transport. Indeed, Eric Hobsbawm has written that piece mastering (a British name for the system) and subcontracting are "almost invariable concomitants of rapid capitalist industrialization in its early stages" (1964: 356).

In the United States, I have found substantial evidence that indicates that inside contracting was widely used. The data I present should be considered as a very minimal statement of its prevalence, not only because of the limitations of my research, but also because the system was so commonly accepted that people at the time often did not think it necessary to note its use. For example, an 1880 publication of the Singer Sewing Machine Company describes the factory and production process in great detail, department by department, building by building, explaining what workers did, how many tons of iron were used each week, how close the tolerances were, and so on. The account does not make any mention of inside contracting, however, even though Singer production was organized around inside contractors (see also Roland, 1897, 12: 997).

Inside contracting dominated the iron and steel industry. In 1910 John Fitch wrote that the contract system "was a method of hiring labor which prevailed in the early eighties and which still exists in some of the independent mills" (1911: 99; see also Roland, 1897, 12: 994; Davis, 1922; Stone, 1974; Montgomery, 1976). Iron and steel plants were among the largest—fifteen of the seventy largest plants in 1900—and most advanced of their day.

Among small arms producers inside contracting was said to be all but universal. In the 1860s the Colt plant employed about 1,500 persons "to whom they pay monthly over $80,000 or nearly a million of dollars a year."

> Almost the entire manual labor of the establishment is performed by contract. The contractors are furnished room, power, material, heat, light—while they furnish muscle and skill—themselves and subordinates being all subject to the immediate government, as prescribed by the code of rules laid down by the company. They number several hundred—some particular manufacturers requiring only their individual exertions, while others employ from one to forty assistants. Many of them are men of more than ordinary ability, some have been connected with the concern since it was first established, and have rendered themselves pecuniarily comfortable by their exertions. (Bishop, 1864, III: 412)

Inside contractors were also used at the Winchester Repeating Arms Company (one of the seventy largest plants in 1900), Remington Arms (227th largest in 1917), as the main form of organization at the U.S. government arsenal at Harper's Ferry, and in exceptional circumstances at the arsenal at Springfield (Deyrup, 1948: 101, 207–9; Buttrick, 1952; Williamson, 1952; Navin, 1950; Nelson, 1975: 7).

Many of the largest and most famous machine shops (factories which themselves produced machines) used inside contracting: Lowell (one of the seventy largest of 1900), Pratt and Whitney (1,200 workers in 1900), and Whitin (1,700 workers in 1900) (Gibb, 1950; Roland, 1897, 12: 995; Navin, 1950: 546).

A miscellaneous set of other important companies, many of which made and assembled interchangeable parts, also used the contracting system: Reed and Barton silversmiths (800 employees in 1887), Baldwin Locomotive (13,000 workers, making it one of the four largest in 1900), Waltham Watch (one of the seventy largest of 1900), and Singer Sewing Machine (more than 4,000 workers in 1900, one of the twenty largest of 1900, used the system from 1863 to 1883) (Gibb, 1943: 70–71, 272; Converse, 1903; Bingham, 1903; Roland, 1896–1897; Moore, 1945; Waltham Watch Company records).

The list of industries and companies where inside contracting was used proves that the system was not confined to backward or small-scale industries. On the contrary, those establishments which are known to have used inside contracting are among the leaders of the U.S. industry of 1860 or 1880. Not only were they among the largest companies of their time, but they were also technological leaders of their day.

Specifically, many of these companies used interchangeable parts. Not only was the "concept of interchangeable parts the basis for mass production which was to revolutionize industry and society" (Ferguson, 1967; see also Lampard, 1967: 303), but interchangeable parts were "the very essence of American technology" (Oliver, 1956: 137). They probably represented the most important American contribution to the technology of the nineteenth century. Before the development of interchangeable parts, if a rifle or a musket malfunctioned during a battle, it was impossible to fix it with a part taken from another gun. Only a trained mechanic with the proper tools could make the part that was needed, and find a way to make the part fit. Unless parts can be interchanged, it is obviously impossible to have mass production in the sense we use the term today.

The development of interchangeable parts, which in accordance with the romantic theory of invention is often erroneously attributed to Eli Whitney (Woodbury, 1960), was actually a long process with many small steps. What was considered interchangeable in one generation would be rejected out of hand by the next generation. According to Charles Fitch, Eli Whitney's standard of interchangeability was within one-thirty-second of an inch, while the standards of 1880 (when Fitch wrote) were within half a thousandth of an inch (1883: 2; see also Roe, 1916: 141; Deyrup, 1948: 194). The precision necessary for full interchangeability could be achieved only through the use of specialized high-quality machinery. Improvements in interchangeability depended on the continuous development of new and better machinery, techniques and gauges, for only in this way could standards of accuracy be improved.

This continuing improvement in interchangeability is not the kind of thing that makes its way into general history texts. It involved a myriad of "small" improvements, the more important of which are the substance of histories of technology, the less important of which are forgotten. This development of, and improvement in, interchangeability took place above all in the small arms industry, which pioneered successive advances in measurements, gauges, and standards of interchangeability. The arms industry necessarily worked hand in hand with machine shops and the machine-tool industry. Increases in precision (and therefore in interchangeability) were possible only through improvements in the machinery that produced the parts. This is to say that interchangeable parts were pioneered and developed in precisely those industries that are known to have relied on inside contracting. Small arms were produced almost entirely under the contracting system and most of the important machine shops are known to have used contractors. The first industries to follow small arms in the use of interchangeable parts also relied on contractors. The Waltham Watch Company was the first company anywhere in the world to produce watches through extensive use of machinery and interchangeability, and is said to have refined the system to new levels of accuracy. Locomotives were first made from interchangeable parts by Baldwin Locomotive. In sewing machines Singer was the most important company from the early 1860s on. The first typewriters were produced by Remington, which had excess capacity after the Civil War and no demand for its rifles. The places which are known to have used inside contracting were on the cutting edge of capitalist industry of 1860 or 1880. They were not only among the largest enterprises, they were also the most advanced technologically. It was these industries which were looked to as examples of the best the United States could produce.

In fact, these were almost the only industries in which the United States technology led the rest of the world. At the Crystal Palace exhibition in London in 1851, the American exhibits were at first the object of scorn. Soon, however, the American exhibits made of interchangeable parts began to attract attention and admiration—the McCormick reaper, Hobbs' locks, Robbins and Lawrence's rifles ("the various parts made to interchange" as stated in the official catalogue) (Rosenberg, 1969: 7, 17).

> There was one American exhibit which exceeded all others in capturing the fascinated attention of visitors: Colt's repeating pistols. . . . Colonel Colt himself was accorded the singular honour of an invitation to address the Institute of Civil Engineers—apparently the first American to be so honoured. . . . The meeting was something of a major

event. It was attended by high ranking members of the British military establishment, eminent members of the engineering profession, and by such American dignitaries as Abbott Lawrence, the American ambassador, and Robert James Walker, former Secretary of the U.S. Treasury. (Ibid.: 15–17)

The British, in fact, were so impressed by the American exhibits that they named interchangeable parts "the American system." As a direct result of the exhibition, the British sent a high level committee of trained observers to study the American arms industry and suggest improvements for British arsenals. The British ended up buying 20,000 interchangeable Enfield rifles and 157 machines for the manufacture of arms (Roe, 1916: 138). With this machinery the British began to produce interchangeable parts for themselves.

Technological Change and Mass Production

Contracting dominated many of the largest and most advanced firms of the mid- to late nineteenth century. The system was especially prevalent in those industries that were most technologically advanced. It might still be argued, however, that contractors had difficulty with technological change, that these were the leading industries despite the presence of contractors, not because of them.

In fact, however, observers at the time saw contractors as the cause of technological improvement in these industries. It was obviously to a contractor's advantage to find a way to cut costs, since the price from the company was fixed, at least for a year or so. When the Singer company introduced new machinery they also introduced the contract system:

> These contractors were entirely in control of the work. They received with the contract small tools enough to equip the machine tools in their own departments, but the use of these small tools was optional with them; each contractor kept up his own tools, and, if he desired improvements in the tools, made them himself with his own tool-

makers, of which each contractor kept a larger or smaller force at his
own expense. (Roland, 1897, 12: 997)*

Contractors made use of their resources to good effect. A 1904
study by the Bureau of Labor reported that "The statement of one of
the manufacturers of a New England town as to the operation of the
contract system in his plant was to the effect that the contractors and
subcontractors under the old regime had invented nearly every
labor-saving machine in his establishment" (U.S. Commissioner of
Labor, 1905: 136). Probably the best study of the interchangeable
parts industries in the United States was made for the Bureau of the
Census in 1880 by special agent Charles Fitch, who concluded that
the invention of the special machine tools used in the small arms,
sewing machine, and related industries resulted from the system of
contract labor (Deyrup, 1948: 149). According to Fitch:

> It is to their [the inside contractors] interest and profit to increase the
> productiveness as largely as possible, and to the devices of this class, in
> the development of minor details to secure the greatest result from
> the smallest outlay, the improvement in productive efficiency in this
> and in kindred manufactures is largely due. The system of employing
> head machinists by piecework or contract may almost be esteemed as a
> germinant principle in the development of special machinery and a
> higher productive efficiency in the manufacture. (Quoted in ibid.: 149)

Some of these improvements resulted in significant new devices
which were patented. For example, Henry Woodmancy, one of the
contractors at the Whitin Machine Works, made a number of inventions, and assigned the patents to the company in return for particularly liberal contract rates (Navin, 1950: 143). But in many cases the
improvements were the kind of "minor" tinkering that never get
patented, and yet are a crucial part of continuing improvements in
productivity. For example, a foreman at the government arsenal at
Springfield, where contracting was not used, was sent to study
Remington, where contracting was used, and reported:

> In looking over the works of Remington & Co., it is easily seen how
> they accomplish so much, with such limited facilities. In the first place,

---

*The same situation existed at Winchester. "Most of the contractors were excellent
and ingenious mechanics, who operated their own machine shops and had enough
time to experiment" (Williamson, 1952: 89).

the work is all contracted to a few men. These men make their own tools and fixtures. . . . These contractors are good mechanics, and are always studying to make improvements, by which they can simplify the operations, and produce more work, thus increasing their profits. In starting the milling of the frame, they had the same trouble that we found in getting power enough to drive the mills for the purpose of cutting out the inside. But instead of increasing the size and width of the pullies, they reversed the cone pully on the counter shaft over the machine, thereby running two belts over the two larger grades of the cone they increased the power sufficiently to overcome the difficulty. I mention this as one of the many operations that might be cited, showing the simplicity with which they accomplish an object, and save expense. (Deyrup, 1948: 208)

The result of these continuing improvements was an equally continuous fall in the prices of the items contractors produced. Contractors were called such because they contracted with the company to produce certain goods at a stated price. The company and the contractor bargained over this price, which was periodically adjusted (usually once a year). The new price was almost always lower than the old price. Henry Roland, in an article which basically opposed the use of the contract system, admitted that "its use insures a constant reduction in the cost-price of work." Harold Williamson constructed an index of the rates received by contractors at the Winchester Repeating Arms Company. This index dramatically documents the extent to which contractors improved productivity and cut costs: it dropped from 100 in 1880 to 71.6 in 1890 to 51.0 in 1900. In just twenty years contractors cut their prices in half.

Contractors were not simply innovators. Their contemporaries credited them with being good managers as well. They reached this conclusion on the basis of examples such as this one from the Pratt and Whitney machine shop:

In case of an order for some half-dozen machines which could not be undertaken by the contractor who usually built them, as his department was full, the order was given to another department filled with workmen of a slightly higher grade than those employed by the contractor to whose department the job ordinarily would have gone, with the result of 70 per cent increase in cost over the contractor's rate, while the work was not up to the contractor's standard. Here were better mechanics, taking them at a machine-shop estimate, and in a high-grade shop with the best facilities procurable, thoroughly experienced in the special line to which the lot of machines demanded belong; and yet these good men in this good shop produced inferior work at a very greatly increased cost-price. It was such instances as these which gave the contract system its prestige, and kept it in force for many years, in spite of the certain features inseparable from the system and extremely unpleasant to managers. (Roland, 1897, 12:995)

Similarly, an article by John Converse tells of an incident at the Baldwin Locomotive Works where a broken elevator prevented a contractor from doing his work. "The contractor was losing money, as he could not turn out his tanks. The elevator was running inside two days; in the ordinary course of events two weeks would probably have been taken to put it in working order" (1903: 664). These examples were offered by knowledgeable observers as representative of the typical experience with contracting.

While the companies and industries that used inside contracting were advanced for their day, and produced precision equipment, it might still be argued they did so only by creating fine hand-crafted individual objects. This view is implicit in Arthur Stinchcombe's work, for example. Stinchcombe offers what could be taken as an acceptable definition of bureaucratic production:

> [It] may be defined by the criterion that *both* the product *and* the work process are planned in advance *by persons not on the work crew*. Among the elements of the work process planned are: (1) the location at which a particular task will be done, (2) the movement of tools, of materials, and of workers to this work place, and the most efficient arrangement of these work-place characteristics, (3) sometimes the particular movements to be performed in getting the task done, (4) the schedules and time allotments for particular operations, and (5) inspection criteria for particular operations (as opposed to inspection criteria for final products). (1959: 170)

While this is a reasonable definition of *bureaucratic* production, Stinchcombe calls it a definition of *mass* production, thereby implying that it would be impossible to mass produce if people on the work crew made the basic decisions.* Contractors (who were on the

---

*Note that Stinchcombe has taken the problem of whether mass production must be bureaucratic production and simply defined it out of existence (a typical sociologist's ploy). Oddly, the article is titled "Bureaucratic and Craft Administration of Production," but offers no definition of bureaucratic production.

work crew) and their workers made all the decisions Stinchcombe enumerates (in varying degrees, depending on the industry, company, etc.), and so by Stinchcombe's definition cannot have represented a form of mass production. Daniel Nelson, a historian, also has implied that contracting was incompatible with mass production:

> In firms that expanded slowly and continued to require highly skilled shop workers at crucial points, the [contract] system was retained, often into the twentieth century. In other companies that increased output and adopted mass production methods more rapidly, the contract system soon fell into disfavor. (1975: 37)

Historical evidence demonstrates that inside contracting, a non-bureaucratic system, was capable of mass production and rapid increases in output. At Winchester, for example, half of the gun shop consisted of contractors and their employees. Winchester production in 1880 was 26,000 guns; in 1890 it was 79,000; in 1900 it was 164,000; and in 1904 (the last year before contractors began to be gradually phased out) it was 225,000: a production increase of more than 800 percent in twenty-five years (Williamson, 1952: 460, 478). A second example is that of the Singer Sewing Machine Company, which sold 21,000 machines in 1863. In that year the company introduced new machinery and inside contracting as the means of organizing production. Perhaps contractors were seen as necessary to get the full benefit of the machinery; in any case contractors were introduced at the time that the technology became *more* complex. In four years sales doubled, in two years more they doubled again, and again the following two years, so that in 1871 Singer sold 181,260 sewing machines. It took seven more years for sales to double again, reaching 356,432 in 1878, and the next year the figure was 431,167 (Singer Sewing Machine, 1880: 34; Roland, 1897, 12: 997).* To place these figures in perspective, it is useful to realize that the General Motors Lordstown plant, famed for its efficiency, produced 323,000 Vegas in 1971 (Rothschild, 1973: 69).

It should be emphasized, moreover, that not only are there

---

*Another example of mass production and rapid increases in output under inside contracting is the Colt company during the Civil War: output went from 73,000 guns in 1861 to 188,000 in 1863. The Springfield Armory introduced contracting specifically to achieve a rapid increase in output; once the increase was achieved contracting was again phased out (Deyrup, 1948: 182, 197).

numerous examples of inside contracting being used for this kind of mass production, but the items produced were sophisticated machines made out of high-precision interchangeable parts. Singer insisted that their machines were precise "to the thousandth part of an inch" (Singer Sewing Machine, 1880: 70), and standards in the arms industry were even more rigorous (Fitch, 1883; Smith, 1885). How then could this be done? Was inside contracting a form of bureaucratic production?

The system of inside contracting definitely was a hierarchical one, in terms of decision making and regulation, as the rest of this chapter will document. However, hierarchy is not synonymous with bureaucracy. Bureaucracy is a Weberian ideal type; the question is not whether it is present or absent, but rather the degree to which the characteristics of bureaucracy are present, the extent of bureaucratization. Most of the characteristics of bureaucracy were either absent or only minimally present in the system of inside contracting. A key factor that distinguishes bureaucratic from nonbureaucratic systems is whether production decisions are made by members of the work crew or by full-time officials who themselves do no production. Contractors were actively involved in production, and most of the basic decisions about production were made by people (including contractors) who themselves produced the goods. There were very few rules which applied to contractors, essentially no chain of authority to regulate or limit the coercive means at the disposal of contractors, no methodical provision by central authority "for the regular and continuous fulfillment of these duties and for the execution of the corresponding rights" (Weber, 1958: 196), and often no written records by the larger enterprise on the activities of the contractor's unit. Central authority in general was virtually absent from inside contracting. Above the contractors there was usually only a superintendent with a couple of assistants, and even the superintendent served primarily to coordinate the contractors, not to control or direct them. All these fundamental aspects of bureaucracy were absent or only mimimally present in the system of inside contracting.

Closely related to the presence of a central authority is the degree of overall centralization. Studies of bureaucratic organizations attempt to assess the degree of centralization or decentralization by determining at what level decisions are made. How high in the organization do you have to go before an official has the complete right to hire or fire someone, to give raises, to spend money (and how much), without checking with any higher official? Are there rules that have to be followed (for example, regarding hiring relatives)? In the inside contracting system essentially any and all such decisions could be made by the first level above the worker, by a contractor who might supervise only two or three employees. And no one could question the contractor's right to make any decision, no matter how outrageous it might appear. The system was therefore extremely decentralized. Today it is difficult to find any employee with this degree of autonomy: even the head of a multinational division (for example, within General Motors the president of Chevrolet), would be subject to more rules and would be answerable for many decisions (i.e., hiring relatives at high salaries).

Since inside contracting was not bureaucratic, modern organizational specialists would have trouble understanding how it could mass produce and especially how it could mass produce items made of interchangeable parts. For interchangeability to work each piece had to be identical, and mesh with any other piece. To further complicate matters, frequently several contractors worked on the same item. At Winchester, "for example, gun barrels first had to be forged, then drilled, machined, filed, fitted with sights, and finally either blued or browned. At Winchester a separate contractor was in charge of each of these operations by 1880" (Buttrick, 1952: 208). This obviously made it difficult to locate the difficulty if any problems developed. Despite this, contracting, with its very loose central control, produced the goods. It could do so because pieces were made to such exacting standards (one-thousandth of an inch or closer), and because the company always inspected the work after each operation, whether the part was made by contractors or by ordinary day laborers. No company could trust contractors, foremen, or individual workers to produce parts which were always acceptable. The company itself always hired inspectors who checked the work between each of the operations, and the worker or contractor received credit only for those pieces which passed inspection. Usually contractors were charged a penalty for those pieces which did not pass, since this meant that the earlier work of others had also been wasted. For example, while the government arsenal at Springfield resisted the introduction of the contract system, it did so because it feared "conflicting loyalties rather than inferior workmanship, since the type of workers employed and the form of inspection used were the same under both systems" (Deyrup, 1948: 161).

The autonomy of contracting units regarding production decisions, the weakness of the central regulating authority, and the degree of decentralization of decision making are politically significant as indications (very partial and inadequate) of what a socialist society could do. All the bureaucratic layers which exist today obviously were not necessary to coordinate the work and produce the goods.

Scale of Operations

The basic facts about inside contracting—the extensive use of the system, the advanced character of the industries where it was employed, and the ability of contractors to generate technological change—not only demonstrate its historic importance but also provide solid evidence against the view that bureaucracy is necessary in order to use sophisticated machinery or achieve mass production. For a political assessment of the system we need to understand its class relations: to what extent did contractors act as managers or capitalists, and to what extent as privileged workers? To begin to answer this, consider the size of contract units and the scale of operations. A contractor with a hundred or more employees and with earnings six or ten times those of his average employee presumably did more managing than producing. On the other hand, a contractor with one or two employees probably did more producing than managing.

At the Waltham Watch Company during the period 1867–1870 the superintendent received $250 a month, and the up-and-coming person who soon afterward became superintendent received $292 a month. These were the highest salaries, and with the exception of five contractors to be discussed, no one received as much as $400 in *any* month during these four years. Unfortunately, the only data we have for Waltham Watch is the gross amounts received by each contractor. The company simply delivered this sum to the contractor: it made no attempt to determine or record how many employees the contractor had, what wages they received, or how much the contractor kept for himself. The lowest paid of these five contractors received an *average* of more than $500 a month, and four of the five received an average of well over $1,000 a month.* During 1869 and 1870 E. H. Owen received about $5,000 a month at a time when the highest salaried official earned less than $300 a month. Since the company required no further accounting, it had no formal way of knowing, nor can I know, whether E. H. Owen had fifty employees earning an average of $100 a month each, or two hundred employees earning an average of $25 a month each. Nor was the company likely to know whether Owen himself was earning $1,000 or $15,000 a year.

The Waltham Watch data thus emphasize the large size of some contracting units. Without this solid payroll data, Henry Roland's account of the situation at Singer Sewing Machine during the 1870s might appear unbelievable. According to Roland, "while some of the very small contractors made as little as $2,000 per year, some of the larger ones, running two hundred or more men each, made more than $10,000 a year" (1897, 12: 997). Unquestionably these are large figures, both for the number of workers and for the earnings of the contractor, but Singer was one of the largest, fastest growing, and most fabulously profitable companies of the age. E. H. Owen at Waltham Watch received over $60,000 in 1870, which would have allowed him to hire one hundred workers at $500 a year each (a good wage at the time), and still keep $10,000 for himself. Obviously, contractors running operations of this size have to be seen more as managers than as workers.

Company records for Winchester rifle confirm the large size of some contracting units, and also offer evidence on the earnings of both contractors and their employees. However, this data also demonstrate that not all contractors were this kind of semimanager. In addition to five large contractors (with forty employees and incomes

---

*In 1870, for example, Charles Moore received $8,091, James T. Shepard received $19,947, J. B. Gooding $35,578, Leonard Greene $30,011, and E. H. Owen $61,579. Similar but generally slightly lower figures were recorded for 1867, 1868, and 1869 (Waltham Watch Company records).

of \$5,000), there were also eight medium and five small contractors, the latter averaging just two employees and earning only \$1,400.

Table 3.1
Winchester Repeating Arms Company Gun Shop Contractors, 1881–1889

	Large	Medium	Small
Average number of contractors	5	8	5
Average annual total received by contractors	\$35,900	\$9,500	\$2,700
Average annual number of workers	43	11	2
Average annual pay of workers	\$ 700	\$ 650	\$ 570
Average annual income of contractors	\$ 4,800	\$1,740	\$1,430

Source: Adapted from Williamson (1952: 480) and Buttrick (1952: 216).

The Whitin Machine Works records emphasize a point which is suggested by the earlier data: contractors were not necessarily high-pay quasi-capitalists (see Table 3.2). Many job workers worked more or less alone, either without any help or with only a couple of employees. While such an arrangement might be very different from that of a contractor with forty or one hundred employees, in both cases the person was classified as a job worker or contractor. The contractor who worked with a single assistant is as much a part of the reality as the giant units with one hundred employees. The complete range of sizes, down to and including contractors with no employees, is one aspect of the situation which must be stressed.

Table 3.2
Whitin Machine Works 1874

Total received by contractor	Number of contractors	Contractors' average income	Average number of employees*
Below \$2,000	8	\$ 952	0.5
\$2,000-\$5,999	14	\$1,575	5.0
\$6,000 and above	9	\$1,640	14.0

Source: Payroll, job work, and contractor-employee record books, Whitin Machine Works Collection, Baker Library, Harvard University.
*Three contracts were shared by two people. In those cases I have considered all of the employees together as one unit, but have split the job work earnings in half, adding half to the wages received by each of the two contractors.

The complementary aspect which must also be stressed is that the largest units were often as large as the average enterprises of the 1870s and 1880s, when manufacturing concerns were far smaller than they are today (although even today a business with one hundred employees would not be considered negligible). The average number of employees for all industries in 1870 was only eight, and in 1880 it was less than eleven. Even in the industries with the largest units, many contracting units were about the same size as whole companies: in 1880 the average foundry and machine shop had twenty-nine employees, the average sewing machine company had ninety employees, firearms had one hundred twenty-four, iron and steel had one hundred forty, and watches (not including Waltham) had one hundred forty (U.S. Census of Manufactures, 1880). While contractors were not the equivalent of independent businesses since they had little of their own capital involved, they were responsible for more than just employee supervision. They selected and maintained the machinery used, planned and routed the work, controlled inventory, ordered materials, hired and fired workers, and so on, in addition to their responsibilities for production per se.

Related to the problem of the scale of inside contracting is the question of the relative importance of contracting in those factories where it was used. Contracting always coexisted with regular day-wage employees working under foremen. In the three companies whose records I have examined, contractors employed about one-quarter (Waltham), one-third (Whitin), and one-half (Winchester) of the total workforce.*

Understanding Contractors in Class Terms

Any analysis of inside contracting's significance must include not only the parameters of the system—the mechanics of its operation,

---

*Daniel Nelson says, "At the Winchester Company no more than half the total employees were ever under the contract system at one time" (1975: 36). This statement is contradicted by the only existing evidence, which shows that in thirteen out of fourteen years from 1881–1894 gun shop contractors had more than half the gun shop payroll. Since no records survive for the ammunition shop (though it is known to have used contracting), it is plainly inappropriate to compare gun shop contractors to total employment (Williamson, 1952: 478).

the extent of its use, the characteristics of the industries in which it was used, and the size of units—but also the class relations involved. Some people have tended to see inside contractors as workers, others as managers. In fact, of course, contractors were both workers and managers (as all students of the system recognize to one degree or another).

A current political debate focuses on the issue of what is variously called "the professional-managerial class" or "contradictory locations within class relations" (Ehrenreich and Ehrenreich, 1979; Wright, 1978). In this debate, as in much other discussion of class in the modern world, people often imply (or explicitly state) that class used to be a clear and unequivocal concept—almost everyone could be unmistakably identified as belonging in one of two (or three or four) classes—but now the situation is muddled; class is no longer such a useful term because there are so many people who cannot be clearly classified. The only nineteenth-century group which is seen as not easily classified into one of the two main camps is the petty bourgeoisie, and they are fairly easily demarcated.

The system of inside contracting shows that class has never been a simple concept. There has never been a golden age for Marxist academics when everyone could without effort be pigeonholed, when class as a concept was so unmistakably accurate that no thought was required and no problems encountered.

Contractors were in a supremely contradictory situation within class relations: on the one hand they managed workers and made a profit on each piece produced; on the other hand they often did production work, were generally regarded by capitalists as more-or-less workers, and they bargained antagonistically over contract prices in much the way that pieceworkers do. Contractors were capitalists in relation to their employees and workers in relation to their employers. The contradictory nature of the situation is a useful starting point, but it is not really a question of "class location." The term implies that there is a (structural) map identifying each class on the basis of certain enumerated characteristics or variables. No matter how well this is done,* it inevitably tends to make class a static

---

*Erik Olin Wright provides a good attempt to do what should not be done. Wright is aware that class is a relationship and he explicitly cautions:

It is important not to interpret the categories in these typologies as constituting discrete, empirical "groups." This would certainly be a violation of Poulantzas's (structural) category, instead of a dynamic relation. At the most, "class location" provides a rough and tentative beginning. From then on, however, progress is to be made by analyzing the historical dynamic in order to see what happened over time, rather than by refining static categories.

In any case, although contractors were pulled both ways, it would be a mistake to locate them as either workers or managers. To do so is to attempt to impose twentieth-century categories and modes of thought on a nineteenth-century world. It is anachronistic to say, as does Daniel Nelson, that "puddlers and rollers were also basically workers rather than managers" (1975: 39). This distinction assumes that workers do not manage and managers do not work, whereas the basic point about craft production in general and inside contracting in particular, a point which must be grasped if nineteenth-century work is to be understood, is that skilled workers controlled the details of the work process. They planned the work and they did the work, they supervised and they obeyed. Even when discussing inside contractors one cannot draw a clear line between "a manager" and "workers." Small inside contractors might not have even a single full-time helper, while large contractors might have more than one hundred employees, with a complete range between these extremes. A modern tendency is to specify criteria that will allow us to clearly designate some contractors as workers and others as managers or capitalists, perhaps with a middle range yet to be determined.

In one sense this is a useful approach, but a nineteenth-century observer would have been more likely to classify all of these people as contractors, and this approach also captures an important part of the nineteenth-century reality. As David Montgomery (1972) has shown, people in the mid-nineteenth century did not think in terms of a working class and a capitalist class. During the 1860s and 1870s in the United States, people were likely to think in terms of "producers" or "labor"—including workers, contractors, and factory owners—and oppose them to "speculators" or "financial monopolists"—including

---

view of social classes. The purpose of the typologies is to highlight the relationships among the various criteria, not to turn the analysis of classes and class struggle into a static exercise in categorization. (1978: 44, 46)

Yet ultimately this is what he (and Poulantzas) does. The great fault of such analyses is precisely their static quality.

bankers and railroad magnates. The widespread existence of inside contractors was undoubtedly one of the factors leading to this kind of terminology, and the way of viewing the world which it suggests.

Most of the rest of this chapter attempts to understand the contracting system in class terms. There are several parts to this analysis. First, inside contracting is compared to the helper system, which was very similar in important ways, and yet significantly different. Second, the wages and earnings of contractors and their employees are compared, and it is demonstrated that there were very large differences. Third, more descriptive information on the relations between contractors and employees is introduced. To avoid the conclusion that contractors were essentially managers, the next section focuses on the relations of contractors with top managers and owners, a situation in which contractors appear as workers. Finally, the system of inside contracting is assessed more generally, and the problem of why it was ended is analyzed.

Two alternative positions can be identified in modern analyses of inside contracting. In Katherine Stone's and David Montgomery's work the helper system and contracting are viewed as one basis of, and important evidence for, workers' strong position in the nineteenth century. There were many different forms of contracting, and the variant on which they focus was considerably more collective and less hierarchical than the contracting that is my main focus. As presented by Stone and Montgomery, the common form of contracting in the steel industry involved a contract with the work group as a whole; the work group then decided on what proportion of the total each of them was to receive (although the shares were far from equal). Another variation, fairly similar to this, existed at the Baldwin Locomotive Works of Philadelphia, at Reed and Barton silversmiths, and in the machine shop of the Winchester Repeating Arms Company. There were no fixed, permanent contractors; rather, any senior employee could contract for a particular job or for a limited period of time. The contractor would pick employees from among those already working in the shop; their wages were then charged against the contractor's account. The contractor could set the employees' wages, but obviously he could not pay them lower wages than they were accustomed to, or else they would not be willing to work with him. A worker might well be the contractor in charge for one job, and the employee of another contractor for the next job (Buttrick, 1952: 216–17; Bingham, 1903: 40–41; Converse, 1903: 663–64). Stone and Montgomery thus focus on contracting as a source of strength for workers, a basis of what can in some sense be considered a form of workers' control. For the kinds of contracting they consider this is a reasonable characterization and useful starting point.

A very different analysis is offered by John Foster (1974). Foster's analysis is particularly appropriate to my main focus, permanent contractors who received much higher incomes than their workers, although to a lesser extent the same approach can (and should) be applied to all forms of contracting. Foster argues that contractors were an aristocracy of labor, a group of workers with high wages and an incentive to support capitalism. These contract workers then served as taskmasters and pacesetters for the rest of the workforce. Though contractors might appear to be similar to the old craft elite, there is a crucial difference: "instead of enforcing discipline against the management they were now to do so on its behalf" (Foster, 1974: 231).

Foster argues that the rise of contracting in England between 1840 and 1860 was related to changes in the labor force and the methods of production. During the period that contracting was introduced, the proportion of skilled workers "in the Oldham industry declined from about 70 to 40 percent (with equivalent increases in the number of labouring and semi-skilled jobs). The number of juvenile jobs also went up" (ibid.: 227). In at least a couple of important instances, there were strikes against the introduction of the contract system. Less skilled workers were more militant than, and opposed to, skilled workers. Contractors and other skilled workers lived lives apart from the rest of the working class, orienting themselves to and becoming a part of a different culture. These were the people who attended church, taught in Sunday schools, and participated in the temperance and adult education movements. Temperance kept them out of the key institution of the working-class culture, the pub. Sunday school and adult education gave them opportunities to learn what the bourgeoisie wanted to teach them.

Foster's argument is interesting and persuasive,* and serves as a

---

*Unfortunately, the evidence he presents is only suggestive, not adequate to substantiate his claims. It seems clear from his own presentation that the situation was somewhat more complicated than he indicates.

useful counterpoise to the dominant view in the U.S. left, which sees contracting as strong evidence for workers' control. However, I think Foster tends to lose sight of the important point that aristocrats of labor are still *laborers*. They do not simply become agents of capital, "enforcing discipline . . . on its behalf." To regard them in this way is to make as serious an error as is made by Katherine Stone when she refers to skilled workers and capitalists as "partners in production." It seems to me that the basis for an understanding of the helper system and inside contracting must be a recognition that they represented an attempt to control the craft system *from the inside*. Capitalists left the craft system basically intact, but attempted to give selected workers a special incentive to cooperate with capital and management.

The nature of this strategy is crucial. As this chapter will attempt to show, contractors came from the working class and were viewed in important ways as part of the working class (to the extent that such a conception began to emerge). Their technical training and initial workplace socialization came from workers. Moreover, as contractors their relationship to capital continued to be basically antagonistic, and capitalists at least continued to view contractors primarily as workers. Thus, while contractors may be viewed as agents of control, they are totally different than capital's current agents. Today lower level white collar personnel (to some extent) as well as engineers, professionals, managers, and supervisors are very sharply differentiated from workers. The technical training and the general socialization of the key agents of control takes place in schools, outside of the workplace, in a social setting that is shaped by capital, not workers.

The Helper System

There is no clear line separating inside contracting and the helper system, and the people involved did not necessarily see them as separate, but at the extremes the differences are clear. A contractor who simply supervised the work of fifty or one hundred subordinates is clearly different from a skilled worker who was assisted by one helper. In the glass bottle industry, for example, each glass blower used to have a "mold boy" and a "cleaner-off": "The mold boy operates the molds into which the glass is blown, and the cleaner-off removes the particles of glass that adhere to the blower's rod" (Ashworth, 1915: 30). The glass blower could not do the work without help, though of course the help could have come from other trained glass blowers, working each position in rotation. If these workers were hired by the company, and paid by the company, then there would be only a slight resemblance to inside contracting. However, frequently these helpers were both hired and paid by the skilled worker, to whom they were solely responsible. Since such skilled workers were usually paid on a piecework basis, the worker was in a sense a small inside contractor.

There are two reasons not to regard such skilled workers as contractors. First, the scale of operations was usually small—such workers almost never had more than half a dozen helpers, and in many cases only one. Second, these skilled workers were usually strong union members. Many of the strongest unions of the nineteenth century were organized by mule spinners, glass bottle blowers, potters, puddlers, rollers, and molders, all of whom used helpers in their work. Journeymen who controlled the hiring and pay of their helpers often used these powers to coerce the helpers into joining and supporting the union.

Skilled workers not only planned the work, they also directed and controlled the labor of unskilled workers.

> Iron molders, glass blowers, coopers, paper machine tenders, locomotive engineers, mule spinners, boiler makers, pipe fitters, typographers, jiggermen in potteries, coal miners, iron rollers, puddlers and heaters, the operation of McKay or Goodyear stitching machines in shoe factories, and, in many instances, journeymen machinists and fitters in metal works exercised broad discretion in the direction of their own work and that of their helpers. They often hired and fired their own helpers and paid the latter some fixed portion of their own earnings. (Montgomery, 1976: 487–88)

The extent of this control was indicated by John Ashworth, who noted that "for years there has been a clause in the national constitution [of the Amalgamated Association of Iron, Steel, and Tin Workers] providing that 'all men are to have the privilege of hiring their own helpers without dictation from the management'" (1915: 75).

Skilled workers had various options they could adopt in regard to helpers. One might expect them to want as many helpers as possible, so as to do only the most skilled work, thus maximizing their own earnings and reducing the amount of heavy or dirty work they themselves had to do. Had skilled craft workers adopted such a strategy (and it was appealing to some) they would have been on the way to becoming inside contractors, and would truly have been artistocrats of labor, participating in the exploitation of their fellow workers, collaborating with employers in attempts at speed-up. It might appear that the more they controlled and directed their helpers, the more control the skilled workers had of their own work, and the stronger their position vis à vis capital. This is approximately David Montgomery's position when he argues that "the functional autonomy of craftsmen rested [in part] on the supervision which they gave to one or more helpers" (1976: 487). In contrast, many craft workers of the time recognized the helper system as an attack on their autonomy, not a support of it. Employers were the ones who favored the use of helpers, thus preventing craft workers from practicing all aspects of the trade, restricting them to the work defined as "most highly skilled," and coercing them to become pacesetters and low-level managers. Craft workers, and especially craft unions, generally opposed and tried to limit the use of helpers, insisting they do the work themselves (Ashworth, 1915: 16–18, 76). Glass bottle blowers, window glass workers, steel rollers, molders, plumbers, steamfitters, and machinists all tried to restrict the use of helpers.

Unions generally insisted that the employer pay the helper, so the journeyman would not have any material incentive to maximize production. For example, the *Iron Molders' Journal* of 1873 declared:

> We desire here and now to say that it is against the spirit and intent of the law, is against justice and common sense, is, in fact, unconstitutional for any member of the Iron Molders' International Union to employ a helper and pay him out of his earnings. No helper can be employed unless paid by the proprietor of the shop, and no piece molder can run a helper, whether employed by himself or his employer. (Quoted in ibid.: 68)

This struggle to limit or eliminate the use of helpers took place not simply between workers and capitalists, but within the working class itself. Individual journeymen often wanted to maximize their own earnings; the craft as a whole tried to collectively force its members to be workers only, with no material incentive to exploit other workers or maximize output. For example, the machinists' union provided that "'journeymen members refusing to do any kind of work belonging to the trade simply because it may be rough or dirty shall be subject to a fine or expulsion'" (ibid.: 39). It is important to note both sides of what is involved in this rule: on the one hand, some machinists plainly tried to avoid rough or dirty work and have helpers do it for them; on the other hand, the union as a whole was opposed to this practice, and insisted that its members do all the work, both pleasant and unpleasant, skilled and unskilled, which belonged to the trade. Such a policy helped avoid divisions in the workforce, maintain solidarity in the face of employer offensives, control access to the trade, and reduce employer incentives to introduce new technology (since the new machine would have to be run by a full-pay craft worker, not a low-pay helper).

Relations of Contractors and Employees

Unlike skilled workers who collectively limited the number of helpers in an attempt to increase solidarity, permanent contractors took on wage workers, thereby gaining a strong material incentive to enforce discipline and maximum output. Such contractors were separated from their employees in income, power, autonomy, and prestige. Payroll data on the comparative earnings of contractors and their employees give some illustration of this separation, as long as we remember that the numbers are only an indication of the relationship, not a measure of the categories called classes.

The best records for this purpose are those of the Whitin Machine Works, in Whitinsville, Massachusetts, one of the largest nineteenth-century manufacturers of textile machinery in the United States, with 574 employees on its May 1869 payroll. Thirty-three of these people were contractors, and they employed about 150 full-time workers, so that about one-third of the workers were either contractors or their employees. About one-third of the total workforce

Table 3.3
Whitin Machine Works
Inside Contractors and their Employees, 1874

Name	Total received by contractor and employees	Contractor			Contractors' Employees	
		total income	wage	job work	number	average wage
William Taylor	$ 333	$ 333	$ 192	$ 141	1	$406
Theodore Lawton	480	480	331	149	1−	390
A. W. Paine	901	901	514	387		
George B. Searles	1,030	919	391	528	.5	($111)
Welcome Hewitt	1,575	1,403	730	673	.3	($172)
Lewis Smith	1,635	1,229	489	740	1	$406
A. W. Thomas	1,789	1,399	571	828	1−	390
John H. Aldrich	1,913	917	220	697	1+	823
George P. Fisher	2,497	1,834	665	1,169	1.3	500
O. B. Moulton	2,582	674+	524	150+[a]	6	318
Joseph G. Allen	2,779	1,626	643	983	2	577
Henry C. Peck	2,790	966	670	296	3	608
Joshua T. Carter	2,863	1,718	625	1,093	2+	520
Orrin Wade	2,945	1,161	522	639	5	356
John and		809	433	376[b]		
Abraham Schofield	3,457	942	566	376[b]	4	426
James Hopkins	3,519	1,825	634	1,191	3	565
B. L. M. Smith	3,709	1,553	485	1,068	7	308
Cyrus F. Baker	3,739	1,706	589	1,117	3	678

Name	Total received by contractor and employees	Contractor total income	Contractor wage	job work	Contractors' Employees number	average wage
Robert Foster	$ 4,274	$2,005	$658	$1,347	12	331
Carlos Heath	4,737	2,351	473	1,878	4	596
Willard Hopkins	5,790	2,565	473	2,092	6	537
John Harrington	5,870	1,897	489	1,408	12	331
Warren Smith	6,059	3,034	545	2,489	8.5	353
Frederick Houghton	6,198	1,436	384	1,052	10	476
J. H. Burbank and		780	567	213[b]		
John Flannigan	6,486	718	505	213[b]	16	312
David Smith[c]	7,018	1,093	445	649	13	500
Oscar Taft	8,334	2,142	573	1,569	12	516
George L. Bathrick	9,530	1,884	535	1,349	22	348
C. H. Warfield[c]	11,179	1,759	551	1,208	23	400
Henry Woodmancy	11,414	1,516	520	996	16	619
James and		1,825	478	1,347[b]		
Charles Pollock	15,223	1,853	506	1,347[b]	23	502

Source: Payroll, job work, and contractor-employee record books, Whitin Machine Works collection, Baker Library, Harvard University.

a. Job work records for O. B. Moulton have only one entry for 1874. The rest of the records are apparently missing, but it is possible that this is all that he earned.

b. In those cases where two people shared one contract, I have divided the job work earnings evenly between them, though I have no way of knowing if the two contractors agreed on an even division, or if one of the two (say, the father) was the senior partner, perhaps taking all of the job work earnings, and the other (say, the son) was the junior partner.

c. David Smith and C. H. Warfield shared a contract for part of the year. I have divided everything from that period equally, and added it to their record in the last half of the year.

earned $2 or more per day (only 2 percent earned $3 or more), and I
have taken this as an indication of skilled labor. The lowest wage
frequently found in the shops was 63¢ a day.* Two dollars a day, six
days a week, all year long would produce earnings of about $600, but
given the irregularity of employment I have taken average earnings
of $500 as a rough indication of skilled work.

Table 3.3 shows the earnings of Whitin contractors and their
employees for the year 1874. The first column, "total received by
contractor and his employees," indicates the size of the total unit,
though at Whitin the employees received their wages directly from
the company paymaster, so the contractor did not actually handle all
this money. The next group of three columns gives the contractor's
total income for the year, and breaks this down into the day-wage
and job-work totals. The contractor was guaranteed the day wage
even if he lost money on job work. The "job work" column gives the
amount the contractor had left after his and his employees' wages
were deducted from the total value of what they had produced (that
is, job work is the excess of the contractor's sales to the company
over costs incurred). Finally, the last two columns show the average
number of employees and their average wage. Estimates of the
average number of employees should be treated with some caution,
since there was considerable turnover, variation in the number of
days worked per month, and many employees who fairly regularly
worked many days fewer than the rest of the unit.

As the table indicates, the total sum involved in the various
contracting units varied considerably, with two contractors receiving
less than $500 and three receiving more then $10,000. On the other
hand, there is very little variation in the *wages* received by contractors. All but the smallest contractors earned wages of about
$500 a year, the same figure I have taken as an indication of a
skilled worker. The earnings from *job work* (their profits as con-

---

*The reason for the odd wage rates is that the wages were expressed in shillings and
pence, not dollars, even though this was the United States in the 1860s and 1870s. A
rate of 12 s. was $2 a day; the lowest rate was 3s.9d., or 63¢ a day. Although the rates
were expressed in shillings and pence, the totals were given in dollars.

Also note that these wage rates should not be compared to those elsewhere without
remembering that the Whitin Machine Works was in a small town, not a metropolitan
area, and most of the housing was provided by the company at comparatively moderate cost (for more detail on procedures see Clawson, 1978: 293 ff.).

tractors) show considerable variation, from less than $300 to more than $3,000.

At least for this kind of contracting—which was probably as prevalent as the group contract found in much of the steel industry— it is clear that contractors were well above the bulk of the working class in terms of income, whether we want to characterize them as aristocrats of labor or as quasi-managers. Although contractors had many very highly skilled employees, only one employee of a contractor earned $750 or more in 1874, while thirty out of thirty-four contractors did so.* The mean income for contractors was $1,408; the median was $1,436. Since the highest wage found anywhere on the payroll was $4 a day, the *most* that a salaried employee could have earned is $1,250 (working six days a week, fifty-two weeks a year), or less than the *average* contractor. The average contractor made more than three times as much as the average employee. This is not simply a statistical artifact, the result of a few contractors making a lot of money: in every instance the contractor made substantially more than even his highest paid employee, and in all but two instances the contractor made more than twice as much as his average employee. At Winchester Repeating Arms Company the income differences were even greater than at Whitin, because some contractors ran larger operations than any at Whitin. Even small contractors, with an average of two employees, received well over twice what their employees earned ($1,430 compared to $570). As can be seen from Table 3.1, large contractors, with an average of more than forty employees, earned almost seven times as much as their average employee ($4,800 compared to $700).

These large differences in earnings make it extremely unlikely that contractors were being paid for their skill in producing goods, i.e., as workers. If they had been, there would be no sharp discontinuities between the earnings of the most highly skilled workers and those of contractors. The large break in earnings indicates that contractors' earnings were due largely to their supervision and direction of other workers. Thus a fundamental basis of the high incomes received by contractors was that they were not simply receiving an

---

*The one employee who did may have been about to become a contractor, replacing the person he worked for. The four who did not include one contractor for whom data on job work earnings are missing; two of the other three had no employees.

income for their own production; they were receiving a part of the surplus value produced by workers under their direction.

Marxists measure exploitation in terms of the rate of surplus value, which is equal to surplus labor divided by necessary labor. Ignoring substantial theoretical difficulties, this could be quantified in terms of the categories in the Whitin payroll as job-work earnings divided by employees' wages, if it is assumed that the contractor's wage was equal to the value of the goods he produced and his job-work earnings came from his employees' surplus labor.* This assumption does not hold for every contractor, and is not particularly meaningful for those with two or less employees, since these contractors probably produced their full share of the goods and their job-work earnings included surplus value which they produced. Leaving aside contractors with two employees or less, the rates of surplus value are still remarkably high. In only four cases is the rate of surplus value below 20 percent, and in only two cases is it 10 percent or less. More commonly, it is 50 percent or more. For example, Willard Hopkins had job-work earnings of $2,092 from total employee wages (six workers) of $3,225, for a rate of surplus value of 65 percent. John Harrington had job-work earnings of $1,408 from twelve employees who earned a total of $3,973, for a rate of surplus value of 35 percent. Plainly, contractors have to be seen as participating to a significant degree in the exploitation of their employees. The job-work earnings can only be understood as surplus value; they are far too high to represent the value of the contractor's labor power.

At the same time it is important to remember that the contractors received only a part of the surplus value produced by their workers, and probably not the largest part. The Whitins did not operate the company for the benefit of their contractors. The company made a substantial profit, which also came from the surplus value produced by its workers. Profit records do not begin until 1876, but in the

---

*This assumes that a contractor's day wage was equal to the value of all he produced, not just the value of his labor power. Since contractors' day wages were about average for skilled workers, if the contractor produced full time and did no managing (which would happen if he had no employees) he would produce a significant amount of the surplus value which he received as job-work earnings. On the other hand, if a contractor managed full time and did no production, not only his job-work earnings but his day wage also represented surplus value.

period 1876–1885 (ten years) the company declared dividends averaging $115,200 a year. In addition, the net worth increased in this period by $451,000, so that total estimated company profits were $160,300 per year. Since employment during this period continued at about the same level, this meant that the company made average profits of more than $250 per employee per year (compared to average employee earnings of under $500 a year, a rate of surplus value of more than 50 percent), in *addition* to the surplus value which the contractors kept. Even this is not the full measure of the surplus value extracted from Whitin workers: beyond this the state as well was supported out of surplus value, some of which came from Whitin workers (Navin, 1950).

This large difference in incomes was paralleled by a large difference in power. On an assembly line today, both foreman and employee are hired by the personnel office of the company, at wage rates set by some higher level in the company. The methods of production are determined by the technology of the line; innovations in technology are made by production engineers. Even the speed of the line is determined at a higher level. Decisions about layoffs follow rules negotiated between the company and the unions. The foreman almost always lacks the unilateral power to fire.

By contrast, the contractor of 1870 personally hired all his employees, in most cases without having to follow *any* rules or guidelines. Control over hiring gave the contractor great power both in his family and in the community at large:

A contractor would hire those who lived near his own home, and in many cases the names of half a dozen of his own relatives were on the payroll. For this reason, a large contractor was an important figure in his neighborhood. It was not at all unusual for a youngster who wished to become an apprentice to a contractor, to mow the latter's lawn and do all sorts of odd jobs for the privilege. (Williamson, 1952: 91)

The contractors of 1870 also had unilateral power to set employee wages. They often paid one or more of their employees more than they paid themselves; most paid at least one employee as much as they themselves earned. Wage rates were governed by custom or rules—in any case no employee at Whitin received more than $3 a day or less than 50¢ a day—but contractors could and did give their employees extra pay, perhaps as a piecework bonus, perhaps as a way of sharing job work earnings. About one-third of all contractors gave extra pay to at least some employees, sometimes comparatively insignificant sums, in a few cases almost as much as the wage itself. In general, people with high daily wage rates were much more likely to earn extra pay than those with low daily rates. The two contractors who paid out the largest sum in extra pay (Carlos Heath, four employees, an average of $110 each; Henry Woodmancy, sixteen employees, an average of $135 each) were also two of the contractors whose employees had the highest average wage.

Contractors had control over work assignments (as do foremen today, to a limited extent) and training. At a time when work experience was a far more important qualification than education, the contractor could decide which employees should be trained as skilled workers and which should do routine work. The significance of this is clear, since contractors were recognized as an important force in training skilled mechanics.

While contractors had some power to control inventory, they were also very dependent on the company's production. The earnings of contractors, especially large contractors, fluctuated widely from year to year, depending on business conditions. At the Whitin Machine Works, this is Henry Woodmancy's income for the years 1888 to 1891:

| 1888 — $5,216.51 | 1890 — $6,277.35 |
| 1889 — $7,931.78 | 1891 — $3,254.21 |

At Winchester, the earnings of large contractors went from an average of less than $3,000 in 1881 to an average of more than $6,000 in 1884, stayed over $4,000 for a few years, dropped to almost $2,000 in 1889, stayed low for many years, then climbed to more than $10,000 in 1898 (Buttrick, 1952: 212).

It is possible that companies forced contractors to bear the brunt of recessions, thereby lessening the effect on their own profits. For example, at the Waltham Watch Company, the annual report dated March 27, 1862, explains the policy of 1861:

> The object this year has not been to make money, which with about one third of the usual sales was clearly impossible, but rather so to conduct the factory as not to create new debt, to keep in employ the

principal hands and to lose by such contracted operations as little as might be.

The loss as proved by the accounts has been $4,010.85, that it is not larger, is owing in a great degree to the extreme generosity of the contract hands, who with but one or two exceptions in recognition of the extraordinary state of things, allowed their contracts to be suspended during the entire year and accepted from one quarter to one half less pay than that to which the company was legally bound. At least ten thousand dollars have been saved to the company by these worthy unselfish men. The officers also voluntarily abated a similar proportion of the salaries to which they were entitled. (Quoted in Moore, 1945: 42)

The evidence for this is not at all clear, however. Workers in general usually bore the brunt of a recession, and the presence of contractors may not have made much difference; the fall in the contractors' income would be only a dramatic illustration of what would have taken place anyway. At Waltham Watch, for example, in every depression the company made drastic cuts in workers' wages, introduced new machinery, increased the pace of labor, and so on. In the depression of 1857 the factory was closed down for a month, and reopened with wages cut in half. The same general policy was followed in the depression of the 1870s and in 1891 (ibid.: 30, 73–75, 82–85).

There was a wide gulf in income between contractors and even the most highly skilled workers. But was it these skilled workers whom the contractors supervised? Daniel Nelson has made such a claim: "In the arms industry, as in others, jobs assigned to contractors involved difficult precision work and demanded highly skilled workmen and close supervision" (1975: 36). John Duncan argued exactly the opposite, claiming that contractors fix "wages at the lowest possible point the men will agree to take," so that "unless the work is of such a nature that a rather low type of worker can be employed and taught the tasks to be done" the system would not work (1911: 219). The Whitin data allow us to see whether contracting was confined to jobs done by highly skilled workmen, as Nelson argues, or was limited to unskilled work, as Duncan claims. The evidence clearly shows that both are wrong. Duncan is completely off the mark—eleven contractors paid average wages of more than $500 per year, the figure I have taken as an indication of skilled work and an amount earned by the top third of the workers in the plant.

On the other hand, against Nelson, there were eight contractors who paid average wages of less than $360 a year, and even this figure conceals the large number of employees at very low wages. For example, B. L. M. Smith had seven employees, whose average was $308 for the year. Of his seven employees, one was paid $2.50 a day, one $1.67 a day, and five were paid at the lowest rate in the works, 63¢ a day. Assuming that wage rates are in any way a guide to the skill level of the employees, it is not tenable to argue that contractors supervised only skilled workers.* Other evidence confirms the wage data: contractors were used in situations where items were mass produced out of interchangeable parts; while this work was certainly not mindless or simply repetitive, it is likely to have been more routinized than other production, and is definitely not a case of contractors running operations whose main purpose was research and development. Another indication of the "unskilled" nature of contract work is that contractors often supervised women: this was apparently the case both at Waltham Watch and in the ammunition shop at Winchester rifle.† The inability to specify what sort of work contracting controlled is itself a significant finding: contracting was not a specialized tool, but a perfectly normal method of organizing production, which could work well for any type of work problem.

The data on incomes show that there was a gulf between contractors and their employees. Good information on the subjective aspects of relations between contractors and their employees is difficult to find: this information was obviously not likely to become part of any official records. There are, however, certain kinds of quantitative data which at least indicate some of the factors which must have shaped class relations. Two factors in particular emphasize

---

*Nor can it be claimed, as Nelson does, that contracting persisted when companies required "highly skilled shop workers at crucial points" (1975: 36) but disappeared quickly otherwise. B. L. M. Smith, the contractor whose employees earned the *lowest* wage, was one of the last four contractors left at the Whitin Machine Works (Navin, 1950: 149). Also note that since many contractors had more than forty employees it seems inappropriate to characterize it as designed to ensure "close supervision."

†Obviously there is nothing about women themselves to indicate that the work they did was unskilled, but in the social context we can assume that work done by women was at least considered to be relatively unskilled.

the likelihood of noneconomic ties between contractors and their employees, and thus the contradictory situation of the contractors: on the one hand, driven by economic motives and realities to exploit their workers; on the other hand, connected to their employees by many different kinds of social relations such that they had to take account of each other in more than economic terms.

The first factor emphasizing the noneconomic ties of contractors and their employees is data about who contractors hired. Aside from the obvious (but as yet undocumented) fact that contractors tended to hire their friends, they also hired their relatives. About one contractor in five had someone with the same last name as the contractor on the payroll. This is of course a minimal estimate of the hiring of relatives, since contractors might have hired their in-laws, nephews, cousins, or other affinal kin, which would not appear from the last names. Contractors often paid their relatives very high wages, even those who had little experience or who worked irregularly. For example, in 1874 Joseph Allen's employee John Allen received $3 a day (which put him in the top 2 percent of the plant's employees) even though he had not worked anywhere in the plant five years earlier, and probably did not have much experience or seniority. Contractors also hired the relatives of other contractors, in what may often have been reciprocal arrangements. The fact that a contractor's employees included his friends, his friend's children, his own children, his brothers, his neighbors, and so on, must have served to check the extent to which the relationship could be one of naked exploitation. In addition, it is not unlikely that many employees boarded with the contractors for whom they worked (Katz, 1975; Modell and Hareven, 1973; Nelli, 1970: 56–66; Gibb, 1943: 136). People probably had many different kinds of social relations, and had to take account of each other in more than economic terms. In many ways a contractor probably should be compared not just to a foreman, but also to the head of a patriarchal household.

A second factor creating noneconomic ties between contractors and their employees was the fact that contractors had once been skilled workers, and skilled workers could reasonably hope to become contractors. At any given time, about one-sixth of the workers earning $2 a day or more were also contractors. The evidence clearly indicates that it was such highly paid workers who became contractors. Despite the rewards available, contractors were not former company officials or the college educated children of stockholders. In 1874, at the Whitin Machine Works, nine people were contractors who had not been so in 1869. Eight of these nine had been on the company payroll as wage workers in 1869, the employees of other contractors. People who were employees together must frequently have formed friendships, may well have discussed how the unit should be run. For example, when Fred Houghton was promoted to contractor he lowered his own day wage and raised the wages of the other skilled workers in the unit.

Among skilled workers, the possibility of becoming a contractor undoubtedly influenced class relations, since the position and income of a contractor were substantially above those of an ordinary skilled worker. A 1903 article on the Baldwin Locomotive Works attempted to answer a question which the article said had dominated a meeting of the National Civic Federation: "By what singular good fortune, or by what surpassing subtlety and skill, has the Baldwin Locomotive Works been able, in the seventy-two years of its operations, utterly to avoid strikes and all labor troubles, and, with more than 13,000 men on its pay rolls now, to have proved invulnerable to proselyting labor unions?" The answer was twofold: all promotion was from within, and heavy use was made of the contracting system. At Baldwin people contracted for a particular job, called on the foreman for workers (using people already employed in the plant), paid the workers for that job, and then might disband the group. This meant that a large number of people were contractors at one time or another.

> Throughout these sixteen acres of buildings, four and six stories high, there are scores of such small groups of workmen. The contractor, always an elderly man who has spent many years in the shops, and could be entrusted, if need be, with the superintendency of the works, clad in the familiar checked jumpers, sits at his crude desk figuring, or moves among his men keenly calculating how the work goes on.
>
> The men know him, trust him, and respect him. And therein lies the illustration of the inspiration that came to Charles T. Parry, whose workmen know that if they loaf they will hurt the firm, but they will hurt that contractor first, and he is one of them. Shrewd? Indeed, it is a stroke of genius. And then, on the other hand, working in such close

touch with a boss, the men know that their own rights will be protected, that they will have every possible chance for advancement and pay. (Bingham, 1903: 40)

The contracting system makes the contractor as well as his employees less likely to oppose capital: "It is a curious study in human nature to behold how a little authority transforms a man" (ibid.).

Such factors pushed contractors and their employees to cooperate with each other and relate in noneconomic ways, but the contradictory character of their situation meant that other factors pushed contractors to exploit their workers. Most basic was the reality that contractors had a strong material interest in maximizing output, whatever the effect on their employees. For example, when the U.S. government arsenal at Springfield, Massachusetts wanted to introduce a new water-powered machine to turn gun stocks, the workers who had been making stocks feared they would lose their jobs and therefore refused to use the machine, insisting it was worthless. Given the social relations of society and of the plant, the workers had every reason to take this position: if the machinery succeeded it would not lighten their labor or increase their earnings, but many of them would be out of work. The arsenal feared that its workers would successfully sabotage the new stocking machine, and so arsenal officials introduced a contractor, who then had every incentive to make a success of the new machine (Deyrup, 1948: 97).

The extent of mobility from wage labor to contract status may have reduced the economic exploitiveness of contractor-employee relations, but the possibility of permanently escaping the working class by becoming a successful businessman pushed contractors to keep driving their employees. Workers who became contractors had the possibility of using their incomes and positions as contractors to start themselves in business. At least one of the most important machine shops of the nineteenth century, Pratt and Whitney, was started by two former contractors. After a spell as a contractor elsewhere, Francis Pratt joined Amos Whitney at one of the most famous nineteenth century "universities" for the training of mechanics—the Colt arms factory. (Amos Whitney's father also worked at Colt.) In 1854 Whitney and Pratt both left Colt for the Phoenix Iron Works, "where they worked together for ten years, the former as a contractor, the latter as superintendent. Whitney was earning over eight dollars a day when he left Colt and took up the new contract work which offered at the beginning only two dollars a day" (Roe, 1916: 177–78). In 1860 Pratt and Whitney rented space and began manufacturing—but they continued to work at the Phoenix Iron Works. They expanded rapidly and in 1862 took in a third partner, each of the three contributing $1,200. (In 1870, eight years later, the mean capital for all manufacturing establishments was only $8,400, so their enterprise, while small, was not unusually so.) Still Pratt and Whitney continued to work at the Iron Works, with the third partner taking charge of the shop. Not for another two years did they leave their previous positions, which presumably were providing them with money to live on and capital to invest in their new business. The fact that they could hold both jobs simultaneously for four years is obviously an indication of the power contractors had to come and go as they pleased. Pratt and Whitney's business expanded rapidly:

> From $3,600 in 1862 their net assets grew in four years to $75,000, and during the three years following that they earned and put back into the business more than $100,000. In 1869 the Pratt & Whitney Company was formed with a capital of $350,000, later increased to $500,000. In 1893 it was reorganized with a capitalization of $3,000,000. (Ibid.: 179)

The route from skilled worker to contractor, and from contractor to manufacturer, provided real possibilities for upward mobility.*

So far the evidence I have presented on subjective relations all tends to indicate contracting should have been an ideal system from capital's point of view. Contractors apparently had huge incentives to maximize output and keep costs to a minimum, thus ensuring capital an agent in the work group. If personal relations between contractors and employees were good, this could itself be an im-

---

*Herbert Gutman (1976b) has shown that many locomotive, iron, and machinery manufacturers in Patterson, New Jersey in the period 1830–1880 started life as workers. Gutman's article makes no mention of inside contracting, but it seems very likely that many of the people who became successful manufacturers had prepared for this by being inside contractors. As contractors they would have gained experience in managing production, and they would have had the opportunity to accumulate capital far more rapidly than could be done on workers' wages. Contracting was very common in exactly those industries where Gutman found substantial upward mobility, and contracting seems an ideal preparation for beginning a small business. The connection between contracting and mobility in these industries should be investigated.

portant barrier to class-conscious action by workers. The fragmentation of workers among a large number of contractors, with conditions varying greatly from contractor to contractor, must have made it difficult to achieve solidarity. All of these are arguments as to why it would be difficult to unionize under a contracting system, and yet there must be another side to the story, because Henry Roland insisted that while "strikes may be rare under a contract system . . . there is still a feeling of antagonism, growing out of opposing interests, which is unfavorable to the best results" (1897, 12: 996).

Moreover, Winchester took a key step toward abolishing the contract system (specifically, the contractor's power to hire) as a direct response to a union organizing drive. Evidently the fragmentation and personalistic relations made it more difficult to enforce uniform capitalist policies just as they made it harder to achieve working-class solidarity.* The International Association of Machinists "attempt at organization seems to have greatly disturbed the management," which responded by taking control of hiring. The superintendent screened all employees and used a veto power specifically to exclude possible union organizers or militants. "From the beginning [the superintendent's] clerk made a special notation after the names of all those suspected of union activity and all those fired for reasons which would militate against rehiring. The notation used is rather amusing—ROBAL, which is LABOR spelled backwards" (Buttrick, 1952: 218; Williamson, 1952: 135). It seems likely that at least some contractors, many of whom had friends and relatives among the workers, were willing to tolerate the union. It is easy to imagine how difficult it could make life for the company if there were militant union activists who were beyond company discipline (on firing, wages, output, being away from their work, etc.).

Relations of Contractors and Top Officials

A focus on the relations between contractors and their employees emphasizes the large gap between them and indicates the incentives

---

*These contractors may have resembled the small entrepreneurs studied by Herbert Gutman (1976b), people who had personal connections to workers and tended to side with them in strikes.

contractors had to move toward becoming managers or officials rather than workers. Compared to their employees contractors seem much like managers or capitalists, but the contradictory nature of their position is evident in the fact that compared to their employers contractors seem much like particularly powerful and (potentially) troublesome workers.

If a determination were made based solely on income, large contractors at least would be classified as belonging in the same category as the very highest managers and officials. At the Winchester Repeating Arms Company, for example, during the 1880s the average annual income of the president was $14,200, and the average top official made $7,600. Contractors made nearly equivalent sums: the largest contractor made an average of $10,800, and the average large contractor $4,860, incomes which are far closer to top management than to the average worker's $700 or less.*

However, while contractors' incomes and degree of autonomy suggest an equality with management, contractors were apparently seen by workers, and even more so by managers, as being closer to the working class than they were to managers and officials. At the Baldwin Locomotive Works workers would not strike because this would hurt the contractor and "he is one of them" (written by an adviser to management). When George Marston Whitin calculated what income his contractors "should" earn, he referred to contractors sometimes as "job workers," sometimes simply as "workers."

The basic relationship of antagonism centered around the bargaining between contractors and company officials over the contract price, which was in many ways similar to workers (especially pieceworkers) bargaining for higher wages. Periodically, in many cases once a year, the contract price would be reviewed. Either the old price would be allowed to stand, or a new price would be "agreed" upon. If there was an adjustment, the new price was always lower than the old one. Since the company knew very little about how to manufacture the item in question it was difficult to tell if the contrac-

---

*As another comparison, the average stockholder received $3,090 from Winchester dividends, and the two largest stockholders (descendents of the founder) each received $40,000 a year. The stockholders obviously did not do any work to earn their money, and they may well have had other investments. Since the top day wage was only about $5 a day, workers' incomes could not go above about $1,500.

tor and his employees were doing their best or were restricting output and holding back innovations. The contractor's greater knowledge about production was one source of his power in the bargaining process. In some situations the company did not even know what income the contractor was receiving, and when a contractor made a number of different items he could be making a large profit on some items and taking a loss on others.

Contractors knew (just as workers on piecework know) that if their incomes appeared inordinately high, the company would cut their contract price. They therefore tried to keep their apparent profits as low as possible whenever a price cut seemed likely. For the same reasons, a contractor would not want to introduce a technological innovation which reduced the cost of manufacture until after a price for the coming year had been agreed on. Price cuts were an important feature of the contractor's world. For example, in 1869 Cyrus Baker was paid $2.50 for each loom lathe he and his employees finished. In 1870 the rate was cut to $2.25. Though this cut is "only" 10 percent, there are few companies today that could survive an across the board price cut of 10 percent. Moreover, contractors' rates were often cut by substantially more. At Winchester between 1876 and 1880 "the price paid for polishing gun parts was cut over 40 per cent, case hardening and the manufacture of screws and sights each 45 per cent. Drilling and machining barrels, the receiver shop, and the contractors making small parts and gunstocks were similarly dealt with" (Buttrick, 1952: 211). A contractor's ability to keep the company from cutting his prices must have been one of the keys to success in contracting. Without this ability a contractor might soon be poor or out of business, even if he produced high-quality goods, managed his workers well, kept down production costs, and continually made improvements.

The contradictory nature of this bargaining process is best summed up by Henry Roland, writing in 1897 in *Engineering Magazine:*

> First of all, the contractor is and must be supreme in his department; he must fix the wages of his men, must have absolute control of them, must hire and discharge his help at will, and so becomes in effect an independent ruler in the territory of the management. If, as is the case in some shops, the management deals solely with the contractor, and delivers into his hands the savings of his department in a lump sum,

the contractor paying his own men, then the management is wholly ignorant as to the compensation obtained by the contractor himself and of the cost of the work to the contractor, who keeps his own books, and is, in every sense of the word, an independent power, and a power which must obviously be treated as an equal, although actually occupying the anomalous position of a belligerent inferior. The interests of the contractor are directly opposed to those of the management, and the yearly "adjustment" of prices, always involving a reduction of the contractor's prices, is a constant source of perplexity and dissatisfaction to both parties. The management sees the contractor, in spite of the yearly cut in prices, constantly drawing larger pay than he could obtain as a foreman, because he seems always able to improve his methods so as to reduce the cost of his product to himself; hence the management believes that the contractor holds his improvements in reserve, and is, in effect depriving the concern of the use of valuable methods of reducing cost known to himself alone, and kept back to neutralize the effect of future reductions in prices. The contractor is not unmindful of his own efforts in reducing the cost of work, which he rightly believes to have resulted greatly to the benefit of the management, and to justly entitle him to a portion of the increased profits arising from diminutions of cost effected by his skill and ingenuity. Hence the contractor, like the piece-work man whose piece-price is constantly reduced, finally ceases to exert himself, and makes his own gains so small as to ensure himself against reduction. It is very clear, therefore, that the contract system does not tend to develop ideal conditions of harmonious relation between the contractor and the management. . . . (1897, 12: 995–96)

The bargaining with the owner or top official over contract rates put contractors in a position very similar to ordinary workers disputing piece rates. While some factors may have pushed contractors to become like top managers or capitalists, this bargaining process forced contractors to recognize that in important respects they were in a position very similar to ordinary workers, and were often treated accordingly. Moreover, in any dispute over contract rate cuts, the contractor was likely to find allies in his employees (who would wish to avoid having their pay cut) at the same time that he was in conflict with capital.

Contractors' contradictory situation was a result of being middlemen for capitalists who had not yet taken over the full responsibilities of capitalists. In attempting to understand the contradictory nature of inside contracting, and the dynamic of the worker-contractor-capitalist interaction, one of the best places to begin is with Harry Braverman's statement that "such methods of dealing with labor bore the marks of the origins of industrial capitalism in mercantile capitalism, which understood the buying and selling of commodities but not their production, and sought to treat labor like all other commodities" (1974: 63).* For example, if the Waltham Watch Company could contract with P. S. Bartlett to make the "P. S. Bartlett" style watch for $9, and could sell the watches for $12, the company essentially could operate like a merchant not at all concerned with production (the company at that time was actually owned by people who had been and continued to be large-scale merchants). With production costs determined in advance, all the company had to watch was overhead (including machinery), materials, and sales. At the Whitin Machine Works "with the cost of labor pre-determined, the owners found that they had to watch only material costs, especially the cost of pig iron, to know at what level to quote machinery prices" (Navin, 1950: 146). Capitalism, in this form, was simply a matter of buying low and selling high. While bourgeois economists at that time, and even today, understand capitalism in that way, as something that happens in the marketplace, Marx pointed to the *underlying* relation: capitalism as such only emerges when there is buying and selling of that very special commodity, labor power. The success of *any individual* capitalist depends as much on his or her success in the buying and selling of commodities as it does on ability to extract surplus value, but the success of the capitalist *class* can come only through the extraction of surplus value from the working class.

---

*I disagree with some other aspects of Braverman's discussion of inside contracting. Braverman lumps together the putting out and inside contracting systems, and says these "systems were plagued by problems of irregularity of production, loss of materials in transit and through embezzlement, slowness of manufacture, lack of uniformity and uncertainty of the quality of the product. But most of all, they were limited by their inability to change the processes of production" (p. 63). This statement is questionable in its application to the putting out system, but is almost completely inaccurate in its description of inside contracting, as the above chapter attempts to demonstrate. Braverman has here believed conventional sources on subjects that were not central to his investigation. Most of Braverman's brilliant book is distinguished precisely by its rejection of the conventional wisdom, but in this instance he too has fallen prey. This is simply another example of the difficulties in creating a new analysis, and a demonstration of the hegemonic power of the conventional wisdom.

As long as the details of the production process were not under the direct control of capitalists, capitalism was weak and only partially developed. It is not only that the contradictions are more obvious when one group of people do *all* the work of producing (including the planning and coordination) and another group takes most of the benefits. More important than these concerns about legitimation is the actual control of the production process. The fundamental task of capital is to extract surplus value and accumulate capital. Under the system of inside contracting this was done for capital by a quasi-autonomous power, rather than being fully under the control of the capitalist. Thus contracting is essentially a transitional stage.

The dynamic of capitalism is to take more and more control over the labor process (although struggles by workers are a crucial counteracting tendency). This tendency is as evident in the evolution of the contracting system as it is in its eventual replacement and the rise of Taylorism. Originally, the contractor had essentially total control, and the company knew almost nothing about the contractor's operation. At Waltham Watch, for example, the contractor of 1870 was simply given a sum of money based on the contract price and the number of units delivered. The contractor had complete control over this money and paid his employees. The company had no records or formal way of knowing the number of the contractor's employees, their names, their earnings, or how much money the contractor kept for himself. A similar system prevailed at Winchester until the depression of the 1870s. In 1881 Winchester began to keep "full" records, but even then the company only knew how much each employee was to receive as determined by the contractor. It could not tell whether pay was by the day or the piece, how many hours the employee had worked, or how many pieces he or she had produced.* In the absence of records it was obviously very difficult to squeeze the contractors—the company could not even tell which

---

*At Winchester, women were 25 percent of the total workforce, and 50 percent of the workers in ammunition production (Williamson, 1952: 84). This must have had a substantial impact on the relations of contractors and employees in the ammunition shop. Unfortunately, records for the ammunition shop do not survive, though apparently the same set of rules and procedures governed contractors in both the ammunition and gun shops.

contractors had large earnings and which were barely making a living.

Henry Roland provides a clear statement of how and why this system was changed, citing the history of the Singer Sewing Manufacturing Company:

> At first each contractor hired, paid, and discharged his own men; with them the company had no dealings whatever, exercising over them only general authority in the matter of shop regulations. . . . It will be seen that, with this order of things, the management could be kept in almost total ignorance of the real course of affairs in any contractor's department, and, in point of fact, was kept in ignorance so far as the contractors could avoid giving information. . . .
>
> This led very naturally to a close scrutiny of the situation, and resulted, first, in the payment of the contractor's men by the company directly. This looked like a very innocent and unimportant change, but it was really the thin end of the wedge which was ultimately to deprive the contractor of his profits. As soon as the company paid the workmen, it had correct information as to the piece-cost of the work, and could also, of course, discover which pieces were high and which low in price, in view of the labor time consumed in production. Hence the company became able to approximate more closely to the contractor's possibilities of cost reduction for the next year, and so could more intelligently "adjust" or reduce the prices offered in the annual contract. (1897, 12: 998)*

This is a clear statement that bureaucratic record keeping was introduced as part of an attempt to control employees, not to improve the competitiveness of the company's pricing, not to improve the product. Though at first this record keeping and control strategy was very simple, over time it was forced to expand remarkably.

This record keeping allowed the company to gradually reduce the earnings of the contractors. A clear demonstration of this process is the rate-setting procedure at the Whitin Machine Works. George Marston Whitin made no attempt to learn about production so as to

---

*Note once again the opposing approaches adopted by inside contractors and craft unions. Unions insisted that the best approach was to enforce equality and solidarity so that no worker had either the ability or the temptation to put themselves above other workers and/or participate in their exploitation. Contractors attempted to become small-scale capitalists, maximizing their power over their employees. The above quote demonstrates one of the main problems with this approach: big capitalists always tend to drive out small.

establish a "fair" *price* based on a scientific determination of the difficulty of making an item, how well the company could do if it made the part itself, or anything of like kind. Instead Whitin tried to establish a "fair" *income,* the amount a contractor-worker "should" earn, based on his class position. Rates were systematically cut, since Whitin saw no reason why contractors should earn significantly more than skilled workers. Whitin

> gradually reduced the level of jobbing rates until they yielded low net returns. A memorandum book kept during the closing months of 1890 shows clearly how he went about making his reductions. First he estimated what income he thought a certain "job worker x" [contractor x] should receive commensurate with his ability. Then he compared that "fair" income with the income "worker x" was likely to receive during the year at going job rates and under existing business conditions. If it looked as though the "fair" income of "worker x" ought to be 25 per cent less than his "likely" income was going to be, Whitin reduced all the jobbing rates in "worker x's" department by an appropriate amount. (Navin, 1950: 148)

At Winchester the same approach was used: according to Buttrick one of the main difficulties with inside contracting "was the problem of controlling the income earned by each contractor so that income would match the individual's position in the social hierarchy" (Buttrick, 1952: 210).

At Winchester, as at the Whitin Machine Works, as time went on life was made more difficult and less remunerative for contractors. Contracts were renegotiated more regularly and scrutinized more carefully. Contractors' incomes were sharply reduced; contractors became reluctant to bid on certain jobs. "After 1890, the position of some of the large contractors was weakened by dividing the jobs among two or more individuals" (Williamson, 1952: 136). The largest contractor was made the new superintendent, and used his knowledge and experience to weaken the position of contractors. In addition to reducing their incomes, he did this by interfering with contractors' control over their workers. As a first step, "he insisted that every contractor and every worker be on the job when the plant opened in the morning. He had the gates locked one minute after the whistle blew so that late-comers had to walk through his office before going to their jobs" (Buttrick, 1952: 214). Much more important, soon thereafter contractors lost their complete control over hiring (at Whitin around 1890, at Winchester around 1900). Hiring passed from the control of the contractor to the superintendent's office. As previously discussed, at Winchester this was an explicit attempt to control a union organizing drive.

It is important to note how late the system of contracting remained as a major way of organizing production. Though its importance may have begun to decline as early as the 1870s (at Waltham Watch it was ended in the 1870s, and at Singer Sewing Machine in the 1880s), it persisted into the twentieth century at many machine shops, including Pratt and Whitney and the Whitin Machine Works, at Baldwin Locomotive, at many arms factories, including Winchester, and in some of the steel industry. At Winchester, for example, records on the contract system survive only for the gun shop, though the cartridge shop and machine shop also used the contract system. The gun shop had about one-half to two-thirds of total employment. Gun shop contractors alone received 32 percent of the *total* payroll as late as 1904, which probably mean they accounted for *half* the payroll in the gun shop. Thereafter the contracting system was quickly phased out—by 1908 contractors had only 10 percent of the total payroll, in 1912 they had only 7 percent, and in 1914 there were no contractors left. Even after this, however, a variation of the contracting system continued to be used in the machine shop at Winchester "long after the system was discarded elsewhere in the plant" (ibid.: 216), that is, after World War I.

Why was the system of inside contracting abolished? The two most important reasons were, first, the attempt to shift income from contractors to the company, and second, the wish to establish and maintain an "acceptable" social hierarchy. Neither considerations of efficiency nor dissatisfaction with inside contracting's technical capacity to perform the work were significant issues at the time.

The first and most obvious reason was that contractors made a lot more money than would foremen fulfilling approximately the same function. At Winchester large contractors had an average of forty-three employees and earned an average of $4,800 per year; at the Whitin Machine Works contractors had an average of seven employees and earned an average of $1,408 per year. At Whitin the highest pay received by any day-wage employee was $4 a day, and less than 1 percent of the workers received this much. Even had foremen been paid twice what their average employee earned—and by the standards of that day or this those would be high wages for a foreman—they would have been receiving far less than contractors. The savings to the company could easily amount to $20,000, $30,000, or $100,000 a year. Any company would be only too happy to add this much to their annual profit. According to Henry Roland, it was for exactly this reason that Singer ended the contract system. Contractors' earnings "in all cases [were] vastly more than they could have obtained elsewhere for their services" (Roland, 1897, 12: 997). With tighter controls on contracting, "it was true that the price of work was annually reduced, and that the quality of the work steadily improved, but the company did not view the great gains of the contractors with any approach to satisfaction" (ibid.: 998).

It seems clear that since contractors were earning such high incomes, replacing the well-paid contractors by comparatively low-paid foremen should have cut costs, assuming that the company could manage the work as efficiently as the contractor. The only instance that I know of where records were kept is the Winchester Repeating Arms Company.

> Henry Brewer, one of the college-trained executives who had come with the company, was superintendent of the cartridge shop.* He kept a careful record of costs on all jobs during the two or three years after they were taken off contracts and compared it with similar costs under the contract system. According to his account . . . . "I had expected that we would produce the goods cheaper . . . but to my surprise I found that in practically every instance costs were increased. . . . I do not know what the Gun Department experience was but I think it was somewhat similar." (Williamson, 1952: 138)

The problem, obviously, was that the college-educated company executives could not run the work as efficiently as the contractors. The latter were so much more efficient that they could take home large incomes for themselves and still produce the work *cheaper* than the company. However, thanks to Taylorism and the manage-

---

*Note that Brewer's information is about the cartridge shop, where 50 percent of the workers were women, while the only surviving records on contracting at Winchester are for the gun shop.

ment movement, by 1910 "management" (in approximately the sense we use this word today) was able to do *almost* as well as contractors and workers.

However, even had Winchester or other companies known that the abolition of contracting would not cut costs in the short run, they had other reasons to end the system. One of the main reasons did involve technology and technological change, although it was a social not a technical reason. The inside contractor was in total charge of production in an area, and hence was the person to introduce technological changes. He was also the person who benefited from such changes: if his contract price were set for the year and he introduced an innovation in January that halved the cost of production, he would make a fortune during the rest of the year. The company would get no benefit from this technical improvement until the next time that contract prices were "adjusted," that is, lowered. In fact, unless the company was keeping a record of how much the contractor's employees earned (by disbursing the money to each employee per the contractor's order), it might never know that the contractor had found a way to reduce his costs and increase his profits. Thus if technological change were equally rapid under the two systems, and if at a given point in time a company could abolish contracting and replace it with day-wage foremen, there was a considerable incentive to do so: technological change would not be any greater, but the company would get more of the benefit and its employees (specifically, contractors) would get less. Henry Roland offered this as one of the main rationales for abolishing contracting: the experience of the Singer company "shows that, with fixed-pay foremen, the cost reduction is fully as constant and rapid as it was under the contract system, and this saving comes sooner to the owners" (1897, 12: 999).

If the first reason to abolish contracting was to shift income from the contractor to the company, a second powerful reason to eliminate the system was the social anomalies it created. A small part of this problem was the actual and potential variation in the earnings of employees. Since each contractor set his own wage rates, workers doing basically the same work, and possessing roughly comparable skills, might receive very different wages. A successful contractor might pay generous wages while someone who was struggling would pay low wages. This variation might lead to discontent and hostility, which would be directed against the company as well as the contractor.

A much more serious problem, from the point of view of the officials of the company, was the income and social position of the large contractors. Large contractors frequently earned more than high company officials. At Winchester, for example, there was an influx of young, college-trained executives during the 1890s and early 1900s (Williamson, 1952: 137), who earned less than the older, less educated, contractors. This created "a feeling that the large contractor enjoyed an economic and social position in the community that made it more difficult to secure the loyalty and cooperation of the company's own administrative staff" (ibid.: 136). This problem was the reason for the introduction in 1887 of a bonus system for the benefit of the officers.

More than thirty years after contract system was abolished, John Buttrick interviewed management officials who remembered the pre-1914 period. While these people all insisted that trouble with the labor force was the reason for abolishing contracting, "in the course of almost every interview . . . we were told of contractors driving to work in fine carriages, carrying canes, and sporting stickpins. Such men, it turned out, had delegated all the dirty work in their departments to assistants and were 'outmanagering' the managers" (Buttrick, 1952: 217). Some of the large contractors apparently wished to be considered on a par with managers and officials, but the officials were not willing to accept the contractors. At the Winchester plant in 1900, only one company official rode to work—Mr. T. G. Bennett, the president of the company, the founder's son-in-law, and the husband of one of the two largest stockholders (Williamson, 1952: 131, 134). All other company officials walked to work. Some of the contractors, however, "came to work in fancy horse-drawn carriages, wearing frock coats, and sporting diamond stickpins, spats, and gloves. These individuals not uncommonly had sub-foremen under them and supervised their departments at arm's length" (ibid.: 136). During this period, essentially all foremen and the great bulk of superintendents continued to do manual work—teaching and demonstrating, setting up machines, trying out a new process, and similar activities. Dressing up was one way contractors could prove to the world that they did no manual work, and of course the carriage and general splendor demonstrated that they had the income to be above the working class. Company officials resented the contractors and refused to accept them as equals. It is easy to see why officials would want to end a system which produced such rivals for position and prestige, both in the plant and in the community.

The foremen who replaced contractors received much less pay, had much less prestige, and were clearly of lower social standing than company officials. This made it likely that contractors would quit rather than become foremen. At Winchester considerable efforts were made to get contractors to stay on: a bonus system for foremen was made to resemble the profit earned by contractors, foremen were permitted to reject workers sent from the hiring office by the superintendent, and foremen's recommendations were usually enough to get someone hired. "In spite of these rather heroic efforts, over half the contractors quit rather than be transformed into foremen" (Buttrick, 1952: 220). This is the more remarkable when it is remembered that for some years before contracting was actually abolished the system had been under attack, with the earnings and powers of contractors steadily being reduced. At Waltham Watch four of the five large contractors stayed on as foremen after contracting was abolished, but Waltham abolished contracting during the depression of the early 1870s, and other jobs may have been hard to find.

Conclusion

It is interesting to note that many of the attacks on inside contracting would be just as valid if applied to capitalism itself. Thomas Navin has argued that under contracting, it was in the contractor's direct material interest to hold down the wage of his workers, since any wage increase came out of the contractor's pocket.

> No doubt most job workers directed their attention chiefly toward the level of wages they paid their men, for there at least they could watch figures which they knew had a close connection with their dollar income. . . . As long as a job supervisor could dictate how much he was

> willing to pay a man, he was probably slow to grant a raise, for by the very nature of the system, individual raises were virtually taken from the job-worker's pocket. (1950: 143)

Navin's argument is perfectly correct as far as it goes. However, the argument applies with equal force to *any* employment for wages under a capitalist system. If this is an argument against the contract system, it is just as much an argument against the capitalist system.

Henry Roland complained about the subcontractor system, in which the contractor divided up his operations and let them out to subcontractors. According to Roland, "by the subcontractor system the principal contractor became almost an idler, drawing a large sum of money for merely nominal service" (1897, 12: 998). Would Roland say the same thing of a plant superintendent who supervised many foremen or contractors? Would organizational theorists accept this characterization of high company officials and managers (not to mention stockholders)?

The most interesting such example, however, concerns the very question of the contractor's inefficiency. Why should any believer in the capitalist system expect contracting to be inefficient? Yet almost all do. Contracting is simply a system which carries the marketplace right inside the factory. Ordinarily, inside the factory the product of one worker is not a commodity to the next. That is, one worker does not forge a rifle barrel and then sell it to the next worker, who drills it out and sells it to a third, who machines it and sells it to a fourth, and so on. The product usually passes from one worker to another quite routinely, with no financial transaction, sales pressure, or demands for recompense. The worker who has forged the barrels makes no demand at all on the worker who will drill the barrels; he or she just passes them along, without greed or jealousy. In capitalist society outside the factory transactions are not so simple. No one parts with a commodity without receiving its equivalent in value. Supporters of capitalism are as outraged when it is suggested that the marketplace could be brought inside the factory as they are when it is suggested that the market could be taken out of society altogether. It would plainly be "inefficient," "chaotic," "anarchic," to have a factory organized without a strong despotic central power (for even under contracting, workers sold their products to a central capitalist, not to other workers), just as it would be "tyrannical," "inefficient," and "despotic" to have a society without a market.

> The same bourgeois mind which praises division of labour in the workshop, life-long annexation of the labourer to a partial operation, and his complete subjection to capital, as being an organisation of labour that increases its productiveness—that same bourgeois mind denounces with equal vigour every conscious attempt to socially control and regulate the process of production, as an inroad upon such sacred things as the rights of property, freedom and unrestricted play for the bent of the individual capitalist. It is very characteristic that the enthusiastic apologists of the factory system have nothing more damning to urge against a general organisation of the labour of society, than that it would turn all society into one immense factory. . . . In a society with capitalist production, anarchy in the social division of labour and despotism in that of the workshop are mutual conditions the one of the other. (Marx, 1867: 337)

4
Craft Production and Workers' Control

Inside contracting is basically a special instance of the craft system of production which dominated most industry in the mid-nineteenth century. Both historically and analytically, therefore, it might logically be discussed after a consideration of craft production. However, I have presented the material in the reverse order because I have found, from attempts to discuss the subject, that many people find it hard to believe that a craft organization of production was dominant even after the emergence of factory organization and developed capitalist production. Understanding the scale and importance of inside contracting in nineteenth-century industrial America forces us to realize the tremendous differences between that era and this. It then becomes easier to understand the general character of nineteenth-century craft production. In many ways the most significant fact about inside contracting is that it was not considered unusual in the nineteenth century for a simple reason: it did not differ greatly from most of the other production of that time.

Power in the Workplace

The foremen of 1880 were far more similar to the inside contractors of that same year than to the foremen of today, differing from the contractors primarily in that they did not have a direct material interest in the level of production. Foremen obviously wanted a good production record, since this would help to ensure their security and advancement. Moreover, they occasionally received bonuses based on output, but this was infrequent and small in scale. Thus, unlike the case with contractors, the income of foremen did not necessarily increase in relation to the productivity of their workers.

In other ways, however, the powers of the foreman were close to those of inside contractors. Foremen hired and fired their own employees, kept track of the hours they worked, determined their rates of pay, trained them, and controlled layoffs in slack periods. In many cases these powers persisted until World War I, and occasionally beyond. However, a mere thirty years later, in 1945, a study showed that almost all foremen had lost these powers. In only 3.5 percent of the companies surveyed did the foreman have the complete right to hire, in 29.5 percent the foreman had no right to hire, and in 67.0 percent the foreman had the final say after initial interviewing and selection by the personnel department. Similarly, only 10.5 percent of the companies gave their foremen the complete right to discharge, while in over half of all the companies the actual discharge had to be made by the personnel department or the foreman's superior at the foreman's recommendation (in the rest of the cases the foreman could discharge after other forms of consultation). Only one foreman in seven had the complete right to raise pay or promote within his department, and only one foreman in ten had the complete right to discipline (Kolker, 1948: 95–96).

The foremen of the 1880s not only had almost absolute control over labor, they also decided what materials to order. They controlled the inventory of raw materials and necessary equipment, and usually of the finished product as well. It was generally their responsibility to keep track of production in other parts of the shop in order to make sure the needed parts were delivered in time and to expedite delivery when necessary. As late as 1921 outside consultants hired to report on the Waltham Watch Company noted: "We found each foreman operating his department as though it were a plant in itself—he determined largely his own production; hired his own personnel; and he purchased his own materials, largely" (Moore, 1945: 115).

In sum, essentially all aspects of the production process were under the nominal control of foremen. In a 1910 report on a government arsenal, the colonel in charge noted:

It is difficult to enumerate the duties and responsibilities of a foreman. As a rule his duties are not specific beyond seeing that the shop keeps running. He is supposed to see that men are supplied with material to work upon, to assign their jobs, to give instructions as to how the work should be done, to suggest or supply any special tools or fixtures if any are required, to see that the tools in his department are kept in good order and condition, to see that work is delivered from other departments when needed, and that proper effort is being made throughout the shop, to look after discipline, and, in addition to a considerable amount of clerical work, to shoulder many other details which perhaps need not be mentioned. (U.S. House of Representatives, 1912: 112; Wheeler is here quoting his earlier report.)

The foreman was a powerful figure not simply in relation to his workers, but also with respect to higher authority. As with contractors, there was essentially only one level of authority above the foreman. In many cases, each foreman operated what was quite literally a plant unto itself. At the Whitin Machine Works, for example, the departments were

set up on the basis of product rather than of function. All card parts, for example, were made and assembled in one area instead of being turned in one department, milled in another, and ground in a third. Under a single supervisor's direction, a complete machine might be manufactured from castings to the assembly of finished parts—in the case of the more complex machines a separate department might take over the final erection. (Navin, 1950: 139)

What higher authority there was tried to ensure cooperation between foremen, not to give them specific orders or directives on how to run their operations. At Reed and Barton, this task fell to the owners of the company:

One of the functions of Reed and Brabrook was to ensure cooperation between foremen. In many cases this was no easy task, for these czars of production exhibited highly individualistic tendencies and brooked little interference from anyone. . . . Because the foremen were chosen for ability and experience rather than for their qualities of leadership, a certain amount of friction occurred both in and between departments. (Gibb, 1943: 284–85)

When foremen and higher authority did quarrel, it was not necessarily the foreman who lost. Aaron Dennison, the founder of the

Waltham Watch Company (but not the owner) was forced to leave the company because of a dispute with a foreman (Moore, 1945: 45). At Reed and Barton:

> On one occasion superintendent Nathan Lawrence objected to some process which Charles Minchew, boss plater, was using. One word borrowed another. Finally, Minchew ordered Lawrence out, and told him he would kick him out if he came into the department again that month. Lawrence immediately reported the incident to George Brabrook [one of the three top officials]. Thinking it over a moment Brabrook replied, "Well, Mr. Lawrence, the foreman of the plating-room has the reputation of carrying through with his word. If I were you, I think I should keep out of that department for the rest of the month." (Gibb, 1943: 284)

The great powers of foremen made them important figures, both in the shops and in the community at large. In some cases foremen went to considerable lengths to demonstrate their authority and position. At Reed and Barton silversmiths, for example:

> On all occasions [foremen] deported themselves with great dignity, and the foremen customarily reported for work attired in silk hats, cutaway coats, and attendant accessories. Men in the departments always were careful to address their bosses with a respectful "Mr." (Ibid.: 284)

This may have been the exception rather than the rule, however. For example, the Watertown Arsenal hearings (discussed below) make it clear that foremen and workers were usually on friendly terms with a rough egalitarianism which did not deny the foreman's authority. This was important to workers, since a despotic foreman could make life miserable for his employees (see Nelson, 1974b; Ozanne, 1967).

It is important to emphasize that foremen did not attain their positions because of their abilities or training as office workers or managers, but rather because they had been successful and respected skilled workers. Not office clerks or college graduates, but molders, machinists, carpenters, and rollers became foremen. Even as foremen they continued to involve themselves directly with production, rather than just supervising. They set up machines for workers, tried new machinery or processes themselves, and saw this activity as a central part of their job. Katherine Stone has shown that around the turn of the century foremen had to be taught *not* to do these things, but rather to simply direct the work of others (1974: 81). Similarly, when the Watertown Arsenal tried to abolish the craft system and replace it with a Taylor-inspired form of organization, not only the foremen but even the plant superintendent had to be kept from doing work on the shop floor. The colonel in charge testified:

> When [Mr. Nelson] first became head of the planning division [the Taylor system center for directing the work] he was accustomed to the old way of doing things, and the temptation was, of course, to do a great many things on the floor in the old way. The result of that was that sufficient attention on his part was not being given within the planning room, where we thought his efforts were best utilized. (U.S. House of Representatives, 1912: 396)

As George Gibb says, "In the first place, the foreman was a master of his trade. Not only was he the head of the department, but usually he was the best workman in it. That, indeed, constituted the main reason why he had been chosen boss" (1943: 284).

The Power of Workers

In terms of its formal procedures and structures of authority, the labor system of the nineteenth century looks much like that of today: at that time as at this, workers had to obey their foremen, foremen had to obey their superintendents, and superintendents answered to still higher authority. The most easily visible difference is that foremen had almost all the powers now held by a far greater number of managers—personnel directors, research and development scientists, engineers, efficiency experts, inventory controllers, foremen, timekeepers, bookkeepers, and other white-collar workers. Yet this formal difference between nineteenth- and twentieth-century production, important though it undoubtedly is, is less significant than the fact that workers controlled many of the details of the work process.

While nineteenth-century foremen had general control over all aspects of the production process, they could rarely make every decision that was theoretically theirs. For example, on June 10,

1873, iron puddlers in Troy, New York went on strike against an arbitrary foreman, who "had refused to assign a puddler to a furnace he had been working at and insisted he could move or discharge any worker at his pleasure" (Walkowitz, 1974: 431). That is, a strike was provoked when a foreman tried to actually make the decisions which were formally his, since these decisions were normally made by workers.

Hearings of a special committee of the U.S. House of Representatives to investigate the Taylor and other systems of management* indicate the nature of the actual relationship. Testimony at these hearings makes it clear that while workers and foremen preserved the fiction that all decisions were made by the foreman, this was not in fact the case. Undoubtedly foremen accepted the responsibility for all such decisions, and felt that any merit or blame was theirs, but the actual methods and decisions came from the workers—the foreman only gave his approval and endorsement. Colonel Wheeler, in charge of the Watertown Arsenal, listed the many duties of the foreman and went so far as to say:

> "The direct result was . . . that the foreman, instead of performing such work as he was best fitted for, by his mechanical training and experience, was confined to a desk or to an office to such an extent that work on the floor of the shops was greatly neglected, and as a rule, took care of itself." (Quoted in Aitken, 1960: 123)

The actual testimony makes it clear that this was a considerable exaggeration—a part of Wheeler's program of denigrating the old system and praising the system he was introducing—but there is an important measure of truth in this analysis. Many of the foreman's nominal powers were in the hands of the workers.

Officers at Watertown Arsenal were trying to introduce Taylor's scientific management system, which aimed to give each worker explicit instructions on how to do the work; workers resisted. One

---

*This committee was appointed and the hearings held as a result of the opposition of workers at the U.S. government arsenal at Watertown, Massachusetts to attempts of the officers at the arsenal to introduce Taylor's "scientific management." Of the three congressmen, one became secretary of labor and another secretary of commerce, both under President Woodrow Wilson. Thousands of pages of testimony were taken, mostly from people who worked at the government arsenals.

worker testified about an instance where he thought the instructions he was given would not do the job adequately.

> I could not do the work as it should be done, and the foreman came along the floor, and I spoke to him about it, and he said, "How would you do it?" Well, I told him instead of running the heavy chip on the high speed [his instructions] that I would run it at a lower speed with more feed and get better results. So he told me to go ahead, and Mr. Merrick [the scientific management "expert"] came along, and he asked me why I changed it. Well, I told him I had orders from the foreman that I could do it. (U.S. House of Representatives, 1912: 432)

The worker, not the foreman, decided the original method was wrong; the worker, not the foreman, asked to change the method; the worker, not the foreman, suggested an alternative. The foreman, however, gave the needed approval and supported his worker. When the scientific management expert objected, the worker, the foreman, the expert, and the superintendent of the plant all participated in a test. The group of them, according to the worker, "tried the scientific way and we tried the foreman's way"—the "foreman's" way, even though the worker had suggested it—and found the "foreman's" way to work better. "So I believe I was told to leave the machine the way the *foreman* fixed it, or the way *we* changed it to" (ibid.; emphasis added—the two are apparently equivalent). The worker persisted in giving the credit for his own suggestion to the foreman: "So they finally came to the conclusion after all that the foreman was right, and they left it that way."

Other instances of the same phenomenon recur in the testimony. When new shop rules prohibited workers from making their own decisions, they nonetheless were confident enough to first take considerable time and effort to reset the machine, and only afterward ask the foreman's blessing (ibid.: 372, 445).

The fact that workers, not foremen or inside contractors, made most of the decisions which were formally the responsibility of the supervisor, is the reason why I characterize the nineteenth-century labor system as craft production. Harry Braverman has argued that the most crucial distinction concerning labor is not the usual one of blue collar and white collar, not even that between mental and manual labor, but is rather the distinction between those who plan the work and those who carry it out (see Braverman, 1974: especially 315–19). Braverman argues that in the modern corporation these are two very different groups of people, though at one time the same people did both activities. Similarly, Arthur Stinchcombe (1959) uses this distinction as the basis for the differentiation between craft production and bureaucratic administration. In bureaucratic administration the work process as well as the product itself is planned in advance by persons not on the work crew. In craft production, on the other hand, most aspects of the work process are determined by workers in accordance with the empirical lore that makes up craft principles. Craft production depends on the knowledge and skill of people directly involved in the process of production, who both plan and carry out the necessary tasks. Stinchcombe deals only with the construction industry in the mid-twentieth century, which makes the craft system appear to be an isolated instance of limited importance. In fact, however, as Braverman recognizes, most work used to be organized on a craft basis, if by this we mean that the same people planned and executed the work.

As an example of the work process associated with a bureaucratic administration of production, consider modern automobile production. The first decisions are usually made at the very top of the company. Do changing demographic, economic, or competitive factors indicate the need for a new car, and if so, to what image should it appeal (powerful-sexy-sporty versus small-cheap-economical versus whatever)? Some decisions are made and general principles are given to the research and development division which decides on the general design and produces a prototype. Throughout this process the top levels of the company are consulted continually; they usually choose between the various possible options. If the idea is adopted, engineers plan the production of the car. New machinery is created or old machinery is reset. Engineers plan the sequence of operations, and if necessary the factory is reorganized (or a new factory is built). Efficiency experts determine the exact movements that each worker should make. Even the speed of the line is set by high officials. The quality of the cars is determined by high-level decisions about the materials used, the operations to be performed, and the length of time workers are to be given for each operation. No one on the shop floor, not even the foremen, need plan any aspect of the work process. All the workers need to do is stand at their machines and work, doing the same operation over and over. The company would feel that something had gone seriously wrong if this work required any but the most minimal thought.* The company doesn't want worker input even if it could help improve the quality or construction of the car (see Watson, 1971). The number of units produced, the level of inventory, and so on are decided on by economists, executives, and inventory control personnel.

This paradigm of modern production is in stark contrast to nineteenth-century craft production. In the nineteenth century, workers, foremen, or inside contractors—all of whom were directly and intimately involved in the actual process of production—would frequently be the ones to introduce a new product or design. At the Waltham Watch Company, the "C. T. Parker" and "P. S. Bartlett" watches were named for the inside contractors who designed and produced them. When the Whitin Machine Works found that it was legally required to pay a royalty for the use of any spindle showing freedom at its bolster bearing, the company wanted to devise a new spindle in order to avoid the royalty payment. This new spindle was designed for the company not by an independent expert or a college trained engineer, but by one of the company's own inside contractors (Navin, 1950: 194). At the Winchester Repeating Arms Company, until 1886, when a laboratory was introduced, the development and production of priming mixtures was entrusted to the primer shop foreman, "who had long experience in the work." He tried out new mixtures empirically, and recorded the results and formulas in a "little black book." "This information was available only to the foreman, who kept it a closely guarded secret," with the result that high management didn't dare fire him (Williamson, 1952: 143). At Reed and Barton silversmiths foremen "passed judgment upon new designs" (Gibb, 1943: 284). In all these cases, even the

---

*Even here, it is not possible to kill all human initiative and creativity, though capitalism has done its best to do so. Workers find ways to win at least some slight degree of control over their speed; often workers find new and better ways to do the work, sometimes even designing new tools and equipment for the purpose. (These new methods must be kept secret from the company, or workers would be required to increase their output accordingly.) (See Walker and Guest, 1952; Houbolt and Kusterer, 1977; Garson, 1975; Chapter Seven below.)

products to be manufactured were decided on by people directly involved in the production process.

Whether or not workers designed the product, they did plan the work process. At an early period, before the Civil War, workers were simply given a pattern musket, for example, told to make duplicate parts that would interchange, and left to plan the work.

By the 1911 hearings at the Watertown Arsenal, there was a well-developed system of drawings and limit gauges. The foreman was given a set of drawings for the parts his workers were to make; he then decided who should make each part (which involved selecting the machinery to be used), and distributed the drawings to the appropriate workers. The use of drawings, specifications, and gauges did not mean that the worker's skill and expertise were no longer necessary, however. In order to know how to make the part, machinists had to study the blueprints and drawings. It was impossible to say how long it should take to understand any particular drawing, so the men had to be left alone until they understood what needed to be done.

> When a man has got a job of work, he will very often take the drawing out and lay it before him on the bench, and I have seen a half hour's time and an hour's time spent entirely with the man's face over the drawing. . . . Now, as foreman of the room I can not take the drawing away from the man, but I must wait until the man understands it. You know that some men are able to grasp those things quicker than other men and I must wait until they see the things clearly. (U.S. House of Representatives, 1912: 319)

There was no way that such a worker could be rushed. If he did not understand the drawing, he would be almost certain to ruin an expensive and valuable piece of work. Understanding the drawings was not by any means a simple or mechanical task: "if the drawings are not made in detail, if they are made in assembled groups, in sections, or in some other way, they [workers] certainly have got to have foresight to read them" (ibid.: 319). Workers did not simply have a hard time understanding the drawings, did not simply have to have the foresight to plan the work carefully, they had to use their knowledge and experience to supply information that was not on the drawings but which was crucial to the successful completion of the job.*

> *Mr. Redfield.* Is it your experience that drawings are commonly blind in the respect that matters are omitted from them which it is assumed the mechanic will himself supply but which are an important part of the work?
>
> *Mr. MacKean.* There are some cases of that kind in a great many of our drawings. (Ibid.: 319)

Workers who spent an hour studying a drawing might also quite justifiably want to talk to other workers about the problem, get their advice, check to be sure they had made the correct interpretation.

The "blind" drawings of the Watertown Arsenal, which required the workers to perform operations and make parts even though these were not called for on the drawings, were not by any means an example of mismanagement. Congressman Redfield was himself a manufacturer, and later secretary of commerce in Woodrow Wilson's cabinet. The very fact that he knew to ask about this practice indicates that it was typical. The common practice was to give workers instructions which, if interpreted and executed in literal fashion, would lead to total disaster. For example, in an 1885 article in the *American Machinist* Oberlin Smith suggested an innovation for use in "average" machine shops. (Guns, sewing machines, locks, and the like already made use of limit gauges which took care of the problem he was dealing with, he explained.) When a shaft had to go into a hole, the common practice at that time was to instruct the workers to make both the shaft and the hole one inch wide. As Smith pointed out, actually the workers would not do so, or the shaft could not fit into the hole. Either the hole or the shaft had to be out of specification; it could make a difference which one was. Smith's suggestion was that workers be instructed to make a hole of one inch and a shaft of .999 inches, with a maximum variation of .0004 inch, so that even

---

*It would be a mistake to believe that this was simply a result of the primitive nature of production and blueprints in 1911. Even in modern automobile production, despite all the caution and effort that goes into planning, engineers do not foresee all the problems involved in the layout of the production process. Once production actually begins, workers keep finding bugs and problems. This is one of the main reasons why the first cars produced for any new model are always full of bugs and assembly defects.

with the smallest permissible hole and the largest permissible shaft there would still be .0002 inch of looseness. "It is obvious that such a system would produce much better results than the present one of instructing the workman to make a hole of one inch and a shaft of one inch, leaving him to disobey orders by using his individual judgment as to the variations" (1885: 1).

At the same time that the worker studied the drawing, he was planning the work and deciding how to set up and run the machine. For example, the same amount of material could be removed on a lathe at a slow speed with a deep cut as could be achieved at a higher speed with less cut. Mathematically these two choices might be equal, but in actual practice they were not. Workers had to use their skill and expertise to determine the optimum relationship between all of the variables which had to be considered—the speed, feed, depth of cut, shape, sharpness, and temper of the tool used, the hardness of the material, the amount of power applied to the machine, the desired quality of the finish, and so on. These decisions were all part of the worker's job. When Frederick Taylor wanted to incorporate in his system a way to make these determinations for the workers, he was forced to create a slide rule which took into consideration sixteen different variables (U.S. House of Representatives, 1912: 449). Mr. Nelson, the master mechanic (plant superintendent) at the Watertown Arsenal, saw the ability to make these decisions as the difference between a skilled and a semiskilled worker.

> *The Chairman.* Is it your judgment that matters of that kind, of speed and feed, should be determined with some latitude left to the workman himself?
>
> *Mr. Nelson.* Yes, to a mechanic.
>
> *The Chairman.* Working in conjunction with his foreman?
>
> *Mr. Nelson.* If I used a handy man* I believe I should dictate the speed and feed for him.
>
> *The Chairman.* But if you use a skilled workman you think his judgment ought to be utilized?
>
> *Mr. Nelson.* His judgment ought to be utilized.

---

*"Handy man" (or sometimes "specialist") was the term used by machinists to denote what we today call a semiskilled worker.

The Chairman. You suppose when you employ a skilled workman at the wages of a skilled workman that you are paying him for his skill, do you not?

Mr. Nelson. I am paying him for his skill.

The Chairman. But if you were using a handy man you would expect to have to direct him?

Mr. Nelson. I would expect to direct him and lay out a routine for him to work to. (Ibid.: 509)

So far this discussion of nineteenth-century production has described the production of a new item, which of course involves more variability and requires more skill and planning than does ordinary routinized production. But even "ordinary" and "routine" work situations required a great deal of planning and skill by the production worker. To begin with, it would be a mistake to view the "ordinary" mass production situation as one in which nothing changed for a period of twenty years. For example, during the 1860s and 1870s Singer doubled its production of sewing machines about every four years, and this can hardly have been done without drastic changes in the work process. In general, the nineteenth century was a period of rapid advances in machinery, methods, and technology, which involved frequent changes in the nature of day-to-day work. Even aside from increases in output or changes in technology, nineteenth- as well as twentieth-century industry introduced new models, styles, and products. In 1889 there were only two typewriter companies; by 1909 there were eighty-nine separate companies (Bliven, 1954: 94–95). Edward Hess, one of the employees of Royal Typewriter, was granted 140 patents on various typewriter features (ibid.: 90). New models and features were constantly being introduced. In the eight years from 1858 to 1865 the Waltham Watch Company introduced five new styles of watch. By 1881 they made twenty-one grades, in 1886, thirty-six grades, in 1891, forty grades and in 1896, forty-five grades (Moore, 1945: 77). This focuses only on the companies which mass produced the most standardized products. For companies that made larger and more variable items, such as machine shops or locomotive works, there was probably even more variation. In bureaucratic production planning for a new item is the responsibility of engineers, research and development scientists, and other nonproduction workers, so that the development of new products generally does not significantly involve production workers. In the nineteenth century the development of these products, and the decisions about how to begin production, were far more likely to be made by shop-floor workers. Instead of having a minority of employees who do nothing but develop new products, as is the case today, a much larger number of workers had at least some significant involvement with planning the production of new items.

Even when the product remained the same, variation was possible in a number of other elements of the work process. For a machinist, for example, the quality of the castings he was given to machine might vary tremendously, and this variation might demand adjustments on the part of the machinist. Similarly, in an age when iron and steel quality was much less standardized than it is today, the hardness of the metal could vary significantly from week to week, and this again required adjustments. For other kinds of workers, for example, iron puddlers, the variations in the materials could be the key element in the production process. Pig iron containing silicon, sulphur, and phosphorous—impurities which made the iron brittle—would be put into a puddling furnace and a fire, made by burning bituminous coal, would be stoked for roughly thirty minutes, until it melted the iron. James J. Davis' account gives a feel for the way in which even during "routine" production an iron puddler had to combine judgment and knowledge on the one hand with physical strength and skill on the other.

> For the next seven minutes I "thickened the heat up" by adding iron oxide to the bath. This was in the form of roll scale. The furnace continued in full blast till that was melted. The liquid metal in the hearth is called slag. The iron oxide is put in it to make it more basic for the chemical reaction that is to take place. Adding the roll scale had cooled the charge, and it was thick like hoecake batter. I now thoroughly mixed it with a rabble which is like a long iron hoe. . . .

> My purpose in slackening my heat as soon as the pig iron was melted was to oxidize the phosphorous and sulphur ahead of the carbon. Just as alcohol vaporizes at a lower heat than water, so sulphur and phosphorous oxidize at a lower heat than carbon. When this reaction begins I see light flames breaking through the lake of molten slag in my

furnace. . . . The flames are caused by the burning of carbon monoxide from the oxidation of carbon. The slag is basic and takes the sulphur and phosphorous into combination, thus ending its combination with the iron. The purpose now is to oxidize the carbon, too, without reducing the phosphorous and sulphur and causing them to return to the iron. We want the pure iron to begin crystallizing out of the bath like butter from the churning buttermilk.

More and more of the carbon gas comes out of the puddle, and as it bubbles out the charge is agitated by its escape and the "boil" is in progress. It is not real boiling like the boiling of a teakettle. When a teakettle boils the water turns to bubbles of vapor and goes up in the air to turn to water again when it gets cold. But in the boiling iron puddle a chemical change is taking place. The iron is not going up in vapor. The carbon and the oxygen are. This formation of gas in the molten puddle causes the whole charge to boil up like an ice-cream soda. The slag overflows. Redder than strawberry syrup and as hot as the fiery lake in Hades it flows over the rim of the hearth and out through the slag-hole. My helper has pushed up a buggy there to receive it. More than an eighth and sometimes a quarter of the weight of the pig iron flows off in slag and is carted away. . . .

For twenty-five minutes while the boil goes on I stir it constantly with my long iron rabble. . . . Little spikes of pure iron like frost sparks glow white-hot and stick out of the churning slag. These must be stirred under at once; the long stream of flame from the grate plays over the puddle, and the pure iron if lapped by these gases would be oxidized—burned up.

Pasty masses of iron form at the bottom of the puddle. There they would stick and become chilled if they were not constantly stirred. The whole charge must be mixed and mixed as it steadily thickens so that it will be uniform throughout. . . .

The charge which I have been kneading in my furnace now has "come to nature," the stringy sponge of pure iron is separating from the slag. The "balling" of this sponge into three loaves is a task that occupies from ten to fifteen minutes. . . . I am balling it into three parts of equal weight. If the charge is six hundred pounds, each of my balls must weigh exactly two hundred pounds. . . . I must get the three balls, or blooms, out of the furnace and into the squeezer while the slag is still liquid so that it can be squeezed out of the iron.

From cold pig iron to finished blooms is a process that takes from an hour and ten minutes, to an hour and forty minutes, depending on the speed and skill of the puddler, and the kind of iron. (1922: 90–113)

Great strength and the ability to endure the terrible heat were necessary in order to do the job, but the key element was the worker's skill and judgment. How much coal to shovel in the fire, how to regulate the vents to get the best draught, how much iron oxide to add, how to stir, how much slag to draw off, how to make three equal balls at the right time, how to get them out and into the squeezer at the right time, these were all elements which varied with each batch. Although the product was always wrought iron, and the raw materials were always pig iron, coal, and iron oxide, and although the methods stayed much the same for many years, the worker was constantly planning the production process.

For machinists, after making all of the decisions about how to do the work and setting up the machine, the worker still had to fit up for the job. Colonel Wheeler quoted a management expert's report on some other, nongovernmental, shop in order to illustrate a frequent practice, one which he believed to exist at the Watertown Arsenal in 1910:

> In the usual shop, with some machines lying idle, if a man at a machine wants a dog or a bolt or a clamp the easiest way for him to get it is to go to the nearest idle machine and help himself; and this is what he usually does, except that he usually takes two, if available, and stows one away near his machine for possible future use. When the idle machine is wanted, much time is lost in supplying it with the necessary equipment. Again, a new man is taken on and put at one of the idle machines and given a job; he does not know the shop and he hunts around for the necessary equipment. . . . He goes from one man to another, trying to get the necessary equipment. (U.S. House of Representatives, 1912: 113)

This is obviously a hostile description of the situation, and neither Colonel Wheeler's nor the "expert's" assessment of the efficiency of the system can be accepted as unbiased. It does indicate, however, that it was the worker's responsibility to get the necessary parts, and it shows the extent to which sociability and cooperation were *necessary* in order for workers to do their jobs well.

In the system described above there is no reference to central storerooms. In fact, such storerooms almost always existed. In the

1870s and 1880s these storerooms were generally open to all workers, who could simply take what they wanted. As time went on the controls over these rooms were generally increased. For example, at the Watertown Arsenal in 1911 the bolt and strap room was still left open. "Each man is allowed to go in there or send a helper in there and take what he wishes and return it when he is through using it." This was because bolts and straps were comparatively inexpensive. Until the introduction of the new management system, "as far as possible each machine had a full complement of tools excepting special tools." If workers needed special tools, or were missing tools which they should have had, they either borrowed them from other machinists, or got them from the toolroom. Under the new management system introduced around 1910, the policy was "to keep all tools in the tool room and draw tools only as required by check" (ibid.: 318, 331). Even this system obviously allowed the worker to walk to the toolroom when necessary. The aim of scientific management was, as far as possible, to have the necessary tool for each job brought to the machine by unskilled workers.

In addition to securing the necessary tools and equipment, workers might also need to take the time to have their tools sharpened and tempered. It used to be the custom for the machinist himself to go to the shop and have his tool tempered and wait there while it was being done. Rather than having tools sharpened to standard specifications and available to workers when needed, workers would take their tools and have them ground and tempered to the specific requirements of the job they had before them. Obviously, considerable time was "lost" (from a capitalist point of view, that is; the worker probably enjoyed the break and the opportunity to talk to other workers) waiting for tools to be prepared, but there were compensating advantages. For one thing, such tools would do the work better, since they were adapted to the particular material, speed, and so on that the job required. Perhaps as important, this meant that the tools—even though owned by the company—stayed with the worker, so that "under the old system when a man got a good lathe tool or a good planer tool, it was the custom to take care of that tool, and he thought almost as much of it as he did of the dollars he earned" (ibid.: 333).

Workers had still other miscellaneous duties and responsibilities connected with the production process. If their machines did not work properly it was up to them, with the assistance of their foreman, to fix them. These were the sorts of situations when foremen worked on the shop floor, putting their knowledge and experience to use in difficult or unusual situations. Nonetheless, workers frequently knew more than their foremen:

> The machine went wrong and we worked on the machine quite a while before we found out the cause of its actions. . . . The foreman did not understand the machine any more than myself, he was unable to show me what was the matter with it until we worked on it between us and I found out the cause myself. (Ibid.: 443, 445)

On this particular job, because of the problems with the machine, it took the machinist "three or four days to rig up," and he worked on the job for three weeks in total.

Substantial time was spent on activities other than working at the machines in ordinary production. Workers insisted that they had to be allowed sufficient time "to attend to any accidents that might take place, such as the slipping of belts, or the breaking of the machines, or anything of that sort." When the management of the Rock Island Arsenal set the piece rates, they allowed a worker "about two hours for grinding tools, etc.," although they argued that this was "an excessive amount." Workers opposed setting any production limits, arguing:

> A man is not a machine, and even a machine does not always maintain the same speed or power. Tools will get dull and have to be taken out of the machine, ground, and reset; belts break and have to be repaired. Sometimes the nonproductive movements that are necessary are quite as great as the productive ones and sometimes more so. (Ibid.: 839)

The power that workers had over the process of production made it difficult for management to control them. It was impossible to specify in advance how long it should take a worker to understand a particular blueprint or drawing, and it was pointless to hurry the worker since errors of understanding could prove extremely costly. Workers studying drawings would probably want to talk to other workers to check their understanding. Doing this could save time and avoid errors—but it also meant that it was hard for management to control workers' movements in the shop, hard for supervisors to know when workers were legitimately discussing the work and when they were "illegitimately" socializing. The problems for management were endless. If one worker were talking to another, this might be a needed consultation about the meaning of a blueprint, it might be a question about the possible location of a tool, or it might simply be socializing. Similarly, a worker wandering around the shop might be engaged in a legitimate search for a necessary tool, might be going for necessary materials or fixtures, might be taking a tool to be sharpened, or might be out visiting. Even a worker sitting around doing nothing could be waiting for a tool to be sharpened or a foreman to find him a new job.

Class Struggle

The dynamic of capitalism forces capitalists to continually increase their efforts to extract the maximum amount of surplus value. In the early nineteenth century employers were not generally rational profit maximizers. Their accounts and controls were in a primitive state, and even relations with employees were not necessarily based on capitalist economic criteria. The companies were small; they were often controlled by people who themselves worked and were intimately involved with workers and the work process. At Reed and Barton, for example, "Charles E. Barton remained a solderer to the end. Henry G. Reed's interests grew broader, but were bounded on one side by the plating vats and on the other by the teaware department and Parkin's designing room" (Gibb, 1943: 147–48). This continued through the 1850s and into the 1860s, even though the company had 125 employees in 1860 and 336 employees in 1865. Perhaps as a result, wages in the factory were set on a social, not a rational capitalist, basis:

> Except for the apprentices no definite wage scales were established in the factory. Wages were a matter of individual bargaining, and the primary determinant of a man's pay was his length of service. A young man turning out ten pieces a day, as compared with one of his older associates who produced eight, could not offer the addi-

tional production as reason for an increase to the older man's level of wages. (Ibid.: 283)

In the early nineteenth century, managers and capitalists were not always clear about the fundamental opposition between their interests and those of their workers. In 1833 Thompsonville carpet weavers went on strike, and "personal relations were so good that some of the strikers were employed by the agent on his farm" (Norton, 1952: 24). Similarly, in the great Lynn shoe strike of 1860, the strike committee of the Mechanics Association "solicited contributions from the bosses to the strike fund. Shoemakers were not surprised when several manufacturers actually subscribed to pay; leading the list was a boss who 'agreed to be taxed $300' " (Dawley, 1976: 83). Capitalists were quick to abandon these orientations, however, as strikes made clear the fundamental opposition. The Thompsonville carpet management broke the strike by bribing the union president with a supervisory position, arresting the other leaders, and importing scabs. The shoe manufacturers, with one exception, did not come through on their pledges to the strike fund. Instead, they broke the strike by hiring scab labor. The workers felt betrayed, with one leader concluding that the strike showed " 'the interest of capital is to get as much labor for as little money as possible' " (quoted in ibid.: 85; Norton, 1952: 25). By 1870 or 1880 all capitalists, and almost all workers, had learned this basic lesson.

Workers, on the other hand, were not nearly so single-minded. Corporations were, and had to be, overwhelmingly concerned with profit maximization. Workers pursued many goals. All other things being equal, they wanted as much money as possible, obviously. But they also wanted shorter work hours, a comfortable work pace which would not leave them exhausted at the end of the day, a chance to socialize during the work process, varied and interesting activity, the opportunity to use their full skill and potential, and a chance to produce quality goods in which they could take pride. All of these and more went into the concept of "a fair day's work for a fair day's pay," a phrase that recurs continually in every late-nineteenth-century discussion of the work day. Custom, in one form or another, was an extremely important force in regulating what workers should and should not do, what they should and should not be paid (see discussion below; Thompson, 1963; Hobsbawm, 1964). Workers had to balance a number of concerns, and the result sometimes emphasized high wages, sometimes short hours, sometimes varied and interesting work, sometimes the opportunity to socialize. These decisions were made not by individual workers, but by the work group as a whole, which struggled to enforce the decisions on the employer and on one another.

Workers' skill and expertise combined with their control over the details of the work process gave them a great deal of leverage in every aspect of this struggle. It was not so much that they would absolutely refuse to do something—although skilled workers were hard to replace, and a work stoppage was a powerful threat. More important, workers could sabotage or evade an order through their control over the productive process. As an example of the problems this posed for management, consider the following case of a dispute at the Watertown Arsenal between the officers in charge (management) and the molders (skilled workers). This particular struggle concerned the quality of the work. In this case—and it was one common nineteenth-century situation—management's complaint was that the workers were turning out work that was too good. The officers in charge wanted lower quality, and therefore cheaper, work produced; the molders resisted and insisted on maintaining standards. Their pride in themselves and their craft demanded it.

Management insisted that it had a right to set the standard of quality, but had to admit that in practice they were unable to do so.

Major Williams. We have a system of inspection for all of those castings, and the castings must pass that inspection to be accepted. We aim, ourselves [management], to set our standard of work.

The Chairman. May I ask, Major, in that connection, whether instructions, oral or written, have been given to the workmen in connection with the finishing of these molds?

Major Williams. Yes, sir; I have given instructions to that effect myself. My own personal experience is they do too much finishing.

The Chairman. Were instructions of that character given to the workmen prior to the time of the introducing of this premium system?

Major Williams. I have been after it for about three years. I have spoken to the workmen about it time and time again. (U.S. House of Representatives, 1912: 134)

The most important part of this dispute concerned the nailing of molds. Ordinary nails were used to reenforce the molds and increase their burden-bearing power. On at least one occasion, management—probably frustrated from years of having instructions ignored—ordered a complete halt in nailing as a test case. Gustave Lawson, a molder employed in the foundry, testified about his experience, under questioning by another molder, John O'Leary, a representative of the union.

Mr. O'Leary. Are you familiar with what is known as a top carriage?

Mr. Lawson. Yes, sir.

Mr. O'Leary. Do you recall some time ago, in the making of these carriages, that some one approached you and suggested or instructed you that you were using too much time in nailing the job?

Mr. Lawson. Yes, sir.

Mr. O'Leary. Who was that person?

Mr. Lawson. Larkin, the foreman of the foundry at that time.

Mr. O'Leary. In carrying out his instructions what did you do?

Mr. Lawson. He came to me at 11 o'clock and he says, "There are orders from Capt. Horsefall that you shall stop nailing the cope," and I says, "Well, Jack," I says, "I won't stop nailing." "Well," he says, "go ahead and stop it." I said, "That is going to hurt my character."

Mr. O'Leary. You mean your reputation as a molder?

Mr. Lawson. Yes, sir. I told him if I stopped nailing that cope my efficiency would be hurt, because that is what we go by here. "Well," he says, "you go ahead and do as I tell you; it is an order from Capt. Horsefall you do so;" and in about a half an hour afterwards he came back and he says, "You start to nailing that again," he says; "part of those castings are almost gone; they have scabs all over them." (Ibid.: 148)

Management was forced to concede that "the nailing of a steel casting is an accepted practice. The thing that we endeavor to control is the number of nails that are put in" (ibid.: 150). While this might appear a trivial saving in time, it was not. Preparation of the mold was a time-consuming operation. Typically, workers who had been taking twelve hours to nail and finish a given quantity of molds were ordered to do this in seven hours, thus requiring them to produce almost twice as much.

The congressional hearings were very loosely run; anyone could ask a question of any witness. One day the hearings were held inside the foundry, and Major Williams, in charge of production, tried to establish by questioning a molder that the reduced nailing had not affected the quality, but in the end was forced to fall back on a reassertion of his authority.

Major Williams. Did you nail that mold?

Mr. Hicklin. Yes, sir.

Major Williams. Has it less nails in it than formerly?

Mr. Hicklin. Well, I was told to reduce the nails, and, of course, I did;* but I have seen some scabs on the castings.

Major Williams. Which castings?

Mr. Hicklin. Well, I have seen several on the gun-lever arms that had scabs on them.

Mr. O'Leary. By scabs you mean what?

Mr. Hicklin. Where it is cut.

Mr. O'Leary. Why does that happen?

Mr. Hicklin. For the want of nailing on.

Major Williams. I would like to state, as being in charge of the shops, that it is my business to determine whether or not the product is satisfactory, and not the molders. (Ibid.: 144–45)

The molders could not agree, however. They were concerned about their reputations as molders, and took pride in producing quality work. Workers did not accept management's right to set the quality and level of output; they would not agree to produce a greater number of lower quality items. One molder, when asked what affect piecework would have on wages, ignored the question and said the problem with piecework was "it makes them [workers] become inferior workmen. . . . And that will be the case for me if I have to be speeded up. I don't think I will stand for it; I value my

---

*Remember that Major Williams had been after the workers for three years, speaking to them time and time again, without success.

reputation yet" (ibid.: 207; see also 279–80). To the molders the relevant fact—which they took trouble to establish at the hearings—was that Major Williams had never been a molder, had no practical experience in the trade, had never worked at the bench or made a mold, and had never been trained in the craft (facts which Major Williams could not deny). As one molder summed up the dispute between Gustave Lawson and the officers in charge (see above):

> Now, the point I wanted to bring out is that a military officer, who is not a molder, would not be competent to instruct a man whom you testify is probably the best molder in the arsenal and recognized as one of the best molders in this vicinity. (Ibid.: 151).

That is, these workers rejected the very concept of management as an occupation and a skill separate from expertise in the work itself.*

It is important to consider disputes about quality, both because they were important in and of themselves and because they reveal the attitudes of the two sides and the nature of the struggle. The main focus of struggle on the shop floor, however, unquestionably concerned the speed of production. Workers decided among themselves on an output level, and enforced it on each other. This was set at what workers considered a reasonable speed of production, a speed considerably below what they knew to be physically possible. Workers put strong social pressure on each other not to exceed the agreed output level, since that would make other workers look bad, and would subject them to strong employer pressure to increase their speed. At the end of World War I, Charles Walker, a Yale graduate, took a job as a common laborer in a steel mill. It took the other workers a while to teach Walker the correct work pace. At first he went too fast, and was encouraged by others to slow down.

> So I slowed up on my wheel-barrow loads, sat on the handles, and spat and talked, till I found I was going too slow. There was a work-rhythm that was neither a dawdle nor a drive; if you expected any comfort in your gang life of twelve hours daily, you had best discover and obey its laws. It might be, from several points of view, an incorrect rhythm, but, at all events, it was a part of the gang mores. And some of its inward reasonableness often appeared before the day was out, or the month, or the year. (Walker, 1922: 93–94)

---

*For a British example of this same sort of dispute at about the same period see Thompson, 1963: 236.

Workers wanted to maintain a comfortable work pace, one which would allow them to live a reasonable life, both at work and at home. Even when they were offered increased wages for higher productivity, they still refused to increase their output.

> *The Chairman.* Have you any objection to the premium system at all?
>
> *Mr. Stackhouse.* Yes, I have objection to it—that to come up with the time on the card I have got to move along pretty lively.
>
> *The Chairman.* But you get additional pay if you do move along faster?
>
> *Mr. Stackhouse.* Yes; but I am satisfied with a day's pay for a day's work, and I don't want to go home at night feeling like I would lay down by the machine when I got through my work. (U.S. House of Representatives, 1912: 302)

Mr. Stackhouse readily admitted that he could work fast enough to meet the output goal set for him, but he did not want to, and extra wages were not enough to change his mind.

In the nineteenth century it was generally accepted as legitimate for ordinary workers to have the kind of control over their work time which today is the special privilege of college professors, top managers, and similar elite personnel. The following somewhat romanticized version of the mid-nineteenth century reality appeared in *Engineering Magazine* in 1896:

> The nearest approach to a strike in the Whitin Shops occurred when the ten-hour law was passed in Massachusetts. The workmen asked for the ten-hour day from the member of the Whitin family at that time in charge, and it was given them, with the information that the works would be fenced in, and provided with locked gates. The working hours had been nominally eleven; if a workman was five or ten minutes late, it was not noticed, and, if a hand wanted a piece of pie in the forenoon, he simply walked out of the shop to his home for it. The mail came to the little post-office across the road from the works at five in the afternoon, and, of course, nothing was more reasonable than that a workman should go over to the office to see if he had any important letters. There are to-day fish in the pond, and fur and feather on the hills about Whitinsville, and in the old days many of the hands took their guns to the shop with them, and a flock of ducks in the pond, or even a muskrat swimming across, was the signal for a shooting expedition. (Roland, 1896, 12: 78–80)

The fence and locked gates, the end of the ability to take a break when and as they chose, caused mass resignations in a form of strike.

An extreme example of this sort of workers' control is that of the hat finishers, who "considered it oppressive to work without breaks," "jealously guarded their right to drink," and stopped work to play.

> When times were dull, they turned their shops into recreation rooms, and played card games, checkers, or quoits; indeed "no finishing room would be complete without a checker board and a deck of cards." Even in busy times, hatters broke up their work with frequent diversions. Salesmen regularly went through the shops selling jewelry or other wares, while job-hunters from outside wandered about renewing old acquaintances.* Meanwhile, the finishers themselves walked through the factories, from department to department, visiting with neighbors and friends. . . .
>
> When work was not piled up too high, hatters left their shops to play baseball or to go on a clambake. Danbury finishers found the lure of the great outdoors to be so strong that they left for picnics even without their bosses' permission during the summer of 1886. So passionate was the Orange men's love for baseball that they played when they had ample work to do. (Bensman, 1979: 109–11; for another example see Deyrup, 1948: 162–63)

By 1911, at the time of the congressional hearings investigating government arsenals, these rights were much less common and generally had been much reduced even where they existed. Even so, Congressman Redfield, himself a manufacturer, and later secretary of commerce, assumed that workers would have rights which workers today would hesitate to ask for. For example, he could not believe that workers were not allowed to go over and look out the windows, and wanted to know if an exception was made at least on circus days. At the Rock Island Arsenal hearings he also had trouble accepting the rules about talking:

> *Mr. Alifas.* Is it not regarded by most of the workmen that it is almost an impossibility for a man to refrain from talking all day long?
>
> *Mr. Gustafson.* Well, the statement is made by my fellow workmen that it is an impossibility for a man to refrain from talking all day long, and that, furthermore, they would not stop. . . .

---

*The hat finishers themselves controlled hiring: to be hired a journeyman had to have another journeyman vouch for him.

Mr. Redfield. I want to get a little clearer understanding for the committee of what this system is. What do you mean by a rule against talking? That, of course, does not mean, as I understand it, that you can carry on long conversations, but do you mean that you are forbidden by this rule from speaking to an adjoining workman?

Mr. Gustafson. It does; anything that does not pertain to your work.

Mr. Redfield. You could not say to him, "That was a fine show we saw at the theater last night"?

Mr. Gustafson. No, sir; you are not supposed to say that.

Mr. Redfield. Now, is that literally so, that you are not supposed to talk about anything at all? Do you want us to understand that you are under a system where the only words that are supposed to pass your lips all day long relate to the actual work of the arsenal?

Mr. Gustafson. Yes, sir; that is what we are given to understand. (U.S. House of Representatives, 1912: 908, 910)

Since in general workers wanted to do "a fair day's work," they resisted instructions that called for too little as well as too much work. A molder at the Watertown Arsenal, for example, testified that he received such instructions. "I felt a little bit ashamed of myself," he said, and he therefore explained to the person in charge how and why he should do more work (ibid.: 247). By the nature of the case, however, it was much more common for workers to resist management pressures to do more than they deemed reasonable. Management pointed to figures showing how much could be done in a few hours (or minutes), and then multiplied those figures out to achieve a day or a week's output level. The workers at the Rock Island Arsenal replied by noting:

A race horse may be able to travel a mile in 2.40 or 2.20 minutes, as the case may be, but it does not follow that he can travel 2 miles in 5.20 or 4.40 minutes, or double the time required to travel the first mile, to say nothing of 8 miles in eight times the 2.40 or 2.20 minutes. Neither can a man keep up a pace for eight hours a day, day after day, the same as he could for 30 minutes or an hour. (Ibid.: 866, statement "of the federated employees of the various shops at the Rock Island Arsenal"; see also U.S. Commissioner of Labor, 1905: 206)

Probably the major shop floor struggles of the period concerned this resistance to production speed-up. When workers were told to do more than the amount decided on by the work group, they often simply refused:

> *Mr. Fitzgerald.* He said he [Merrick, the scientific management expert] wanted that amount per hour?
>
> *Mr. White.* Yes; he said I could do it and he wanted it and that was all there was to it. I told him I was not going to kill myself for him or any other man in order to turn out that amount. (U.S. House of Representatives, 1912: 444)

Another worker explained that he could meet the output goals set for him by a scientific management expert if he worked without resting, but insisted that this was ridiculous:

> He would have to work there every second of the eight hours, and if there is any man who can do that I don't believe I ever saw him. I never saw a man who can stand right in the same place all day and work every instant for eight hours. (Ibid.: 453; see also 509, 516)

As it happens, this was said in 1911, at exactly the time that Henry Ford was creating the assembly line, which forced workers to do what this machinist believed to be impossible and ridiculous.

It is important to understand that, whether the question was one of speed or quality, workers were not simply maximizing their individual pleasure. As a class they enforced, through a variety of social means, policies which they collectively supported. Since the pressure from employers was to increase output to the greatest possible extent, worker activity usually aimed at penalizing workers who produced too much. But workers did not earn power and respect in either the work group or the community by producing inadequate amounts of inferior quality goods. No one more bitterly attacked the craft system than Frederick Taylor (see Chapter Six), but part of Taylor's genius was the fact that he understood that the craft system was an alternative (and viable) social system which regulated production, rather than a simple anarchy which left a void that could easily be filled. Taylor was an upper-class person who went to work in a factory (owned by friends of his), became a machinist, and was almost immediately promoted to foreman, at which time he began his lifelong struggle to destroy the craft system and worker control. Taylor is worth quoting at considerable length, both because of his own importance, and because he provides one of the clearest and most conspicuous descriptions of the way the craft system operated:

> As was usual then, and in fact is still [1911] usual in most of the shops in this country, the shop was really run by the workmen, and not by the bosses. The workmen together had carefully planned just how fast each job should be done, and they had set a pace for each machine throughout the shop, which was limited to about one-third of a good day's work [i.e., the maximum possible]. Every new workman who came into the shop was told at once by the other men exactly how much of each kind of work he was to do, and unless he obeyed these instructions he was sure before long to be driven out of the place by the men.
>
> As soon as the writer was made gang-boss, one after another of the men came to him and talked somewhat as follows:
>
> "Now, Fred, we're very glad to see that you've been made gang-boss. You know the game all right, and we're sure that you're not likely to be a piece-work hog. You come along with us, and everything will be all right, but if you try breaking any of these rates you can be mighty sure that we'll throw you over the fence."
>
> The writer told them plainly that he was now working on the side of the management, and that he proposed to do whatever he could to get a fair day's work out of the lathes. This immediately started a war; in most cases a friendly war, because the men who were under him were his personal friends,* but nonetheless a war, which as time went on grew more and more bitter. The writer used every expedient to make them do a fair day's work, such as discharging or lowering the wages of the more stubborn men who refused to make any improvement, and such as lowering the piece-work price, hiring green men, and personally teaching them how to do the work, with the promise from them that when they had learned how, they would then do a fair day's work. While the men constantly brought such pressure to bear (both inside and outside the works) upon all those who started to increase their output that they were finally compelled to do about as the rest did, or else quit. No one who has not had this experience can have an idea of the bitterness which is gradually developed in such a struggle. In a war of this kind the workmen have one expedient

---

*The "personal friendship" was apparently a figment of Taylor's imagination, or a deliberate lie.

which is usually effective. They use their ingenuity to contrive various ways in which the machines which they are running are broken or damaged—apparently by accident, or in the regular course of work—and this they always lay at the door of the foreman, who has forced them to drive the machine so hard that it is overstrained and is being ruined. And there are few foremen indeed who are able to stand up against the combined pressure of all of the men in the shop. In this case the problem was complicated by the fact that the shop ran both day and night.

The writer had two advantages, however, which are not possessed by the ordinary foreman, and these came, curiously enough, from the fact that he was not the son of a working man.

First, owing to the fact that he happened not to be of working parents, the owners of the company believed that he had the interest of the works more at heart than the other workmen, and they therefore had more confidence in his word than they did in that of the machinists who were under him. So that, when the machinists reported to the Superintendent that the machines were being smashed up because an incompetent foreman was overstraining them, the Superintendent accepted the word of the writer when he said that these men were deliberately breaking their machines as a part of the piece-work war which was going on. . . .

Second. If the writer had been one of the workmen, and had lived where they lived, they would have brought such social pressure to bear on him that it would have been impossible to have stood out against them. He would have been called "scab" and other foul names every time he appeared on the street, his wife would have been abused, and his children would have been stoned. Once or twice he was begged by some of his friends among the workmen not to walk home, about two and a half miles along the lonely path by the side of the railway. He was told that if he continued to do this it would be at the risk of his life. In all such cases, however, a display of timidity is apt to increase rather than diminish the risk, so the writer told these men to say to the other men in the shop that he proposed to walk home every night right up that railway track; that he never had carried and never would carry any weapon of any kind, and that they could shoot and be d——. (1911: 48–52)

As Taylor knew full well, he had succeeded only because he was a member of the upper class: had this not been the case, the owners of the works would not have supported him during the transitional period when his policies were counterproductive. Even more important, had his social life and friendships been rooted in the working-class community, he could not have stood the pressure. Taylor went to the Philadelphia Cricket Club rather than to the corner saloon, he won the struggle for control of the workplace, and still he had doubts as to whether the struggle had been worth it: "For any right-minded man, this success is in no sense a recompense for the bitter relations which he is forced to maintain with all of those around him. Life which is one continuous struggle with other men is hardly worth living" (ibid.: 52).

Class Consciousness Versus Political Consciousness

Historical evidence thus indicates that throughout the nineteenth century workers maintained a high degree of control over the work process, control which they struggled to preserve and enforce, often intentionally evading or circumventing management's wishes and orders. Despite all this, however, workers did not theoretically develop or articulate their right to control the work process. In practice, they often made demands which in effect denied capital's right to control labor. In some ways, for narrow particular situations, they were willing to argue that management had no right to interfere with work. But American workers did not go on to develop an analysis that defended their *right* to control production; much less did they see the need for an international struggle to take the offensive in fighting for worker control of production. With some important exceptions, workers tended to concede that management had a right to give orders that workers should obey. The same workers who conceded management's right to give orders then struggled to evade or sabotage these orders.

Lenin made the distinction between a trade union consciousness, which workers could (he said) attain on their own, and a revolutionary consciousness, which had to be brought to them by a revolutionary party. I have always found this one of the most objectionable parts of Lenin's work. Subsequent vulgarizations of this position (lacking Lenin's revolutionary honesty and willingness to change) have been used to justify some of the crassest and most vulgar sorts of Stalinism. It is a fundamental perversion of Marxism to see consciousness as separate from the process of struggle, and to treat "correct" consciousness as an actual object which can be "given" or "brought" to people by some person, party, or group which somehow stands outside the class struggle.

Nonetheless, I think Lenin was getting at an important distinction, fundamental to an understanding of the American craft system of the late nineteenth and early twentieth centuries. It would be ridiculous to say that workers at this time did not have class consciousness. They were very aware of themselves as a group with interests that were opposed to the interests of managers and employers. They clearly saw the need to unite as a class and enforce on each other collective decisions about the work process, and they succeeded remarkably well in doing do. However, in practice they seem to have accepted the capitalist system, and to have assumed that they would continue to operate within it. In my opinion, this is an impossible position: as long as the capitalist system continues, concessions or reforms won within that system will be short lived and subject to continual attack. Either capital or labor must win the struggle, and workers who believed that they could get along within capitalism, preserving the victories they had won without pushing for the overthrow of capitalism and the creation of socialism, were suffering from a dangerous delusion. The dynamic of the situation is crucial, and unless workers can continually push for new victories and the eventual creation of communism, they are certain to lose.

Nineteenth-century American craft workers, however, conceded that management had the right to give orders. They even conceded that management had a right to know all about the work (U.S. House of Representatives, 1912: 308). Most of the time, when workers were given an order they objected to, they did not refuse to obey it. They might object, but having registered their objection they would then circumvent or sabotage the new procedure, as was done in the case of nailing molds. When workers did refuse to obey an order, they did not usually deny management's right to give orders, they simply claimed that it was impossible to obey the order. For example, when Mr. White was ordered to speed up he claimed that it would not be possible to meet the quota set for him unless he worked continuously, and he claimed this was impossible.

Even when workers denied management's right to know about the work and/or to control the work process, they generally did so on narrow and defensive grounds. For example, during the Watertown Arsenal hearings there was a discussion of the old and new methods of keeping time, which were essentially identical, with the major exception that the new system required workers to clock in and out under the eye of the planning room, while the old system operated on the supposition that workers and foremen could be trusted, so it could be supposed that all the time the card was out the worker had been engaged in the production of that item. The following exchange then ensued between Congressman Redfield (himself the owner of a manufacturing company) and Mr. Crawford, a machinist:

Mr. Redfield. Now, Mr. Crawford, as an illustration of the supposition system take this actual case and tell me how you would meet it on what you yourself call the supposition system. In a certain cotton mill running certain looms, after many years the foreman began to think that there was a lot of time wasted in walking about. He tried but he could not find out. He had no means of measuring, except his supposition. So he got the means of measuring, and he found that his weavers were walking 12 miles a day; and having that knowledge as against his former supposition, he so rearranged his looms that they walked but 3 miles. Now, do you object to his using an instrument to find out that the men were doing 9 miles of useless walking?

Mr. Crawford. Well, I worked at the weaving business myself. That was in my early days before I went into the machine business, and when I worked at the weaving business I was paid by the cut and I don't know what concern it was of my employer's how many miles I walked as long as I got out the work. He was paying me for the work done and not for the time I was employed.

Mr. Redfield. I am very glad to have you tell me how you were paid, but the question that I asked you was whether you objected to having it found out accurately that the weavers were walking 9 useless miles.

Mr. Crawford. Well, under the conditions I described I do not see how they are affected by it at all. I was simply taking it out of my own legs and not out of his pocketbook.

Mr. Redfield. Do you object to having it found out accurately that you are wasting time?

Mr. Crawford. I was not wasting time.

Mr. Redfield. You were not one of those men, perhaps.

Mr. Crawford. I was not wasting time.

Mr. Redfield. Still, I asked the question, do you object in such a case to the manufacturer finding out accurately where waste of that kind is going on; and if so, why do you object?

Mr. Crawford. Well, I will tell you. I think when systems of that kind are introduced they are apt to be abused and abused to the detriment of the workman.

Mr. Redfield. Then it is the abuse you object to rather than the use, is that it?

Mr. Crawford. Abuse and the use both, because the one follows the other. You can not have the one without the other. (Ibid.: 421)

Mr. Crawford obviously had a high degree of class consciousness, a realization of the extent to which his interests were different from, and opposed to, those of his employer (and employers in general). He did not think it was any of his employer's business how he did the work, he objected to his employer finding out how far he walked, and when pushed he even stated that the abuse of the system was inherent in the use of the system. However, these views were apparently unrelated to any general political position: he did not assert labor's right to control work in general, but only under the specific circumstances of piecework, when changes in the work process did not in theory change the cost to the employer; it was only when pushed that he stated the use of the system necessarily involved abuse as well.

The lack of a revolutionary political consciousness was the Achilles heel of the American craft system. Workers had actual control over a whole host of decisions, and to a considerable degree over the work process as a whole, but they did not defend this control as their right. Workers allowed owners (and, to the extent they existed, managers) to issue orders, and would have publicly stated that they were obeying those orders. Workers simply used their control of the details of the production process to circumvent those orders they opposed, relying with false security on their belief that only workers could control the work, so that management's theoretical right to give orders did not in practice amount to anything. By not consciously formulating as a set of political demands the rights of labor to control the work process they were open to any employer offensive based on management's legitimate right to give orders. Once management learned how to do the work, workers had no developed culture or consciousness to deal with a situation in which they were given precise and detailed orders, rather than simply general directives.

Workers' Control: Romanticized or Real?

It would be easy to romanticize the situation described in this and the previous chapter. The late nineteenth century could be viewed as a time when there was "workers' control" of industry, a sort of early socialism. I have argued that workers controlled many details of the work process, had comparatively varied and interesting work, used their expertise and creativity during the work process, and had a great deal of control over the rhythm and activities of the working day. Today, workers do not have these forms of power and control, and many workers and unions would correctly consider them to represent a great victory. For obvious reasons, there is a tendency on the left today to view this period with a kind of nostalgia.

The two authors who have done the best work on this topic, David Montgomery and Katherine Stone, both have at times slipped into this nostalgic and romanticized view of the situation, and an examination of their work therefore provides an opportunity to forestall some possible misunderstandings of my own analysis. Stone's excellent article, "The Origins of Job Structures in the Steel Industry," not only renewed interest in the contract system and attempted to understand its significance as more than a historical curiosity, it also provided a pathbreaking analysis of the system's destruction, and of the creation of a bureaucratic job hierarchy. Stone analyzes the steel industry, but feels that "the conclusions . . . are applicable to many other major industries in the United States" (1974: 93). Montgomery's work on machine production is an important contribution both on a theoretical level and through its rich and detailed evidence.

In the steel industry the contract system seems to have been much more under the control of workers than it was in industries producing interchangeable parts. According to Stone and Montgomery, steelworkers selected representatives through a union who bargained with the plant superintendent. The workers then met together to decide how much each would receive. According to Montgomery:

> The iron rollers of the Columbus Iron Works, in Ohio, have left us a clear record of how they managed their trade in the minute books of their local union from 1873 to 1876. The three twelve-man rolling teams, which constituted the union, negotiated a single tonnage rate with the company for each specific rolling job the company undertook. The workers then decided collectively, among themselves, what portion of that rate should go to each of them (and the shares were far from equal, ranging from 19¼ cents, out of the negotiated $1.13 a ton, for the roller, to 5 cents for the runout hooker), how work should be allocated among them, how many rounds on the rolls should be undertaken per day, what special arrangements should be made for the fiercely hot labors of the hookers during the summer, and how members should be hired and progress through the various ranks of the gang. To put it another way, *all the boss did was to buy the equipment and raw materials and sell the finished product.* (1976: 488–89; emphasis added)

To me, Montgomery has gone too far: his conclusion is not only inaccurate as an assessment of this particular example, but also misleading as a characterization of the general situation. The boss did a great deal, even if the goods could have been produced just as well without him. The capitalist controlled plant openings, closings, size, construction, and location. "To buy the equipment and raw materials" is to control, or exert great influence over, the technology employed. Workers might have considerable power to resist the introduction of new technologies they opposed, but in the steel industry they probably had very little opportunity to introduce technologies: the scale and expense would at a minimum require the owner's cooperation and consent. Therefore, these technologies had to be developed within the framework of a capitalist system, in which profit is more important than workers' comfort or similar considerations. This fact alone meant that change in the work process—and change is an incessant feature of capitalist society—was likely to favor owners rather than workers.

The boss's sale of the finished product gave him a measure of control over the way the steel was distributed or used and, within constraints imposed by the market, over the amount that was produced. More important, the boss kept the proceeds of sales and this amount far exceeded what any worker received. The boss, then, did not provide a simple service in buying the equipment and raw materials and selling the product; rather, this was the basis for a position of great power: control over profits, the accumulation of capital, and the use to which that capital was put. The capitalist's position of power greatly overshadowed any actual contribution he made to the production process.

Stone is even more extreme in her conclusions about the significance of workers' participation in the production process. Under the contract system as it prevailed in steel, she argues, skilled workers were "*partners* in production," and therefore "the problem of worker motivation *did not arise.*" In such a situation skilled workers "set their own pace and work load *without input* from the bosses." How hard workers worked became "an issue of class struggle" only after this system ended (1974: 69–70; emphasis added; see also Brecher and Costello, 1976: 30).

I am not sure what Stone means by saying that skilled workers were "partners" in production. By her account, workers completely organized production and did all the work; capitalists took the product, and kept most of the sale price as their profit. What sort of "partnership" is this? I can understand why Andrew Carnegie liked to say that he and his workers were "partners in production" (Stone, 1974: 64), but the fact that some workers made high wages, and were able to do as they pleased as long as they produced a sufficiently high rate of profit is hardly enough reason for Stone to accept this as a partnership. Capitalists are always saying that workers and capitalists are partners in production, meaning that what benefits one will benefit the other, and workers should therefore do whatever the capitalist wants. Marx exposed the falsehood of this claim, arguing that there were opposing class interests, and showing that when the worker cooperates with capital he or she creates capital and the domination of capital. The harder the worker works, the more capital he or she creates for the owner. Under capitalism, the productivity of labor can be raised only through the accumulation of capital; this means increasing domination of the worker. In such circumstances no partnership is possible.

Stone's assertion that the problem of worker motivation did not arise under the contract system and that how hard workers worked became an issue of class struggle only after it ended would be true only if capitalism worked as its apologists claim, through economic incentives and the operation of a free market. Stone does claim that "the price was determined by the market" (ibid.: 64), but this view is naive. Workers bargained with capitalists to determine the contract price, and the power balance between employers and workers was probably a crucial factor in determining the "market price." This is dramatically illustrated by the fact, reported by Stone herself, that in addition to the sliding scale which pegged the contract price for labor to the selling price of steel, the contracted labor price specified a minimum rate below which wages could not fall, no matter how low the selling price of steel. This provision was absolutely crucial, since " 'the negotiated minimum piece rates . . . became the de facto standard rates for the organized sector of the industry during most of the period from 1880 to the end of the century' " (Doeringer, quoted in ibid.: 65).

It is even more dubious to hold that the sliding scale (or piecework) meant that the intensity of labor was no longer an issue of class struggle. Capitalism has always used force as well as material incentives; wages in general and payment by results in particular have never been enough to make workers strive for the maximum output. Both workers and employers knew that if the intensity of labor increased this would lead to a fall in the contract price, not a rise in wages. The intensity of labor, the question of whether workers were doing all they were capable of, was perhaps the single most important issue of class struggle. This is especially clear for piecework (see Chapter Five), but it was also the case in the contract system in steel. The employers' problem was precisely the difficulty, under these systems, of increasing the intensity of labor.

There are two more fundamental reasons why the nature of workers' control as it existed under the craft and contract systems cannot be regarded as anything but an extremely vague, partial, and inadequate indication of what would be involved in a true system of workers' control. First of all, workers did not control the society at large. In an article criticizing the romanticized view of nineteenth- and early twentieth-century production, Jean Monds argues, "What

Montgomery and Hinton call 'workers' control' is really equivalent to the defensive devices built up by workers through years of struggle at the point of production" (1976: 82). I do not agree with Monds' assessment—many of the practices of craft workers must be seen, both historically and analytically, as much more than defensive practices—but it does serve as an important corrective. The "workers' control" of the 1880s and 1890s took place within a capitalist system, where capitalists controlled the state and workers' victories were always under assault. Comparatively few workers were unionized, capitalists won most of the strikes and decisive confrontations (Homestead, Haymarket and surrounding events, Pullman, etc.), union activists were often effectively blacklisted, and an open shop drive destroyed many of the unions that did exist around 1900. In this context, even the victories workers won were often distorted by the necessity of defending themselves against employer assaults. For example, Stone cites the following passages from a company history to show that the 1889 union contract at Carnegie's Homestead mill "gave the skilled workers authority over every aspect of steel production there":

> Every department and sub-department had its workmen's "committee," with a "chairman" and full corps of officers. . . . During the ensuing three years hardly a day passed that a "committee" did not come forward with some demand or grievance. If a man with a desirable job died or left the works, his position could not be filled without the consent and approval of an Amalgamated committee. . . . The method of apportioning the work of regulating the turns, of altering the machinery, in short, every detail of working the great plant was subject to the interference of some busybody representing the Amalgamated Association. Some of this meddling was specified under the agreement that had been signed by the Carnegies, but much of it was not; it was only in line with the general policy of the union. . . . The heats of a turn were designated, as were the weights of the various charges constituting a heat. The product per worker was limited; the proportion of scrap that might be used in running a furnace was fixed; the quality of pig-iron was stated; the puddler's use of brick and fire clay was forbidden, with exceptions; the labor of assistants was defined; the teaching of other workmen was prohibited, nor might one man lend his tools to another except as provided for. (1974: 64)

This statement does show a great deal of control by workers over the work process, of course, but it also indicates the extremely defensive nature of this control. This myriad of rules would not have been necessary had workers actually had control over the production process. Each rule is an indication that workers were under assault on this issue, and were forced to formulate a rule to prevent an employer policy which they opposed. At the same time, these rules, precisely because they were defensive practices, introduced real inefficiencies into the production process. For example, rules that prohibit the teaching of other workers or the lending of tools may be regarded as necessary to preserve the positions of certain groups of workers, but if workers really were in control they would have no reason to adopt such policies, and plenty of reason to oppose them. Work would be much pleasanter and simpler if people were allowed and encouraged to share both knowledge and equipment.

The limits to "workers' control" are clear in the way the system ended. The end of the contract system in steel did not come from an inability of workers to manage production, nor even because workers lost the struggles on the shop floor. State power was in the hands of capitalists, and this was crucial. As Stone's article documents, the key factor was the Homestead steel strike, which was intentionally provoked by the managers of Andrew Carnegie's Homestead plant. The strike was smashed through violence and state power, the contract system was abolished, and "workers' control" was ended. Capitalists had been unable to defeat the system inside the works, but they did not limit themselves to this kind of economic attack: capitalists controlled the state and used this control against workers.

A second reason why the contract system as it existed in the nineteenth-century United States cannot be regarded as a socialist model of workers' control is the fact that it sustained substantial inequalities among workers. Both foremen and inside contractors possessed, at least nominally, virtually dictatorial powers. Needless to say, both officials were picked by the bosses, not by the workers. Even when workers contracted as a group, the standard practice in steel and not uncommon for machinists, there is every indication that they were not a group of equals. Wage differentials are only one indication of the greater power and privilege of the more highly skilled workers; as is always the case in America, these coincided with racial, sexual, and ethnic cleavages. In other words, "workers' control" meant that a minority of workers—comparatively highly paid, white, male, born in America—controlled work for themselves, and also for a larger number of lower paid, less skilled, largely immigrant workers. Before any assessment of the system can be made, it is important to investigate the relations between skilled and unskilled workers, and the way the system looked from the perspective of the unskilled. Montgomery offers some evidence on this question, but he makes no systematic attempt to consider the implications of the problem. Nor have I found evidence which significantly addresses this issue, and that remains a central weakness in my argument, and an area in need of further research. Undoubtedly there were many instances of craft workers oppressing the unskilled, and other cases where workers maintained solidarity and defended each other. Paul Buhle reports a particularly intriguing example from the Rhode Island Knights of Labor. After a victory on one issue,

> suddenly, the Assembly swelled to more members than any hall in the area could hold. Particular sectors of the plant, such as the female inspectors known as burlars, gained an especial reputation for resisting encroachments on their autonomy. The Assembly moved toward administering the shop-floor life as a whole, by establishing the pace, cooperation between workers, and evaluation of the final product. Supervisors complained that they now lacked the authority only the union could provide in disciplining the work force. Within limits, the Wanskuck Knights had achieved "workers' control." What happened here over a period of months strongly resembles David Montgomery's description of craft workers reasserting their prerogative to conduct the work processes in their own way—except that Wanskuck workers were mostly female, hardly "skilled" by any existing craft definitions, and evidently united across lines of job classifications. (1978: 53)

Until the situation of the unskilled is adequately investigated no full understanding of late nineteenth-century production will be possible. A lack of evidence, however, should not lead us to implicitly deny the reality or significance of the problem.

5

Undermining the Craft System: Early Management

The extent to which craft workers controlled both the technical details of the work process and the social order of the workplace posed serious problems for nineteenth-century capitalists. Marx discussed the (earlier) era of handicrafts as a period when the work possessed no framework other than the skill of the workers and in which capital therefore had difficulties in asserting control. By contrast, Marx said, in the stage of modern industry the machinery itself provides a framework that makes capital to a considerable degree independent of workers' skills. This is not a question of static structures at two different points in time, but of a process. In the period I am studying there was a large amount of machinery, which I have argued was indispensable for capitalist control, but it provided only islands of control in the flow of production. In important ways, the social relations of the late nineteenth-century United States craft system very much resemble Marx's description of the social relations of the handicraft era of the eighteenth century, even though the craft system used large quantities of highly developed machinery. The overall framework of control (which Marx attributed to machinery) emerged only toward the end of the period as scientific management, or Taylorism, developed a bureaucratic framework.

This process involved the gradual creation of management and industrial bureaucracy, phenomena which did not really exist in, say, 1870, but which had a firm foothold by, say, 1920. One index of the increase in management is the number of articles published on the subject during the period from 1870 to 1900, from an average of less than one article per year in the early 1870s to an average of about twenty-five articles a year in the late 1890s (Litterer, 1959: 65–68). Many magazines intended to help develop management methods

167

were founded or expanded during this period, and associations that held meetings and published materials were formed.

This chapter focuses on three aspects of the capitalist effort to undermine the relative autonomy of workers and speed up production: piecework, improved record keeping, and technology. Each of these was inseparable from the development of management, and each was partially successful, in that it weakened or destroyed some part of the craft system. However, these early management initiatives shared a common weakness: they were based, albeit unconsciously, on the assumption that workers (and their immediate supervisors) would continue to control production. These new systems gave capital added weapons to use in pressuring workers, but they continued to rely on workers to make the basic decisions about how to plan and do the work and thus remained dependent on their initiative, skill, and cooperation.

Cumulatively, the early management movement that is the subject of this chapter greatly weakened workers' control over the speed and organization of production, but it was unable to make the qualitative leap to a different system because it had no alternative conception of how production could be organized. Implicitly, it accepted that only workers were capable of making the basic decisions, and therefore workers had to be allowed considerable autonomy and control. This movement provided the necessary foundation for Taylorism, but Taylor's genius lay in the fact that he (based on the experience of the early management movement) made the qualitative leap to a recognition that as long as workers had this degree of knowledge, autonomy, and control, capital would never be able to have things its own way. Therefore, he confronted the need for a different organization of production, based on the creation of a separate group (managers, engineers, clerks) to direct and control the work process. On the one hand, Taylor's system was possible only because of the management movement that preceded him, but on the other hand, the genius and necessity of his contribution can be understood only in contrast to the limited vision of his contemporaries.

Simple Piecework

Probably the major means by which capitalists sought to reduce the power of craft workers was the institution of piecework in place of inside contracting and all-powerful foremen. As Henry Roland noted in 1896: "In most cases the effort now is to replace the contractor by fixed-pay foremen, and to put the hands on piece-rate pay, thus exactly reversing the former method of paying the hands by the day and the contractor by the piece" (1897, 12: 401). In paying workers according to the number of items they produced, management tried to appeal to individual workers, rather than to the group and its leader. Thus they no longer operated through semi-autonomous intermediaries but instead tried to directly control and keep track of individual workers. Before the introduction of piece-work, management had not even tried to monitor the performance of individual workers; "the pressure to produce or set the pace was entirely on the foreman who drove the men" (Kolker, 1948: 91). With the introduction of piecework, the rewards and penalties for performance were directed at the individual worker. The company took more direct control over production, made it more difficult for workers and foremen to make deals and reach informal understandings (Norris, 1899: 576), and so undermined their power indirectly as well as directly. Even in its simplest form piecework was inseparable from increased management record keeping, since it was necessary to record how many pieces were produced by each worker.

In theory, piecework was simple. The company set a fair price for each unit of completed work (say, the average cost on the last few equivalent jobs) and workers were paid according to their output. If workers could increase output, either by extra exertion or by improved methods of their own devising, they would receive higher wages. Capitalists would benefit as well, even if labor costs stayed the same, since the extra output per hour would mean falling unit costs for machinery and output. Thus, even with a constant piece price capitalists would get substantial benefits.*

In practice, piecework never worked this way, since employers always cut the price they paid workers. Capitalists would adjust piece prices to a level that allowed workers to earn somewhat more

---

*A simple example makes the point clear. If workers produced 100 gears a day, and if costs were 3¢ a gear for labor and 3¢ a gear for the use of machinery, buildings, land, and overhead, total costs would be 6¢ a gear. If workers doubled their output their wages would rise from $3 a day to $6 a day, and the cost per gear would fall to 4.5¢ (3¢ for labor, 1.5¢ for machinery, buildings, land, and overhead), a 25 percent reduction in total cost despite a constant labor cost.

than their day wage—so they would continue to have a material interest in high output—but only about one-third more, no matter how great the increase in output. Almost all employers insisted that they would never cut a price once it was set, yet every employer did cut prices. As J. Slater Lewis explained in *Engineering Magazine,* in using piecework

> we obtain, it is true, an immediate definition and limitation of cost, coupled with a strong and direct inducement for the employee to exert his best endeavours to increase and intensify production. At least, this is the theory; but in practice it is a true statement of the result only within very narrow limits. . . . There inevitably comes a time—if the workman continues to improve in skill, or to give evidence of a continuous and successful application of intelligence to his work—when the gains of the workman appear excessive compared with his former earnings as a mere supplier of labour by the hour. The employer would be more than human who did not, at this stage, ask himself the question, "Have I not made a mistake in fixing prices?" When this question is answered affirmatively, a reduction of rates inevitably follows. The suzerain power insists on remodeling the convention, and the result is frequently—not peace, but soreness. (1899: 203)

Employers could cut rates in dozens of ways other than changing the piece price for a worker who continued to perform the same operations. New employees could be assigned to the job at a lower rate while the old workers were transferred elsewhere, information about output on one job could be used to lower the initial price on new work, and any sort of minor change could be made the excuse for large price cuts.

> The gearing up of a machine, or the increase in the number of cutting points, a slight change in the tools, jigs or materials, an equally slight change in the shape or size of the product or in the method of handling it—any of these things may be sufficient. . . . By an extension of this method, entirely new classes of work can be readily created, unskilled tasks lopped off from skilled work and given a new and lower rating, still without cutting the rate. (Hoxie, 1915: 85)

Unless workers collectively restricted output they were likely to find themselves working much harder, producing much more, and earning only slightly higher wages. For example, the Rock Island

Arsenal mass produced McClellan saddles. Until the time of the Spanish-American War (1898), workers receiving a day wage of $2.25 shaved the side bars on eight to ten saddles a day. These workers were then put on piecework at an initial rate of 17¢ a saddle (compared to the day-wage labor cost of 22.5¢ to 28¢). At first the workers could not even make their day rate, but by virtue of hard work, ingenuity and (probably) reducing quality, they soon more than doubled output. The rate was repeatedly cut (from 17¢ to 15¢ to 12¢ to 8¢ and finally to 5¢), and workers continued to increase their output so that by the end they were producing sixty-five to seventy saddles a day, an increase of 650 to 700 percent, for which they received about 50 percent more than their day wage. These rate cuts and this increase in output took place even though the product remained exactly the same and no new machinery or methods were introduced (U.S. House of Representatives, 1912: 824–35). Bitter experience taught workers that this was the typical outcome; their protests are found throughout the pages of these hearings. In a separate investigation, the international president of the machinists' union stated: "I have no record nor do I know of a single instance where piecework or similar plans have been introduced where the prices were not reduced and again reduced and again reduced, until the employee has been urged to his utmost limit mentally and physically" (U.S. Commissioner of Labor, 1905: 121).

Workers quickly developed responses to the piecework system. From cumulative experience they learned that if their earnings exceeded what they would have earned on a day rate by more than a certain percentage, they could expect their rate to be cut. In 1904 at a factory employing 2,700 workers "it was reported [among the employees] that the proprietor had said that the proper earnings for a machinist were about $2.60 per day of ten hours, and with this standard before them the employees endeavored to restrict their earnings to that amount" (ibid.: 208).* As one union official summed up the situation:

---

*Usually workers restricted output by slowing the pace during the working day, but in some cases they did so by leaving when the quota was reached. One employer, whose workers were nonunion and for the most part boys, told the Bureau of Labor:

> When they get their stint done they go home, no matter what the rush may be for the work and no matter what inducement we offer them to stay and do more. You couldn't hire one of those men nor one of those youngsters to do another piece if you offered them four times their regular rate per hour. (U.S. Commissioner of Labor, 1905: 139)

> Pieceworkers know that prices are set according to a day scale. That is, the firm fixes its piece prices so that a man can earn about so much a day. If men earn more the piece price is cut. . . . With such ideas in the heads of employers don't you think the workman is an ass who would kill a job by earning more than the firm will stand? Unions have nothing to do with this. It is human nature, and just as prevalent among nonunion men as among union workmen. (Ibid.: 120)*

With rare exceptions, the only workers who maximized output under a piecework system were those who had not learned the consequences. The worker who reported about McClellan saddles, where a 700 percent increase in output brought only a 50 percent increase in wages, explained they had "always worked on a day rating, and . . . never worked on piecework at any time, and this is the first piecework some of these men had ever done" (U.S. House of Representatives, 1912: 835). In 1904, one company told investigators from the Bureau of Labor of what they saw as an example of restriction of output. They had had a worker, "an officer of the Frame Fitters' Local Union and one of the most arrogant agitators of the bunch," who averaged $2.35 a day. After a successful lockout, he along with many other workers was dismissed.

> He was dismissed permanently when the works started in September, 1901, and a green man put in his place with instructions to work the job for what there was in it, developing during the year what could be done, to pay his helpers $1.75 and $2 per day of 10 hours, and the result has been that without undue exertion he has been able to earn at his individual wage from $36 to $39 per week during the past year. The job was, of course, cut in two for this year and he will continue to earn a very satisfactory wage, amounting to $3 or $3.25 per day from now on. (U.S. Commissioner of Labor, 1905: 204)

As the authors of the government report note: "Here 'a green man . . . with instructions to work the job for what there was in it,' succeeded by his energy, push, and skill, by close attention to the interests of his employer and great fidelity to the trust imposed, in reducing his own earnings 50 percent in 12 months, by doubling the

---

*In public pronouncements employers sometimes denied they did this, but very frequently even they admitted this was the situation (see U.S. House of Representatives, 1912: 823–32, 926–27; U.S. Commissioner of Labor, 1905: 136; Roland, 1897, 14: 227)

output" (ibid.; see also U.S. House of Representatives, 1912: 871).

Workers often claimed that under piecework the employers paid only for what they got, which meant that the workers were working for themselves in a sense, so it was "'nobody's business how much or how little we do'" (quoted in U.S. Commissioner of Labor, 1905: 205). Obviously this was a specious argument. Capitalists thought it was their business how much workers did and made incredible efforts to determine maximum output. When capitalists could prove there was restriction of output they used this to justify a cut in the piece price. A large part of the continuing piecework struggle comprised management attempts to prove that the existing output levels could be increased, since if that could be demonstrated, workers were not generally willing to argue or fight for a lower quota. The simplest and most primitive way of doing so was through some sort of demonstration, either by a manager doing the work, or by persuading a worker to become a rate buster.

The Rock Island Arsenal attempted a management demonstration. However, workers maintained a reasonable work pace—not so fast as they could have worked, but not so slow that they could be challenged easily. In one case, when the workers refused to do a job because they believed the piecework rate had been set too low, the officer in charge did the work in order to show them up. Management concluded that the officer had demonstrated the reasonableness of the rate and wrote this in the only official report of the experiment, but workers came to very different conclusions, as emerged in questioning of Mr. Johnson, a carpenter, by Mr. Alifas, a union spokesman:

> *Mr. Alifas.* I would like to ask the witness whether Captain Lund ever tried to demonstrate that the work could be done in the time that had been set?
>
> *Mr. Johnson.* Yes, sir. Captain Lund did not think we were right in our work, he thought we were not fair. Now this happened on a day when I was absent attending a funeral; I was off in the morning four hours and came back at noon, and he had just gone through the work. He stated to the men that he was a cabinetmaker from the old country and that he knew something about woodwork, and that he was going to show us how to do the work, and that it could be done. And he gets the inspector to get the glue ready and have it fixed and have his material

in shape so that when Mr. Winters held the clock on him he could
go ahead.

I was not there, but when I came back at noon the excitement was
going on and they told me all about it, that he started something about
10 o'clock and he kept it up until noon, and in trying to perform this
work he worked so hard that he just sweat all over, he pulled off his
coat, his vest, collar, and necktie, and he went at it like he was going
into a prize fight; he wanted to demonstrate to us that it could be done.
He was literally soaked with sweat; the sweat ran from his legs and
through his pants and bubbles of sweat stuck out all over his forehead,
and he looked in a fearful shape. And Mr. Winters and the man that
was there figured out the time of Captain Lund's own trial and he was
not able to accomplish more than a few cents over the day rate. . . .

Mr. Alifas. Did the men regard that as being a sort of sweatshop
system if they had to work like that?

Mr. Johnson. They certainly did. (U.S. House of Representatives,
1912: 845)

The work was not good enough to pass inspection, and Captain Lund
himself admitted that he had sweat during the work and been sore
afterward (ibid.: 853). Workers may have been restricting their
output, but as one union official put it, some employers "think the
workman who does not have to go home every night in an ambulance
is restricting his output" (U.S. Commissioner of Labor, 1905: 207).

Management preferred to use rate busters for such demonstrations
because they were more likely to keep at the work than a management demonstrator. Rate busters were the rare exceptions who were
willing to exceed work group quotas even though they realized what
the consequences would be for others. Whereas restriction of output was in the interests of workers as a class, each individual worker
had a large incentive to exceed the quota and become a rate buster. A
rate buster could double his or her income, certainly during a
transitional period, until other workers increased their output, and
possibly permanently if other workers held to the quota (in which
case management might be willing to let the rate stand as cheap
"proof" that they would not cut rates).

The Watertown Arsenal hired such a rate buster, named Edgecomb, and he was one of the factors in the molders' strike that
eventually led to the congressional hearings. He achieved pheno-

menal rates, in part by producing lower quality work, omitting certain finishing or reinforcing steps which other molders considered essential. But this was possible only with management encouragement and assistance: he monopolized the crane, refusing to share it as did the other molders; he took sand that another molder had prepared; and he was allowed to keep his helper continuously when other molders shared helpers. When the foreman tried to challenge this Edgecomb cursed him—normally grounds for discharge, but here overlooked by the officers in charge (U.S. House of Representatives, 1912: 140–226). Until he was eventually dismissed (since he was a Canadian citizen and hence not eligible for government employment), the rates he achieved scared other workers into increasing their output, though they said the extra speed came out of their bones.

Numerous incidents of this kind led workers to develop a class awareness of the need to restrict output. Each individual did not have to have this experience in order for workers as a group to know that unlimited production was a hopeless approach. The concept of class means that workers shared such experiences, and they developed a common viewpoint and approach, a common consciousness, as a basis from which to confront experiences or proposals.* Although workers generally knew that they could have produced substantially more, they understood that it was not in their interests to do so, since in the long run their wages would not increase, but the intensity of labor would increase. The "green man" who managed to cut his piece rate in half by doubling his output, was green not only in the technical aspects of the work, but also in his social understanding of the way the shop operated. In this same shop, most of the workers understood piecework. As a result

> their earnings were remarkably uniform, the range being from $2.58 to $2.62. The reason everywhere given by the men for the limit was to stop the cutting of piece prices. The limit had been in force before the unions were formed, and resulted from the multiplication of such cases as is described above. These men had been "green men" formerly, or their fathers had, and the lesson had been learned, as one

---

*At the Watertown Arsenal hearings, worker after worker explained that he did not believe the arsenal management's claims because of his or others' experiences with piecework on previous jobs, working for private employers.

of them stated, that "unlimited production means unlimited reduction in these piece-price shops." (U.S. Commissioner of Labor, 1905: 204)

Workers not only understood the problem in class terms, they acted as a class to enforce restriction of output. The best evidence of worker success in enforcing output levels is the simple fact that in most cases all of the piecework employees earned essentially the same amount, a result that would be practically impossible if each individual worker independently tried to do his or her best. At the Rock Island Arsenal, for example, records showed that during each of four test days spread over six months, each of the twenty-seven polishers earned a minimum of $3.41 and a maximum of $3.52 for eight hours' work. Earnings for four hours were exactly half of those for eight hours. The harness makers employed drawing the leather covers on bayonet scabbards after they had been rawhided each produced exactly 400 covers in fourteen hours (not 399, not 401). At the Springfield Arsenal, barrel welders, the only group for which there are consistent records, all produced the same number of barrels each month, despite absences, differences in individual ability, and so on (U.S. House of Representatives, 1912: 870–71; Deyrup, 1948: 110). Regulation and restriction of output was so widespread and significant that the Bureau of Labor prepared a special 900-page report on the subject.

This uniformity of output did not just happen by chance. Workers collectively decided on production levels, in many cases through informal discussions, in other cases through formal shop meetings of all the workers (as was done by the hat finishers), in still other instances by elected shop committees (see Bensman, 1979).

> For instance, it is admitted by the polishers in the [Rock Island] Armory that they have a table, actual or understood, giving the number of pieces of each operation that they must polish in order to give them about 43¾ cents per hour, or $3.50 per day; they will do that number and no more. If they are given a number of pieces that is not a multiple of one-half hour's work, as set forth in that table, they will do the multiple number and return the remainder to the inspection room without completing them. (U.S. House of Representatives, 1912: 868)

Workers' moral code and sense of class solidarity required that they refuse to break a rate, even if this meant they lost their own jobs. According to one worker's testimony:

> About 20 years ago I went to work for Brown & Sharpe Manufacturing Co., Rhode Island [one of the most important machine shops in the country]. Before vacation there was a gentleman, I should judge about 50 years old, making a job; getting $1.75 for it. When I came back after two weeks vacation, which they have there in the summer time, the job that this gentleman had made for $1.75 was handed to me, and I was told that it was only $1.50. The job was cut and I wouldn't accept it; I had to quit my job if I didn't make it for $1.50, and I quit. I put my clothes on and I deliberately walked out. (Ibid.: 207)

Not everyone adhered to these standards freely and willingly, since individual workers had strong incentives to exceed the work-group norms. In order to enforce output quotas it was definitely necessary for some workers to pressure and coerce others. At the Rock Island Arsenal, a worker

> was engaged in the manufacture of fencing masks for the purpose of establishing a piece price, it being known by the officer in charge that he was an honest, trustworthy man [read: a rate buster]. Upon the completion of a number of jobs the federated employees of the harness shop tried to force him to turn in two hours more time on each job than it actually took. He stated that he could not stultify himself and was fined $2 [more than half a day's pay] by the union. He would not pay his fine and either resigned or was expelled from the union. (Ibid.: 871)

The officers at Rock Island knew of at least two other cases where workers had been "compelled to resign by petty persecution" because they would not obey the collective decisions of the work group. In other places unions lectured and even fined workers: "fast men are called down by the shop committee, and very often by men not on the committee, and told that they are 'killing the job,' etc." (U.S. Commissioner of Labor, 1905: 112; see also 198–210).*

---

*I have barely touched here on an extremely important question: How did the working-class community constitute itself so that it was able to maintain this degree of control? Deciding on a level of output was much easier than enforcing this level, but the problems were still immense: for example, continuing technological change meant that workers had to continually change their output levels. In the absence of a formal union structure—and a great deal of output restriction took place even where

Despite this self-conscious class activity workers did not generally go on to develop a political analysis or an open defense of their actions in restricting output. Publicly, they claimed that since they did as much work as could reasonably be expected, increases in output would have to come at the expense of quality. For example, one worker claimed: "An increased output when prices are cut does not mean that there were restrictions before; it means that there is now a slighting of the work" (ibid.: 120). It undoubtedly was true that production speed-ups led to strong pressures to reduce quality, and workers preferred to make goods they could be proud of, but to argue that increases in output could come only from decreases in quality is to assume that the intensity of labor cannot be increased, and plainly this was not the case. In most cases, the unions were as unwilling as the workers to argue publicly for restricting output. In one factory, for example, a new worker did a task in thirty-seven hours which had previously been done by a member of the union shop committee in forty-three hours, and was told by the committee to stick to the forty-three hours. When interviewed by the Bureau of Labor the union official said:

> The committee had no right to do anything of the sort. The local lodge and the local business agent of the district would not indorse this for one minute, and if it ever comes to the grand lodge it will certainly not be indorsed. . . . It might just as well be understood, once and for all, that . . . we will not permit, if we know it, any of our lodges or shop committees to restrict or put a limit on a man's day's work for him. (Ibid.: 139)*

---

there were no unions—how did workers reach agreement on production quotas? It is even more amazing that workers were able to enforce the quotas they set. Capitalists had tremendous rewards and sanctions which they did not hesitate to use—not only material incentives from unrestricted production, but also the power to promote or fire. Despite this, the working class was usually able to control output, a testimony to the strength of their culture and communities.

Much more work needs to be done to understand how these processes operated, not only the cultural underpinnings, but the day-to-day enforcement mechanisms. We also need to understand how new workers were socialized to accept these practices, particularly since this was a time of high immigration. To what extent were immigrants coerced and intimidated by skilled "American" workers, and to what extent did they willingly support and become part of this worker structure of control? What was the effect of ethnic, racial, and sexual divisions in the workforce?

*Even in 1900 unions tended to limit class struggle, channeling it into "acceptable" forms, and accepting many of the ground rules proposed by capitalists.

Since there was no openly articulated rationale for reducing output, the piecework struggle turned into a series of holding actions: whatever level of output was achieved quickly became the norm. Management might suspect that workers were restricting output, but however strong their suspicions, suspicion was not usually a sufficient basis to begin what amounted to a war over piece rates, a war involving much disruption and hostility, with management not really knowing what was and what was not possible. Workers were usually successful in resisting piecework, but even occasional slips could cause production rates to be ratcheted upward. David Montgomery cites the fact that in both 1867 and 1902 iron puddlers had production quotas, but there was a 104 percent increase in the quota during the thirty-five-year period (1975: 489). Similarly, a union official reported:

> The restriction of output, or fixing the limits to earnings on piecework, began 10 years or more before there was a union here. In 1863 in these piece shops men used to earn from $4 to $8 a day. The cutting began in the early seventies, perhaps 1869. To-day we do 50 per cent more work for $3 a day. Even the man who earned $8 in 1863, and was never suspected of restricting his output, would have to do more now than he did then to live or to hold his job. (U.S. Commissioner of Labor, 1905: 206)

In both these instances, and in others like them, workers were not necessarily working twice as hard (although that certainly happened): there may have been technological change. In any case, over the long run production quotas did not remain fixed, and the movement was always toward more production.

Piecework was often an effective strategy for capitalists, but it is important to note that it still relied on workers' initiative, ability, and knowledge of the details of the work process; management neither told workers how to do the work, nor offered technical advice and instruction. Piecework in its simplest form, or combined with the use of rate busters, represented an admission by management that it was in practice unable to force workers to obey orders, for if workers had been willing to obey orders, there would have been no need to offer them material incentives to do what they were in any case supposed to do (U.S. House of Representatives: 1912: 99, 164). Management still had little or no role in the production process, other than to pit workers against each other: a main purpose of the system was to destroy the class solidarity of the workers.

Evidence shows that workers realized this. They opposed piecework not only because it led to speed-up, but also because of the jealousy, dissension, and hostility it created. The two were inseparable, of course.

> As a rule, piecework creates jealousy amongst the men, and one fellow will say, "There is a fellow making a quarter more than I am making," and another one will make 35 cents more, and it creates petty jealousy amongst the men, and there will always be one or two in the bunch who will overstep the limit, and it naturally urges the others on, and then they are all going at the same clip. (Ibid.: 832; see also 235)

A former president of the machinists' union made this his major objection to piecework: "It is bound to create an enmity and stir up discord between men . . . in the shops, consequently the men can not be as friendly as they should be" (U.S. Commissioner of Labor, 1905: 115). A worker at the Rock Island Arsenal testified that piecework made everyone concerned with themselves, whereas he hoped "that all brothers will take care of brothers and try to bring them along with them" (U.S. House of Representatives, 1912: 920).

Worker testimony reveals the value placed on cooperation. At the Watertown Arsenal, before the rate buster came, the workers had cooperatively regulated the shops, and had been unconcerned with their personal records if they were doing work that contributed to the shop as a whole. Molders testified that they all shared a single crane to bring heavy material to them, each surrendering it to the others in accordance with accepted custom. The rate buster, however, with management support, refused to yield the crane, holding it idle for long periods so as to be sure to have it available when next he needed it.

Workers gave evidence of further cooperation when one testified that the time card records of the time it had supposedly taken them to do a job might be very inaccurate in any given instance because one worker might have gone to help another without bothering to get stamped off of one job card and on to another (ibid.: 253).

Workers claimed, quite plausibly, that destroying cooperation through piecework created real inefficiencies and obstacles to production. A worker in a government shipyard explained:

They were working under this system and having a certain amount of work to do; each man was endeavoring to get out his amount of work, to get a record of the number of rivets driven, the number of holes drilled, and each individual man was absolutely intent upon getting out the work for his own record. There was absolutely no regard . . . to the other men. . . . It seeemed to be the end and aim of each one to increase his own efficiency. There is where we believe the vital principle comes in—that there should be team work rather than that the individual should get out the greatest, the highest amount of labor; and that it should be by voluntary cooperation with the workers working together in cooperation, and that they should work together in harmony to get out this work. Not only will it make the work better and make it run along more smoothly, but at the same time it will lessen the danger of accident. . . . [Here follows an extended example from his work, showing that since workers were only concerned with their own production they dropped hot rivets, tools, and boards that could—and in come cases did—fall on the men below.] And I want to bring out in that connection that it is not alone the fact that the system is not perfected that causes that, although that might be responsbile for part of it, but at the same time it is inherent in the principles of the system itself. (Ibid.: 527)

Despite the inefficiencies produced by workers pursuing only their own ends, piecework could still be more profitable for capital, if it caused workers to exert more effort without equivalent increases in pay. Thus both capitalists and workers realized the importance of the struggle. As Mark Perlman put it in his study of the machinists' union:

Piecework was not merely "payment by results"; it was predominantly a new concept of the job. . . . The fight against piecework was more than a blind fight against technological development; to the unionists, it was a fight for the preservation of the dignity of the craftsman and such economic bargaining as he possessed. (1961: 28–29)

So widespread, and so crucial, was the struggle against piecework that the head of the machinists' union "estimated that 50 per cent of the strikes and 60 per cent of the strike benefits paid out were associated with the issue" (ibid.: 30–31; see also Norris, 1899: 689 ff.).

In sum, piecework was a prebureaucratic capitalist initiative that attempted to destroy workers' social control of the workplace without putting something else in its place. Instead of workers' cooperative organization of production, loosely coordinated by custom and collective decisions, the piecework system was an attempt to make each worker fight the others for the greatest possible individual output. Such a system was never really achieved, and it probably could not have been made to operate successfully, but to capital this at first seemed the only way to break workers' power and dictate the pace of production.

Record Keeping and the Development of Management

Piecework was only the most visible element of a more general class struggle in which capitalists were attempting to change the management and control of workers and production. Despite its potential, piecework by itself was inadequate and could well make things worse, since it gave workers a strong incentive to hold down the level of production at the same time as management relinquished its theoretical right to complain about the way employees spent their time. Workers plausibly could argue that since they were being paid only for what they produced, it therefore cost capital nothing if they chose to talk, work at a moderate pace, or take a break. As one management expert warned, piecework "is evidently unsatisfactory and dangerous in a weakly organized works with an inexperienced" management (Darlington, 1899a: 449).

To realize the potential in piecework and make it an effective strategy for capital, it was necessary to give workers detailed specifications rather than general directives. Essentially this meant the creation of "management," the necessary basis for a new and different way of directing and controlling production. The emerging category of "managers" were being called on to do new things. The old supervisors tended to coordinate the works loosely; they served as the most skilled workers to help solve particularly difficult problems, and exercised personal power to keep workers to their tasks and to control the work process. Supervisors continued to think in the old ways; in particular, they continued to focus on the formal wage rate. Publications for the emergent group of managers (such as *Engineering Magazine*) repeatedly stressed that wages should no longer by the primary focus of attention. More general aspects of management were far more important:

> Disputes as to wages between employers and workmen are of very much less importance than questions as to restriction of trade and management of works. Supposing half the cost of an engine consisted of the engineers' wages (and, generally speaking, it is less than this), a 5 per cent rise or fall would only mean 2½ percent on the cost, whereas methods or policies which make men work in a less efficient manner may double, or treble, the cost of labour. The settlement of questions as to the difference between piece and time work, of the questions of a greater number of machines being worked by one man, and still more important, of the question of substituting machine for hand labour—these, and numberless other matters that are often in dispute in English workshops, are therefore far more vital than mere rates of wages. (Browne, 1899: 408)

The growing literature on management, which increased from about one article per year in the early 1870s to about twenty-five articles per year in the late 1890s, both reflected the rise of a new breed of managers and itself contributed to this process. These articles often discussed ideas and proposals that today would be seen as obvious. In 1886, however, it was a considerable advance when Henry R. Towne, president of the Yale and Towne Manufacturing Company, presented a paper entitled "The Engineer as Economist" which stressed that engineers had to consider economic costs and benefits as well as engineering efficiency.* Articles on bookkeeping not only presented improved systems, they had to begin by explaining why employers should keep records and how they could make use of them (since most employers did not understand bookkeeping and tended to dismiss it).

Even the basics of how to avoid giving workers an issue to organize around were presented as progressive innovations:

> [At the Yale and Towne lock works] the method now in use for reducing cost is to divide the whole force of workmen† into small

---

*As David Noble (1977) shows, this was only a small part of a widespread movement to have engineers become cost conscious and begin to think like business executives.

†To judge by the pictures accompanying the text, the overwhelming majority of workers were actually women.

groups, in no case embracing all the occupants of any one room, and, by careful observation of the operations of each group, decide upon possible reductions in piece-prices paid to workmen without lowering their total earnings beyond possible recoupment by the use of improved means of production, or by increased diligence on the part of the workmen themselves. The foremen are paid by the day, the workmen by the piece. Change is made in the price paid to only a single group at one time; it is the intention to adjust prices once a year; by using the whole year's time, and hence affecting very few workers at once, this method of reducing piece-prices is followed without difficulty. It probably could not be followed without a new force of hands each year, if the reductions were made on the same day throughout the entire establishment. (Roland, 1896, 12: 408–9)

Such articles, basic as they may appear by the management standards of today, helped capitalists and managers develop a common *class* awareness of the problems facing them and of the range of possible solutions.

The effective use of piecework required capital to make three interrelated changes, which interacted on each other and developed as time went on. Capitalists at this time did not have a clear conception of an alternative to the craft system of organizing production, but the piecemeal changes they introduced led them toward scientific management and bureaucracy. Each of these changes favored the expansion of the emergent group of managers, and the management functions that were their responsibility. First, in order to be able to put workers on piecework, it was necessary that management have a clear idea of the various jobs that needed to be done, how the work was divided, what each worker did, how much time was required for each operation, how the work was laid out, which workers did which jobs, and so forth. Second, if only for payroll purposes, the company had to keep track of the output of individual workers, rather than keeping records only on foremen and their work groups. If nothing else changed, this meant a substantially more elaborate set of records. Third, if capital was to get the maximum benefit from piecework, someone who understood the work process had to study and use these records, in order to determine the ways in which changes could be made and the groups of workers to whom pressure should be applied. The management experts of the time were very much aware that piecework required a complete change in the method of running a shop, and stressed the need for making a set of interrelated changes:

> [Piecework] requires a thorough draughting office system, that the drawings be complete, accurate, and corrected to date, and show all that is to be done on the piece. Also, a highly organized "piecework" office and a system of estimates, observations, records, and comparisons, resulting in a definite knowledge of what length of time the work should take. . . .
>
> The success of these systems depends almost entirely on the thoroughness and accuracy with which the value of operations can be determined, while this in turn depends upon the nature of the work, the organization of the draughting office and "piece-work" office, and upon the methods of dividing the operations into their elements and of recording the results of each ticket, so that the information can be available in various combinations of old elements for new work, for which rates may be required. (Darlington, 1899a: 448–49)

Piecework and related changes required much more elaborate records and multiplied paper work and bureaucracy. Many of the old-style supervisors did not understand the need for these changes, which were intended not simply to have a record of what had happened, but rather to serve as an active tool in controlling production. As J. Slater Lewis explained in "Works Management for Maximum Production":

> A great many persons entirely miss the point of advantage to be gained by a carefully elaborated system of records in the internal administration of works. Old ideas die hard, and, since the cost of operations is still the principal element in such records, it is assumed that to produce more accurate "cost accounts" is the whole end of the reforms proposed. "Our costs are quite sufficient for us; we know what our work costs us in labour and materials; we know what to sell at," is the usual reply one gets when urging the utility of more modern methods. Now, apart from the fact that no system of cost accounts which *merely* registers material and labour is any trustworthy guide to the profitableness—or the reverse—of any particular "line" where the margin of profit is very small, or where widely-different classes of work are concurrently passing through the same shops, the object of modern methods of record is quite other than that of a system of cost accounts. That it fulfills the functions of this is quite true; but it has much more extended and even much more important aims.

> The real object of modern organization is to strengthen the adminis-
> trative arm in its control of routine, and to keep it closely informed as
> to fluctuations in sectional and departmental efficiencies. (1899: 63)

Elaborate records were necessary not because of the need to keep
track of the cost of production, not because price competition with
other capitalists required an exact determination of the best-selling
price, not even in order to decide which lines or items produced
were the most profitable. It was conceded that the old methods of
cost accounting were generally adequate for these purposes. The
demands of the class struggle were what required much more
elaborate records and procedures. If workers were to be controlled,
the speed of production to be forced to its maximum, and costs to be
cut to the minimum, management had to have the information on
what aspects of the work process could be speeded up. This point
was emphasized in an article entitled "Cost Keeping Methods in
Machine Shop and Foundry":

> There are two objective points in cost keeping. The first is the de-
> termination of a price at which the factory production can safely be
> offered on the market; for this purpose, gross sums suffice. The
> second point sought is lessening of production costs, and, to obtain
> this highly desirable result, the most minute attainable subdivision of
> cost is demanded. Hence, in all cases, the beginner in cost keeping is
> inclined to open as few accounts as possible, because gross amounts
> will serve his first purpose of discovering a safe selling price, while the
> experienced cost keeper will subdivide his expense account even
> down to ultimate items. This may appear, at first sight, to be a mere
> slavish regard for minuteness of detail; it really arises from his knowl-
> edge that production expenses cannot be reduced in gross, but must
> be attacked in small parts. A manager cannot reduce expense by
> notifying his subordinates of his general desire to do so; he must
> point out the exact items which shall be lessened, and before he
> can specify any reduction, at any point, he must know all the com-
> ponent parts of the cost of that detail. Hence, the experienced cost
> keeper may divide the expense account into a hundred, or more,
> subordinate accounts, while the inexperienced cost keeper may keep
> his expense in a single account, or, at most, divide it under a very few
> heads. (Roland, 1898, 16: 208)

In beginning the move away from issuing workers only general orders and directives and toward detailed specification and control of particular actions, improved record keeping was a crucial first step. The records could be used with varying degrees of sophistication. To be most effective, they required a manager who knew the details of the work and could issue specific orders about exactly what should be changed. On the simplest level, managers began with the time it took a worker or group of workers to do an operation and compared that with the time it had taken to do the same operation in each past instance, with the aim of insisting that current performance match the best that had been achieved in the past.

Workers responded by themselves keeping records of past output, and trying to ensure that there was no variation that could provide an opening for management demands to increase production (or justification for piece-rate cuts that forced increases in output to maintain earnings). In the simplest case, workers simply prepared a table showing how many pieces they had to produce in a day (or hour, or whatever) in order to make a specified daily wage. When workers made a variety of items, they kept track of their time on each item and fought any cuts in the time allowed: "We always kept our own time in a book and when we had a job come out with a time card we always put down in the book the actual time, and if the job came back and the price was cut we would beat it down to the office and down there they would go back and look up the other one and we would ask why the job was cut" (U.S. House of Representatives, 1912: 304). At the Rock Island Arsenal, one worker explained, "each and every man has a time book where he keeps his time and keeps tab on these things, and I do myself" (ibid.: 807).

A more complex use of the records involved comparing one group of workers to another. Given the way many factories were organized, it was quite possible that there were workers making screws, let us say, in many different areas of the shop (or in a large factory, in entirely different buildings). If the items produced were exactly identical, the comparison was simple. Even if the products differed significantly, a manager who understood the work could compare the two situations. For example, screws come in many different lengths, with varying numbers of threads per inch, with assorted kinds of heads and thicknesses of shank, and so on. If the daily output for workers in one area of the plant was one thousand screws, three inches long, with ten threads to the inch, and in another area of the plant was one thousand screws, one and a half inches long, with ten or fewer threads to the inch, this would indicate that the second group of workers should be studied, and presumably would be pressured to increase their output.

A still more sophisticated use of data from record keeping came with the use of outside consultants, which allowed capitalists to make comparisons even between workers in entirely different areas of the country. For example, at the Watertown Arsenal hearings workers complained about the setting of rates. Dwight Merrick, the $15-a-day Taylor system expert who set the rates,* testified that he knew the work could be done in the time he specified, because he had set hundreds of rates on the sames Jones and Lamson machine at other shops, and men had produced the output he specified† (ibid.: 447). Scientific management carried the process of rate setting to its logical conclusion:

> There are those who make a profession of time study and who tabulate for general use the elementary results. In scientific management shops also records are kept of elementary times derived from their own time study work. These records obtained both within and without the particular shop are coming to be used in the setting of new tasks. . . . The matter, that is to say, becomes an office process. (Hoxie, 1915: 50–51)

Record keeping was also advocated as a way of controlling theft and deception. An article by Henry Roland offered many anecdotes and examples to demonstrate the importance of good record keeping, and of increasing the division of labor by having separate workers in charge of the toolroom and the stores. In one case a folder in a book bindery made an error on twelve thousand sheets.

> [She] took the stitcher and coverer into her confidence, and the three girls, all on piece-work, passed the books through to completion, had their piece-work books checked up with credits for the work, passed

---

*The time-study man was thus halfway between the skilled worker who received $3 or $4 a day and the Taylor system expert who supervised the entire system and received $50 a day (Aitken, 1960: 94, 106).

†The experts undoubtedly made plenty of mistakes, as was demonstrated at the Watertown Arsenal hearings. These records and this experience, however, provided important guides in assessing the problem areas in the shop.

the greater part of the spoiled twelve thousand copies down the soil pipe, and took the remainder out of the bindery at night in their clothes and lunch baskets. (1898, 15: 468)

In the early 1860s the Rock Island Railroad shops in Chicago had seven or eight hundred workers. With the aid of undercover investigators who hired on as workers and were shifted from one part of the shop to another, one Saturday afternoon the company searched many workers as they left the shops, and demanded that all workers give up the keys to their tool boxes.

> More than eight hundred dollars' worth of "company" material was taken from the workmen at that single search, including samples of nearly everything used in making freight and passenger cars and locomotives. Two of the blacksmiths, father and son, Englishmen, two of the best men in the forge-shops, were found to have carried out, by some undiscovered method, an anvil, a large old-fashioned smith's forge bellows, two vises, a large lot of tongs, files, axes, fullers, formers, sets, hammers, and sledges, and, in addition, more than ten tons of bar iron and steel. They intended soon to start a shop on their own account. (Ibid.: 468–69)

Roland offered a dozen other examples of the same sort, all involving deceit and antagonism, none involving catching an innocent and unintended error. While he admitted that in particular instances where small quantities were involved "the time expenditure in keeping the record may be many times more than the value of the material delivered," he insisted that over-all it was necessary to designate special personnel to control materials, dispensing them only on written orders and keeping accurate records.

> These numerous anecdotes are given as showing more plainly and conclusively than any argument could do the absolute necessity of a complete bookkeeping and checking system in the shop and factory, with a sufficient clerical force to carry out all details with promptness. Short accounts make long friends. It is not enough to have a reliable method of handling work and keeping track of it in the shop. There must be frequent balances and actual counts. (Ibid.: 469–70).

Preventing theft through the creation of special toolroom and storeroom clerks—when previously tools and stores had been open for any worker to take what they needed—is one example of a still more "advanced" use of the record keeping inspired by piecework. Once special toolroom clerks had been introduced—largely as a way of controlling theft—it was only another small step to have workers stop coming to get their own tools, and instead hire more helpers or clerks whose job it was to bring the appropriate tools. Another more important step in the same direction was the introduction of unskilled workers whose only job was to grind tools to standard shapes, in place of having skilled workers grind their own tools to the special needs of the particular job they had before them. Once this process began there were many other similar steps which could be taken— one authority held that "the special object of a polishing department is to remove from the lathe hand an operation which can be performed by unskilled labor" (Outerbridge, 1896: 652; see also Orcutt, 1899, 17: 598).

As Harry Braverman (following Nicholas Babbage) has shown, capitalists have an economic incentive to increase the division of labor in this way even if the new system is technically the same as the old system. If eight skilled workers, each paid at the rate of $3.00 a day, and each spending one hour a day grinding tools, can be replaced by seven skilled workers at $3.00 a day and one unskilled worker at $1.50 a day, capitalists can save about six percent of their wage bill. The unskilled worker spends all of his or her time grinding tools, and each of the skilled workers has an extra hour a day to do skilled work. Exactly the same work is done, but the capitalists pay less money for wages.

Or such at least is the theory. In practice, capital only benefits if the new low-paid unskilled workers are kept busy most of the time, and if they are able to save time for skilled workers. For example, the employment of new unskilled workers to bring tools, bolts, straps, and so on to skilled workers could be an effective use of the Babbage principle if managers were able to plan the work so as to keep everyone busy. However, if skilled workers all assembled their tools and materials the first hour of the work day, and if no alternative arrangements were made, the unskilled tool fetchers would have nothing to do after the first hour, and they would not significantly reduce the demand for skilled labor. Since such unskilled workers were almost by definition people who could not do a variety of the required tasks, and were not trained to plan the work and be self-directing, in order for them to be kept busy at their limited tasks, someone else had to plan the work for them and direct their labor. This reinforced the need for the managers who had introduced the unskilled workers. Managers had to be able to understand the work sufficiently to know what would happen when a change was made, had to be able to plan alternative methods, and had to know how to keep and interpret records that could determine the profitability of proposed changes.

Technological Change

Technological change was another weapon that capital used to weaken or attack the craft system. Increases in the division of labor and the introduction of machinery reinforced each other. As capitalists became more knowledgeable about, and more involved in, the labor process they split off various operations which could be done by machinery or unskilled labor. The two went together: unskilled workers were able to do the tool grinding in part because of the development of automatic machinery intended for this purpose; at the same time, developing the machinery made sense because managers were keeping records on work times and calculating how much they could save if unskilled workers ground tools.

There is no question that technological advance brings many important benefits, allows the production of more use values for a given amount of labor, improves the quality of the product, and so on. This is widely recognized, so the point need not be belabored. Less widely recognized, however, is the fact that technology is also a crucially important means by which capitalists attempt to control the labor process. Moreover, the two are related: it is a mistake to begin with an opposition between two different kinds of technological changes, one a "purely technical" advance (whatever that may be) allowing goods to be produced cheaper and with less effort, and the other designed solely to increase the speed of labor and the degree to which the capitalist controls the labor process. The introduction of technology allows the capitalist to undersell other capitalists and capture a larger share of the market, thereby increasing profits and the accumulation of capital. Competition with other capitalists is thus an important spur to continued technological innovation. But this does not affect the argument that technology was used in order to increase the speed of production and better control workers: both are important factors in lowering the cost of production.

This reflects one of the fundamental starting points of Marx's analysis: the twofold nature of the commodity under capitalism. A commodity is and must be both a use value and an exchange value. If a commodity was not useful no one would want it, and it would have no exchange value; if it were useful but no human labor was necessary in order to appropriate it then no one would have any need to exchange for it (as is true, for example, of the air). A commodity must be a unity of both these aspects. Capitalists do not first produce use values and later produce exchange values. It is neither fruitful nor reasonable to look at a given commodity and ask, "Is this primarily a use value or primarily an exchange value?"

Marx emphasized that the commodity could not have this twofold character unless the labor which produced the commodity also had this twofold character. Marx also mentioned the twofold nature of supervision within the capitalist production process—supervision to coordinate work and produce use values as opposed to supervision to control workers and produce a profit. Similarly, in a capitalist system technology has this twofold character. Capitalists introduce technological change because they believe it will aid them in the process of capital accumulation, and the success of such change is measured by its ability to do so; whether it succeeds for technical reasons, or because it reduces wages, or because it increases the intensity of labor, is almost irrelevant to the capitalist.

An obvious but highly important example of the way technology is shaped for capitalist ends is the fact that capitalists made special efforts to reduce the amount of high-paid skilled labor, and to have the new machinery be operated by low-paid unskilled labor. This is reasonable in terms of profit maximization, but with different goals it might be just as reasonable to make special efforts to develop machinery to replace the least interesting work, or the most dangerous work, or the most degrading work. One nineteenth-century expert noted: "It is well known that the planing machine requires the highest skill in its manipulation, if anything like accurate surfaces are desirable and expensive 'fitting' is to be avoided. Consequently it is important to do away with planing as much as possible." In its place the author advocated a different method, the advantage of which was that "by this method the removal of metal is accelerated three or four times, and seventy-five per cent of the work is done by unskilled attendants" (Orcutt, 1899, 16: 706).

That cost was, and is, a very important reason to develop or adopt technologies that use unskilled labor reflects the logic of capitalism, which views workers as tools to be used in capital accumulation. Since workers in a capitalist system are only tools, it is irrational within such a system to consider whether one kind of work is more interesting, pleasant and creative, and helps people to develop these qualities in themselves. If one production process produces a given commodity at 99¢ per piece, but requires workers who are mindless robots, it is still unquestionably superior to another process that produces the same commodity at $1 each, and uses workers who can give free play to their creative abilities. As one turn-of-the-century writer summarized the situation: "Viewing men as tools, every added unused power or ability is a detriment" (Arnold, 1896: 1094). An unskilled worker could grind tools, so a qualified machinist who did so was not using his full powers. To the capitalist, this was a "waste," a positive detriment, since a worker was regarded as a means to the end of increased profits and the further accumulation of capital. For obvious reasons, workers took a different view of the situation; since the work was more interesting and pleasant when they performed a variety of tasks, since there was no technical superiority of one system over another, and since they viewed themselves as human beings rather than as tools for the accumulation of capital, workers preferred the more varied organization of work.

Labor costs were only one part of the use of technology to increase profits. Control can hardly be separated from cost—if capitalists cannot adequately control their workers, workers demand more for themselves and this leads to increasing costs. A series of articles on the technical history of changes in machinery found the greatest advantage of the fully automatic machine tool to be that operators were replaced easily enough that output did not depend on their "whim." By contrast, the skilled operator "is indispensable in the case of the semi-automatic or self-acting machine tool, and . . . is wholly intractable and ungovernable, and can and does make work costs large or small at his own pleasure" (Roland, 1899: 182). This still reflects a concern with cost, but it reiterates the fact that formal wage rates are less important than the extent to which workers control the work process and their own time.

Workers' struggles could have a giant impact on the extent to which machinery was developed or adopted. On the one hand, the existing wages helped determine whether or not it was profitable to introduce machinery. Suppose machinery could be devised to do a given job for $750. If the workers doing that job were receiving $500, the machinery would not be introduced; if workers managed to increase their wages to $1,000 by militant struggle, the machinery would then become profitable.

On the other hand, workers' struggle for control of one or another aspect of production could limit the extent to which capital introduced machinery and new methods. Turn-of-the-century management literature carried many articles comparing American and European (especially British) workers, with the unvarying theme that American workers were far more willing to accept new methods and new machinery. For example, in 1899 one author reported:

> A large American manufacturer is sending large quantities of a superior article to England. That shipments may be made in a more compact form, he has established works in England for putting together parts machined in America. On a recent visit to the English factory, he observed the manner in which the work was done. Calling the foreman to one side, he told him that he could show the workmen how they could, with the same effort and working the same number of hours, earn from 25 to 30 per cent more in wages, and asked if it would not be advisable to do so. The foreman thought it was a good idea, and spoke to the men. On calling next day, much to the surprise of the American, not a man was at work, and it was three days before work was resumed, and then only on the condition that no innovations would be attempted. (Orcutt, 1899, 16: 929)

Obviously, in such a shop workers could simply prevent the introduction of new machinery (at least for a time—if other workers allowed the introduction of the machinery soon all shops would have to do so or go bankrupt). Even if the machinery could be introduced in Europe, capitalists had less reason to do so:

It is a fact, verified by statistics and the statements of many American makers of machinery who have successfully introduced their machines into European countries, that, under European conditions and when handled by European workmen, American labor-saving and automatic machinery turns out from 30 to 50 per cent less than is produced by the same machinery in America. I am told that the royalties on the McKay boot-stitching machines, paid on the products turned out, are one-third less from the machines in operation in European countries than from those in operation in America. I know that, on certain machines for the production of bicycle parts, operations which are regularly performed in America in from six to seven minutes usually take from ten to twelve minutes in the hands of European operatives. This is due chiefly to inefficient labor and the want of properly-trained tool makers to keep the machines in a high state of efficiency. It is also stated that the product of the Singer works at Glasgow is no greater than that of the works in America, although they employ one thousand more operatives. (Orcutt, 1899, 16: 927–28; see also 17: 391)

Thus the nature of the workforce obviously had a giant impact on the development and introduction of technological innovations: machinery would be introduced at a slower rate in Britain, since the machine cost as much but brought smaller benefits. One writer argued that these "racial traits" had to be a primary consideration in designing machinery (Williams, 1895: 96).*

Workers' struggles could thus slow the rate at which technological innovations were introduced. They could also propel capitalists into introducing machinery that otherwise would not have been developed, or not developed for many more years. In extreme cases the desire to control workers could outweigh capitalists' concern for technological efficiency and lead to actions that seem "irrational" from the point of view of marketplace capitalism. The struggles at McCormick Harvester in the 1880s indicate that one great advantage of labor-saving machinery—the fact that it "never goes on strike" (Orcutt, 1899, 16: 707)—could override considerations of operating cost.

McCormick Harvester was one of the largest and most fabulously

---

*Americans are a race, Englishmen are a race, Germans are a race, and so on—a use of the term "race" that has gone out of fashion, but one which is no less justifiable than the belief that the differences between American whites and American blacks are "racial" in a biological sense.

profitable companies of the late nineteenth century.* Molders made up only about 10 percent of the workforce, but at least in terms of wages they were the pacesetters for the entire workforce. Since the wage increases they won were granted immediately to all the other workers as well, the extra money received by molders was only a fraction of the cost of raising molders' wages.

During the depression of 1884–1885 the management cut wages, despite the fact that the company had posted record profits of $1.75 million (71 percent net on the stated capital investment). In the spring production rush the molders called a strike just for molders. The company was confident of victory, and welcomed the opportunity to teach the workers "a lesson." Molders' sense of class consciousness and class solidarity was strong enough that at first the company was unable to recruit any molders to work in the factory, as emerges from the following two telegrams:

> To J. F. Utley, Agent, Sterling, Illinois:
> The gentleman you sent in to us as a Molder, Mr. Jas. McBride, did not remain over an hour or two until he packed his valise and skipped. We took special pains to get him into the Works by his riding with Mr. McCormick in his buggy. We can hardly imagine his purpose in coming at our expense and taking the course which he did. If you are able to do so try and collect back his Rail Road fare.

> To Tom Braden, Agent, Des Moines, Iowa:
> Out of the lot of men you sent us yesterday but two of them showed up in Chicago. Mr. C. Allen and his brother, the balance having deserted on the way. We find it is not safe to ship these critters at our expense unless nailed up in a box car or chained. We were unable to get the Messrs. Allen inside our gate today, and presume that before we shall be able to do so they will also disappear. (Quoted in Ozanne, 1967: 15)

After some time and much effort, the company managed to recruit twenty-five scab molders to replace the ninety striking molders. Until this time molder pickets had allowed all other workers to enter the plant, only keeping out molders. At this time they called out all

---

*In 1900 McCormick was one of the twenty largest U.S. companies, with more than 4,000 workers. The successor company, International Harvester, is still one of the thirty largest industrials.

workers, who responded in huge numbers, and the strike was very effective. Pickets beat up would-be scabs, trolley drivers refused to bring workers into the plant, Pinkerton agents were beaten and were unable to keep the gates open, the police and politicians refused to help the company. The company remained adamant, but at this point

> Chicago capitalists became thoroughly alarmed lest this rising tide of union defiance start a general conflagration. At this juncture, Philip D. Armour, capitalist elder and head of the well-known meat-packing firm, tactfully notified young McCormick that he would like to talk with him. In a friendly way, Armour discussed several strikes which he had experienced. He bluntly told the young executive that the public was holding him to blame since there had been no such occurrence in his father's time. Armour then advised him to settle the strike even if it meant paying the men what they asked, since the situation was developing into "open war." (Ibid.: 17)

The strike had become serious and widespread enough that, in the opinion of an important capitalist leader, all of Chicago faced at least the possibility of "open war." McCormick immediately settled the strike, ending by having to concede all the demands at issue.

Given that the molders were well organized and militant, that they led the rest of the workforce, and that the company found it virtually impossible to hire molders who would side with the company instead of the union, the company decided it would have to find a way to completely dispense with molders, or else continue to wrestle with an organized and militant workforce. Young McCormick concluded, "'I do not think we will be troubled by the same thing again if we take proper steps to weed out the bad element among the men,'" (quoted in Ozanne, 1967: 20) and he made it clear that the "bad element" meant the molders. The only possibility seemed to be machinery, and within two weeks the company was making plans to use machinery to replace all of the molders. The company had not previously intended to use molding machines, and there was no assurance that the machines would be able to do the job. Nevertheless, the company spent $500,000 (at a time when skilled machinists earned $3 a day) on molding machinery, and three months later closed the foundry for two months in order to install the machines. Since the purpose of the machines was not to cut costs but rather to smash the union, the company did not buy one or two machines to test their effectiveness. The initial purchase, made just weeks after the strike ended, included enough machines to handle total production. The machines were so inadequate that it was unclear whether they could be made to work at all; they produced poor quality castings, and fifteen molders had to be hired "when it became evident that the molding machines could not produce certain types of castings" (ibid.: 21).*

Moreover, in addition to the high cost of the machinery itself, its adoption, rather than lessening labor costs, more than doubled the cost of labor, since so many unskilled workers were required. Foundry labor costs increased from $3,000 a week with skilled molders and no machines to $8,000 a week after machines replaced the skilled workers; in terms of percentage of payroll costs, foundry labor increased from 18.8 percent before the machines to 31.0 percent after the introduction of machinery.

Bad as the machines were, they were good enough to allow McCormick to smash the molders union. In 1886, a year after the first strike, the molders, who by then were no longer employees, had managed to unionize about 1,000 other workers (out of a total workforce of 1,380). The second strike made it crystal clear that the company's overriding goal was to break the molders' power: three of four strike demands, including one for a substantial wage increase, were conceded. The only demand on which the company would not compromise was a closed shop for molders. Even though they had won their own demands the other workers voted to strike in support of the molders, and a long bitter strike ensued, which the company eventually won.† Profits for the year were less than half what they had been before (down by more than $1 million), but the company had thoroughly smashed worker opposition.

People often find this example disturbing and believe it to run counter to any explanation except one based on McCormick's personal psychology. McCormick, it is said, did not smash the workers

---

*The molding machines were abandoned after three years, and the company sued the manufacturer in an attempt to recover its investment (Ozanne, 1967: 27).

†Toward the end of this strike strikers attacked scabs and smashed plant windows, and the police responded by killing two strikers and wounding several. A meeting called to protest police brutality was held at Haymarket Square. At this meeting a bomb was thrown, killing seven police. The thrower was never found, but four anarchist leaders were hanged, and there was a wave of repression.

because that would allow him to make more money; he smashed the workers even though this reduced his profits. I would argue, however, that McCormick operated well within the bounds of capitalist rationality. The general manager had welcomed the first strike, saying "we have many men employed who have been with us for years without a lesson" in the futility of resistance against the company (quoted in Ozanne, 1967: 14). When workers won the first strike it taught everyone concerned a very different lesson. McCormick probably expected the machinery to work better than it did; nonetheless, he was quite rational to believe that it was worth $1 million to teach the workers that when push came to shove the company, not the workers, would win. Otherwise, the company would have paid even greater costs over the next several years in various kinds of low-visibility, nondramatic inability to force its workers to obey company orders.

Machinery was obviously a very powerful weapon in capital's attack on the craft system—Marx called machinery "the most powerful weapon for repressing strikes" (1867: 410)—but it was not a complete solution. First of all, machinery could not simply be conjured up at will to meet any problems: McCormick's molding machines produced much lower quality, at much higher cost, and a less profitable company could not have afforded to use them. Capitalists often would have liked machinery to replace particularly intractable or high-paid workers, but frequently there was nothing available. Beyond this, however, the introduction of new machinery did not by itself necessarily lead to the anticipated benefits.

The modern view of machinery and its inherent potential for control of workers is dominated by the image of the assembly line. On an assembly line, by far the most important task of foremen and supervisors is simply to be sure that workers remain at their jobs, because if they do so the assembly line will determine most other aspects of the work process. If a worker's job is to put on the left rear wheel and tighten it down, and a string of cars comes off the line without their left rear wheels, or without the bolts having been tightened, it is very easy for management to tell what the problem is.

But the assembly line, a creation of the early twentieth century, was a qualitative breakthrough. Its use as a symbol of machinery in general leads us to overestimate the extent to which nineteenth-century machinery controlled the work process. Machinery was widely used, often very sophisticated, and much of it even automatic. But these machines existed as isolated parts of the work process, connected only through the activities of workers; there were very few connections between one machine and another. Even if a machine was fully automatic, when the product came out of that machine it still had to be transported to the next machine and set up in that machine—even if the next machine was fully automatic. Machinery could solve the problem of controlling the speed of production for one particular operation, but capitalists had not yet developed machinery to the point where it controlled speed for the shop as a whole. As a result, one expert cautioned:

> It is not merely sufficient that the technical portion of such operations be modernised. Automatic and stop-machines will not of themselves produce either a large or an exact ouput, but must be themselves made part of a system arranged to suit the changed conditions of work in order that their real superiority may become available. (Lewis, 1899: 67)

And another expert warned that "the whole establishment must be brought into harmony with this class of machinery, or its introduction will not be productive of the best results" (Orcutt, 1899, 16: 707).

The fact that sophisticated machinery existed as isolated islands in the production process, combined with the very different moral and social atmosphere in the workshops, meant that there could be tremendous variations in the amounts produced. Even on automatic machinery, the set-up process often required considerable skill, and the worker could not be rushed. One worker explained the ways he could slight the work even though the machine was fully automatic, and other workers made it clear that when they had been assigned to operate that machine they had spoiled work simply through a lack of skill or experience (U.S. House of Representatives, 1912: 282, 284).

Machinery was introduced to control labor and the speed of production. By having certain rules built into the machine—the quality of output, the speed at which the machine was to operate, and so on—the need for supervision and control was reduced. At the same time, the more machinery was used, the more important it became to control workers and increase the division of labor. If a worker was paid 30¢ an hour and the machinery (and other overhead) cost the capitalist another 10¢ an hour, an hour the worker spent talking or sitting around cost the capitalist 40¢. However, if extensive new machinery were introduced, even if the worker's wages stayed constant at 30¢ an hour (and they might well increase because of the added responsibility), the machine cost could increase to 30¢ an hour, in which case an hour the worker spent doing what he or she wanted could cost capital 60¢, a 50 percent increase. The same logic coerced capital to increase the division of labor as it introduced new machinery. If skilled workers spent an hour a day doing things that could have been done by unskilled workers (finding tools and equipment, grinding tools, moving the work to the next station) capital could always cut its wage bill by using unskilled workers to do these things. However, when the cost of machinery and overhead became an important part of total costs, capital had a double incentive to use unskilled labor, since the skilled worker doing these other things was not using his or her machine, and the cost of the idle machine might be as great as the wage differential between skilled and unskilled labor. The cost of the machinery made it more important than ever to have close supervision, so that the full benefit could be drawn from the machinery. Machinery, introduced as a solution to the labor problem, became itself the most important reason to increase attention to the labor problem. To take an extreme case, it could literally be more profitable for a capitalist to employ a second worker whose only job was to make sure the first worker stayed at work continuously. If there were a ten-hour work day, and the machine cost $20 a day, and wages were $3 a day, then a worker who spent two hours a day away from the machine (for any purpose, including needed work activity) cost the company $4 a day in unused capacity on the machine. This would make it worthwhile for the company to hire an extra worker for the entire day simply to make sure that the first worker stayed at work continuously. While I do not mean to suggest that such an example—or such a solution—was historically significant, it is important to indicate the way in which machinery changed the economics of supervision. This was the context in which Taylorism emerged.

6
Scientific Management and the Dictatorship of the Bourgeoisie

I have argued that while piecework, improved record keeping, and technology all weakened the craft system, both separately and together, they were not completely successful in destroying that system. Employers of course constrained workers in various ways, and demanded that the goals of capital accumulation be met, but within this general framework, employers continued to assume that for the most part workers would direct and control the work process—which is to say that employers themselves in some sense accepted the foundation of the craft system. As long as this was true, changes produced only temporary solutions; only an alternative method of organizing production could provide a "final solution."

One individual stands far above all others in the contribution he made to solving this critical problem facing the capitalist class. Frederick Winslow Taylor at once excelled in three different respects: (1) he produced by far the best analysis of the existing situation, an understanding of the nature of the problem confronting employers; (2) he developed the solution for this problem, an alternative means of organizing and structuring the production process and the relations of production; and (3) he was himself the most important person directing the implementation of the policies he proposed. Frederick Taylor was the Napoleon of the war against craft production, directing some battles himself and acting through lieutenants in other cases, but he was more than that. He was also the theoretician who comprehended the situation and explained the solutions to the problems that had baffled so many before him. Taylor represented the unification of theory and practice in the cause of the capitalist class.

While it is crucial to understand Taylor's unique place in the struggle to control production, it is just as important to realize that he cannot be viewed in isolation. As the last chapter demonstrated, there was a management movement before Taylor came to prominence. A number of journals were concerned with the question of management, and dozens of authors produced hundreds of articles on the subject. Taylor participated in this movement almost from its very beginnings, serving as a commentator at the session of the American Society of Mechanical Engineers at which Henry Towne delivered "The Engineer as Economist," the paper that more than any other marks the large-scale beginnings of the management movement. Initially, however, Taylor was only a minor participant; it was ten years before he delivered a paper of his own.

By the early 1900s Taylor had become the dominant figure in the management movement. Robert Hoxie's 1915 investigation of management systems for the Industrial Commission begins by noting:

> Mr. Taylor is usually credited with being the founder of scientific management and has been almost universally recognized as its leading exponent. . . . In fact, the Taylor system has been and still is regarded in most quarters as scientific management par excellence and practically identified with the more inclusive term. (1915: 7)

Similarly, the congressional investigation of government arsenals, the testimony from which I have quoted so frequently in these pages, was titled "A Special House Committee to Investigate the Taylor and Other Systems of Shop Management." Although Taylor did not coin the term "scientific management"—it was invented by Louis Brandeis in a railroad rate dispute—the term quickly became totally identified with Taylor's policies.*

Taylor not only dominated the management movement of his own time; his methods and theories continue to be by far the most important in determining the organization of industry today. Harry Braverman has stated this position most clearly and forcefully:

> It is impossible to overestimate the importance of the scientific management movement in the shaping of the modern corporation and indeed all institutions of capitalist society which carry on labor processes. The popular notion that Taylorism has been "superseded"

---

*Copley claims that Taylor originally used the term in discussions with Brandeis, and Brandeis picked up the term from Taylor.

by later schools of industrial psychology or "human relations," that it "failed"—because of Taylor's amateurish and naive views of human motivation or because it brought about a storm of labor opposition or because Taylor and various successors antagonized workers and sometimes management as well—or that it is "outmoded" because certain Taylorian specifics like functional foremanship or his incentive-pay schemes have been discarded for more sophisticated methods: all these represent a woeful misreading of the actual dynamics of the development of management.

The successors to Taylor are to be found in engineering and work design, and in top management; the successors to Munsterberg and Mayo are to be found in personnel departments and schools of industrial psychology and sociology. . . . If Taylorism does not exist as a separate school today, that is because, apart from the bad odor of the name, it is no longer the property of a faction, since its fundamental teachings have become the bedrock of all work design. (1974: 86–87)

These remarks of Braverman's have been widely questioned; they are worth quoting at length because in many cases they anticipate subsequent criticisms and refute them in advance. Braverman has precisely understood the essence of Taylorism; his critics have for the most part failed to understand what it was about, although Braverman told them clearly and well. While I will not deal with the nature of modern work processes, I hope that by clarifying the situation that existed before Taylor, and by emphasizing what was different and significant about Taylorism, I will demonstrate the truth of Braverman's insights.

One comment needs to be made at once, however: Braverman's words, at least in my reading of them, refer only to the fact that Taylorism dominates modern *management,* is the strategy pursued by *capital.* The contrast drawn is between Taylorism and any other form of management orientation. As Braverman himself acknowledged, his work did not examine workers' consciousness and struggles, did not attempt to assess how successful capital was in imposing its wishes on the shop floor. Thus, it may well be true that the organization of modern factories does not correspond to Taylorism in its pure form, and this is an important point. It is not, however, a refutation of Braverman, who insists only that Taylorism dominates engineering, work design, and top management—which together make up only one side of the work process.

Even in the period before 1920, Taylor's system had a giant impact on American industry. Some of Braverman's critics have argued that Taylorism was influential only as an ideology, not as a practice. Were this the case we would expect Taylor's works to have been widely disseminated to a popular audience, but not taken seriously by engineers and managers. The reverse was true: his writings were not bestsellers, but they were taken seriously by the people in a position to put the ideas into practice. Most of his papers were delivered to an audience of engineers, and printed in the major engineering journal *Transactions* of the American Society of Mechanical Engineering. *Engineering Magazine,* the leading journal of the management movement, almost never reprinted articles that had appeared elsewhere, but it did so for Taylor's first major article, stating: "We regard it as one of the most valuable contributions that have ever been given to technical literature, and by reason of that fact . . . we deem it eminently fitting to accord the paper that distinction which its importance and originality unquestionably merit" (1896: 690).

While Taylor's published books and papers were very influential, they were only one of the ways in which his ideas were spread, and the ideas were less important than the widespread introduction of the system. Taylor's ideas were put into practice at a number of important companies. Taylor himself introduced his system at many places, including the Midvale Steel Works (where he was employed for many years as chief engineer), the sixth largest company in 1917, and the Bethlehem Steel Corporation, the third largest company in 1917. Fairly early on Taylor retired from actual direction of the implementation of his system, but continued to select disciples to do these tasks. Taylor corresponded with these disciples and discussed with them the detailed plans for particular companies. The inner circle of Taylor disciples introduced his system at Westinghouse Electric (no. 17 in 1917), Jones and Laughlin Steel (no. 19), Pullman (no. 25), American Locomotive (no. 62), Winchester Repeating Arms (no. 144), Curtis Publishing (no. 166), Remington Typewriter (no. 182), Plymouth Cordage Company (no. 238), Amoskeag Mills (no. 292), Yale and Towne (no. 388), a number of the largest railroads (which are not classified in lists of top industrials), and more than 35 other companies which I have not been able to identify as among the top 500 of the period (Nelson, 1974a, 1975; Navin, 1950).*

This only begins to list the companies that introduced some of Taylor's ideas, including only those that followed the experts' directions and introduced the more-or-less complete Taylor system. A number of other management consultants believed that they were introducing Taylor's system (perhaps with some modifications) but were not accepted by Taylor, either because of a lack of purity in introducing the system in its entirety, or because of personality conflicts. Some of these experts, such as Frank Gilbreth or Harrington Emerson, were important figures in their own right. Taylor was constantly being asked to recommend experts to help in the installation of his system, "and when it came down to cases in these years, it always proved that Taylor had only four experts to recommend; namely, Barth, Gantt, Hathaway, and Cooke." The demand for Taylor's system was so great, however,

> that men who once had been employed under [Taylor], and at the best knew only a few features of his system, were, even in the period between 1906 and 1910, setting themselves up as full-fledged Taylor experts; while regular engineers who professed to be his friends and to honor him for his achievements were in secret telling business men they could introduce his methods without his "elaborate ritual"; that is, could get the same results by taking "short cuts" which would save much time and money. (Copley, 1923, II: 356–57)

A further important source of Taylor's influence was his personal contacts with engineers and businessmen. Taylor saw himself as a missionary or prophet, and was always eager to tell people about his system. Even in the 1880s, a Baldwin Locomotive Works (no. 4 in 1900) executive who rode the same train noted that Taylor was always telling a group of people about his system at Midvale (ibid., I: 170). In his later years, once he began to be famous, Taylor established himself in a residence, called Boxly, and invited all who were interested to visit him.

> Among the pilgrims to Boxly were engineers, industrial and college executives, men and women interested in all phases of educational and social work, army and navy officers, representatives of other govern-

---

*They may have been so, since there are many problems of identification involved. This is a minimum list of top companies introducing Taylorism.

ment departments, and editors and writers. At first they came singly and in small groups. But later, especially after 1910, they often came in parties of as many as twenty-five or thirty. Regular days eventually were set for their comings; usually they gathered twice a week; the hour appointed being in the forenoon so that they would have plenty of time for visiting the Tabor and Link-Belt plants in the afternoon [where the Taylor system had been installed]. (Ibid., II: 283)

The talk Taylor delivered at these visits became standardized, and lasted for more than two hours of rapid-fire delivery, during which the audience was not allowed to interrupt. Only at the end were they allowed to ask questions. For those who were interested in his system Taylor happily offered free advice—"the day hardly was long enough to hold the time that he would spend with them" (ibid.: 286–87). For example, Taylor spent a lot of time over a period of years advising the Packard Motor Car Company (no. 121 in 1917) about his system (ibid.: 353–55).

Taylor's influence also spread through various institutions. One of the people who came to hear Taylor's lecture was Edwin F. Gay, the first dean of Harvard's Graduate School of Business Administration. As a result of this visit to Boxly, together with conversations with Taylor supporters, Gay decided to base Harvard's program on the Taylor system.

Taylor himself opposed the idea, since he believed his system should be taught in workshops, not universities, but when Harvard went ahead anyway he gave his grudging acquiescence, helping to determine the curriculum and eventually giving a series of lectures. By the time he lectured at Harvard his works were so well known (and he was so repetitious), that the bulk of his time was devoted to answering questions. Dartmouth's business school also made the Taylor system "the basic element of its instruction in management," sponsoring a three-day conference for 300 participants, mostly businessmen and engineers, with Taylor as the lead speaker (ibid.: 353, 392).

Finally, Taylor and his followers came to dominate the American Society of Mechanical Engineers (Taylor was its president in 1906), the leading professional association, through which engineers at a host of companies and in most of the leading engineering schools were exposed to Taylor's work and principles.

The result of this widespread influence was that elements of Taylorism found their way into companies where no certified Taylor system expert introduced them. Consider, for example, one or two of the threads connecting Taylor to the auto industry:

> In 1909 [Taylor] made a speech of more than four hours at the Packard plant, deeply impressing the head of the corporation, H.B. Joy, and other officials. Packard at once instituted or accelerated scientific job analyses, and by 1913 the plant had been largely "Taylorized." Late the following year Taylor again visited Detroit, this time addressing more than six hundred superintendents, foremen, and others drawn from industries all over the city. He was told that quite off their own bats, without special prompting or counsel, several Detroit manufacturers had anticipated his ideas. "This is most interesting," Taylor commented, "as being almost the first instance in which a group of manufacturers had undertaken to install the principles of scientific management without the aid of experts." (Nevins and Hill, 1954: 468)

Similar developments took place at Ford.

> Of the group interested in the development of moving assembly lines, Clarence W. Avery had the broadest grasp of the subject and showed the most intelligent initiative. . . . He read widely, knew the latest European and American advances in engineering, and kept in touch with the ideas of men like Fredrick W. Taylor. In his fifteen years with the company he was to rise to be foreman, superintendent, and chief development engineer. "Among us all," writes one of the experimental room staff, "he was known as pushing the assembly line." (Ibid.: 474)

Between about 1880 or 1890 and 1920 or 1930 the organization of production in American industry was transformed. The changes made—from some sort of workers' control of the details of the work process to the creation of management that gave specific orders, directed the work, and monitored the details of performance—are what are crucial, and who in particular gets the credit (or blame) is in some sense unimportant. But during the period these changes were taking hold Taylor was the dominant figure, and certainly his contemporaries saw his contribution as central and overriding. In assessing Taylor's importance it must be understood that the period in which he lived, the period in which his system was most a focus of controversy, is not necessarily the period in which the system was most rapidly or most widely adopted. Thinkers do not necessarily have the greatest impact during their lifetimes, nor do revolutions work their changes in a few brief years. No one would so limit an assessment of Marx's importance, for example. I think Richard Edwards (1979) in his analysis of the ongoing struggle for control of the workplace, misses the importance of Taylorism for just this reason, considering it a failed experiment from which much was learned. Yet when Edwards describes "the predominant system of control [in capitalist organizations today], giving shape and logic to the firm's organization" he calls this "bureaucratic control" and says that it "constituted the most important change wrought by the modern corporation in the labor process." The "bureaucratic control" that Edwards finds to be so important has its foundations in Taylorism, and is in fact simply a modern refinement of that which Taylor originated and introduced.

Taylor's Background

Since Taylor's analysis of the problem facing management, and his recommendations for solving it, came out of his background and experience, his life and work are worth considering at some length.

Frederick Winslow Taylor came from an old and respected family of Philadelphians, part of a group which came close to being an American aristocracy. His grandfather was a merchant who had amassed a fortune in trade with the East Indies and retired at thirty-eight to a country estate of four hundred acres, whereupon he became the largest landholder in Bristol County and a prominent banker. His father graduated from Princeton in 1840, took an M.A. at the same university, and was admitted to the bar in Philadelphia in 1844. His brief and half-hearted law practice was soon abandoned, and he lived as "a gentleman of leisure, the Philadelphia counterpart of the English 'squire' " (Kakar, 1970: 12–13). By the time Fred was eighteen he had traveled widely in Europe with his parents, had been to school in Paris and Berlin, spoke French and German fluently, had graduated at the head of his class at Exeter, and had passed his entrance examinations for Harvard with honors.

However, he complained of failing eyesight that made it impossible to study and decided to forego Harvard to become an apprentice patternmaker and machinist. Late in 1874, at the age of eighteen, Taylor started work at the Enterprise Hydraulic Works, a small pump manufacturer, owned by social acquaintances of his family (ibid.: 28, 36). Taylor worked without pay the first year, for $1.50 a week the second and third years, and for $3.00 a week the fourth year. (At that time the average wage at the Whitin Machine Works was about $1.50 a *day*.) At the same time, however, Taylor lived with his parents in one of the most exclusive parts of Philadelphia, was a member of the Philadelphia Cricket Club, played tennis and cricket with his old friends, sang tenor in a choral society, took part in amateur theatricals, and took summer vacations camping with others in his social circle. After completing his apprenticeship, Taylor went to work as an unskilled laborer at Midvale Steel. The owners were friends of his father—Fred always addressed one as "Uncle William," and the other's son, Fred's doubles partner in tennis, was later his brother-in-law (ibid.: 41). After a brief stint as a clerk, Taylor worked as a machinist for two months, and then was promoted to gang boss. Within six years he went from gang boss to foreman of the machine shop, to master mechanic in charge of repairs and maintenance throughout the works, to chief draftsman, to chief engineer. "Evidently his later promotions mainly represented the taking on of additional duties, for at all times he remained the operative head of the machine shop" (Copley, 1923, I: 116). Taylor undoubtedly had important abilities, but his promotions were primarily because he was a friend of the owners; in fact Fred and his doubles partner "had great dreams of eventually controlling Midvale" (ibid.: 117). (These dreams were destroyed in 1886 when his friend's father sold his share of the company.)

Taylor's unique situation, an upper-class social background combined with a number of years in the shop as an ordinary worker, was crucial for the development of his system. While Taylor worked, he apparently tried to identify with the workers, at least in external mannerisms. "He imitated their dress and manners and always regretted that he could not learn to chew tobacco. More important, to the consternation of his Puritan family and friends, he learned to swear" (Kakar, 1970: 36). On the one hand, Taylor was perfectly capable of realizing that workers were human beings very much like his schoolmates and upper-class social acquaintances. In later years, in a lecture at the Harvard Graduate School of Business Administration, Taylor explained:

> Now, I assume that most of you gentlemen are not the sons of working men, and that you have not yourselves worked during any long period of time, at least, with working men, and on the same level with them. The fact is, that in all essential matters, they are just the same as you and I are. The working man and the college professor have fundamentally the same feelings, the same motives, the same ambitions, the same failings, the same virtues. And a moment's thought must convince any one of the truth of this fact, since the college professors of the present are universally the descendants of the working men of the past, while the descendants of the college professor are sure, in the course of time, to again return to the working classes. We are all of the same clay, and essentially of the same mental as well as physical fibre. . . . Any man who is intimately acquainted with the working classes of the United States must have profound respect for them. (Quoted in ibid.: 37)

On the other hand, Taylor was equally capable of some of the most outrageous remarks about workers, stating that they were opposed to all change simply because it was change, calling them too stupid to understand the science of such work as shoveling or loading pig iron, explaining that the average pig-iron handler was too stupid to learn to shovel (let alone become a machinist or manager), declaring that high wages would be wasted in dissipation, and the like. It would be too simple to say that one position was his real view and the other was for public purposes; Taylor was capable of thinking and acting on either of these contradictory positions.

Whatever view he held about workers' intellect and ability, Taylor never adopted their social outlook, attitude toward work, or political orientation. As long as Taylor was a worker, he obeyed the social code of the work group and restricted output. He might have done some more than others, but "not enough to cause my brother workmen to feel that I was breaking rates and making a hog of myself, as they would put it" (quoted in Copley, 1923,

I: 157).* But as soon as Taylor became gang boss, which happened shortly after he started work at Midvale, he began a war to destroy the restriction of output. In Taylor's own words:

> We who were the workmen of [the machine shop of the Midvale Steel Works] had the quantity output carefully agreed upon for everything that was turned out in the shop. We limited the output to about, I should think, one-third of what we could very well have done. We felt justified in doing this, owing to the piecework system—that is, owing to the necessity for soldiering under the piecework system—which I pointed out in my testimony yesterday.

> As soon as I became gang boss the men who were working under me and who, of course, knew that I was onto the whole game of soldiering or deliberately restricting output, came to me at once and said, "Now, Fred, you are not going to be a damn piecework hog, are you?" I said, "If you fellows mean you are afraid I am going to try to get a larger output from these lathes" I said, "Yes; I do propose to get more work out." I said, "You must remember I have been square with you fellows up to now and worked with you. I have not broken a single rate. I have been on your side of the fence. But now I have accepted a job under the management of this company and I am on the other side of the fence, and I will tell you perfectly frankly that I am going to try to get a bigger output from those lathes." They answered, "Then, you are going to be a damn hog." (1912: 79–80)

Taylor was great enough to learn from his experience as a worker that there were two sides to the fence. Both sides were rational, both sides pursued their own interests, but he, Frederick Winslow Taylor, was unequivocally on the side of managers and capitalists.

Taylor's Analysis

The system Taylor devised to break the power of workers was developed during years of struggle with the workers of Midvale Steel.

---

*Taylor later said he was mistaken to have restricted output. Even if his rate were cut, he should have kept on striving for maximum output: "I was wrong. It would have paid me and the other people [his fellow workmen] to have taken our cut and gone right ahead" (quoted in Copley, 1923, I: 214).

This bitter struggle was probably the most important experience in Taylor's life, and he returns to it again and again in his writings. It was the foundation for his analysis of the problem confronting the capitalist class.

Taylor's analysis of the situation that existed before his system shows the nature of the problem as capitalists saw it. In considering Taylor's analysis it is again important to emphasize the extent to which Taylor dominated the management movement of his time. A description of the existing situation and the problem facing management featured prominently in all of Taylor's writings and talks, and these were the main source of his influence. To cite Taylor is not the equivalent of quoting some obscure slaveholder's reservations about slavery: it is to cite the person who was accepted at the time, accepted above all by capitalists themselves, as the foremost analyst of the problem confronting the capitalist class. Taylor demonstrably articulated and developed the consciousness of the capitalist class, and based on this analysis went on to lead capitalists in a major change. A presentation of Taylor's analysis can serve as a summary of what I have been trying to demonstrate in the last three chapters.

To begin with, Taylor frankly recognized that workers possessed more knowledge of the production process than did management. Taylor noted that the management of his day implicitly accepted this fact, along with the fact that workers would control the details of the work process. More important, he saw that this was inherent in the organization of that work process.

> This mass of rule-of-thumb or traditional knowledge may be said to be the principal asset or possession of every tradesman. Now, in the best of the ordinary types of management, the managers recognize frankly the fact that the 500 or 1000 workmen, included in the twenty to thirty trades, who are under them, possess this mass of traditional knowledge, a large part of which is not in the possession of the management. The management, of course, includes foremen and superintendents, who themselves have been in most cases first-class workers at their trades. And yet these foremen and superintendents know, better than anyone else, that their own knowledge and personal skill falls far short of the combined knowledge and dexterity of all the workmen under them. The most experienced managers therefore frankly place before their workmen the problem of doing the work in

the best and most economical way. They recognize the task before them as that of inducing each workman to use his best endeavors, his hardest work, all his traditional knowledge, his skill, his ingenuity, and his good will—in a word, his "initiative," so as to yield the largest possible return to his employer. The problem before the management, then, may be briefly said to be that of obtaining the best *initiative* of every workman. And the writer uses the word "initiative" in its broadest sense, to cover all of the good qualities sought for from the men. (Taylor, 1911: 32–33)

As long as workers knew more than managers, as long as workers made crucial decisions about how to do the work, management would have to find a way to get workers' voluntary cooperation.

Piecework was an attempt to make it in workers' financial interest to cooperate with their employers in achieving the maximum possible output. However, since employers were ignorant of the actual time it took to do the work, it was in the interests of the worker to "soldier," or take longer to do the work than was in fact necessary (ibid.: 18). Taylor did not try to deny what his experience as a worker had taught him: restriction of output was a sensible, rational policy from the workers' point of view.

This loafing or soldiering proceeds from two causes. First, from the natural instinct and tendency of the men to take it easy, which may be called natural soldiering. Second, from more intricate second thought and reasoning caused by their relations with other men, which may be called systematic soldiering. . . .

The natural laziness of men is serious, but by far the greatest evil from which both workmen and employers are suffering is the *systematic soldiering* which is almost universal under all of the ordinary schemes of management and which results from a careful study on the part of the workmen of what will promote their best interests. . . .

The greater part of the *systematic soldiering* is done by the men with the deliberate object of keeping their employers ignorant of how fast work can be done. So universal is soldiering for this purpose that hardly a competent workman can be found in a large establishment, whether he works by the day or on piece work, contract work, or under any of the ordinary systems, who does not devote a considerable part of his time to studying just how slow he can work and still convince his employer that he is going at a good pace.

The causes for this are, briefly, that practically all employers determine upon a maximum sum which they feel it is right for each of their classes of employees to earn per day, whether their men work by the day or piece.

Each workman soon finds out about what this figure is for his particular case, and he also realizes that when his employer is convinced that a man is capable of doing more work than he has done, he will find sooner or later some way of compelling him to do it with little or no increase of pay.

Employers derive their knowledge of how much of a given class of work can be done in a day from either their own experience, which has frequently grown hazy with age, from casual and unsystematic observation of their men, or at best from records which are kept, showing the quickest time in which each job has been done. In many cases the employer will feel almost certain that a given job can be done faster than it has been, but he rarely cares to take the drastic measures necessary to force men to do it in the quickest time, unless he has an actual record proving conclusively how fast the work can be done.

It evidently becomes for each man's interest, then, to see that no job is done faster than it has been in the past. The younger and less experienced men are taught this by their elders, and all possible persuasion and social pressure is brought to bear upon the greedy and selfish men to keep them from making new records which result in temporarily increasing their wages, while all those who come after them are made to work harder for the same old pay. . . .

It is under piece work that the art of systematic soldiering is thoroughly developed; after a workman has had the price per piece of the work he is doing lowered two or three times as a result of his having worked harder and increased his output, he is likely entirely to lose sight of his employer's side of the case and become imbued with a grim determination to have no more cuts if soldiering can prevent it. Unfortunately for the character of the workman, soldiering involves a deliberate attempt to mislead and deceive his employer, and thus upright and straightforward workmen are compelled to become more or less hypocritical. The employer is soon looked upon as an antagonist, if not an enemy. (1903; repeated 1911: 19–24)

Taylor considered these points so important that he repeated them word for word in both his major books. He was thus willing to admit what many employers tried to conceal, that capitalists restricted wages to the maximum which they thought workers "should" earn. Rate busters are admitted to be "greedy and selfish men." In one of his accounts of the struggle at Midvale, Taylor recounted:

> His workman friends came to him continually and asked him, in a personal, friendly way, whether he would advise them, for their own best interest, to turn out more work. And, as a truthful man, he had to tell them that if he were in their place he would fight against turning out any more work, just as they were doing, because under the piecework system they would be allowed to earn no more wages than they had been earning, and yet they would be made to work harder. (1911: 52)

Taylor, however, was not a worker. He was a manager, an engineer, and both from social background and personal preference he was completely on the side of capital. Recognizing that workers behaved rationally did not cause Taylor to side with the workers. On the contrary, it was part of his attempt to understand the work process in order to better control workers in the interests of capital; it was a fundamental reason why his analysis was superior to the analyses of other management experts of the time. On the basis of modern accounts of Taylor's system or of the problems with workers' control, we would expect Taylor to have located the problem in workers' inability to handle sophisticated processes and advanced technology. In his early works, which were presented as papers at the American Society of Mechanical Engineers and were addressed almost exclusively to an audience of engineers and shop managers, Taylor hardly mentions this as a problem. As he became more prominent, and his writings became a source of controversy and contention, he argued that "scientific management" would develop the "one best way" of doing the work, a way that would be superior to the average methods then prevailing, but this argument always occupied a subsidiary place. Taylor not only admitted but proclaimed that the main reason for his system was that workers, acting as a self-conscious social class, deliberately restricted output to an agreed-upon level. Since, as Taylor admitted, workers were being reasonable in deliberately restricting output, there was no point in trying to reason with them.

The only solution, therefore, was to change the nature of the work by creating "management," something which up to that point had had only a protean existence. The first step in this process was for management to learn what workers already knew: "The first of these principles of scientific management is the deliberate gathering in on the part of those on the management's side of all of the great mass of traditional knowledge, which in the past has been in the hands of the workmen" (Taylor, 1912: 40). Taylor readily admitted that "the knowledge which the workmen had . . . was in many cases quite as exact as that which is finally obtained by the management" (ibid.: 41): he did not say that workers lacked adequate knowledge to produce the goods well, or call on management to systematize and perfect the knowledge necessary for production but which no one as yet possessed. No—the problem was that workers had the knowledge. If there was to be a science of management at all it was necessary that management learn what workers already knew.

Why did management need to acquire this knowledge? Because as things then stood workers controlled the work process. "The underlying philosophy of all of the old systems of management in common use makes it imperative that each workman shall be left with the final responsibility for doing his job practically as he thinks best, with comparatively little help and advice from the management" (Taylor, 1911: 25).

As long as this was true, Taylor said, workplace authority would be divided. Workers would decide on the level of output and the methods of production they thought best. In order to overcome this "the management must take over and perform much of the work which is now left to the men; almost every act of the workman should be preceded by one or more preparatory acts of the management" (ibid.: 26). Taylor is explicitly calling here for the creation (or vast expansion) of what can only be called bureaucracy in industry; he is doing so because it will allow tighter control of workers' activity, hence of the speed of production, hence of the rate of exploitation and capital accumulation. The creation of bureaucracy is not something which Taylor cherished in the abstract, but something to which he was driven because of successful worker resistance to all his (and others) previous attempts to increase the speed of production.

For management to take over work that previously had been done by workers involved planning the work in advance, hence creating a planning room, a central focus wherever Taylor introduced his system. "All possible brain work should be removed from the shop and centered in the planning or laying-out department" (1903: 98). "Brain work," i.e., planning and making decisions, necessarily involves control over many details of the work process, and workers used this control to further their own aims, as well as those of their employers. By removing brain work from the shop floor, workers could be controlled in a way that had never before been possible.

The planning room did not necessarily mean changes in the work or in the order in which it was done. It merely enabled management to specify in advance exactly what each worker was required to do. Workers received a detailed set of written instructions specifying these tasks and how long they should take. Frequently the instructions required workers to do exactly what they had done before, but even if the machine was set up in the same way and used the same speeds and feeds, these were now determined by the planning room, not the production worker (or the foreman). Elaborate records and bookkeeping were called for both to develop these specifications and to be sure that workers did exactly as they were ordered. Even if nothing else changed (and frequently nothing else did change) this was a revolution in the work process.

This new organization of work required the creation or expansion of bureaucracy:

> The fourth [and last] of the principles of scientific management is perhaps the most difficult of all of the four principles of scientific management for the average man to understand. It consists of an almost equal division of the actual work of the establishment between the workmen, on the one hand, and the management, on the other hand. That is, the work which under the old type of management practically all was done by the workman, under the new is divided into two great divisions, and one of these divisions is deliberately handed over to those on the management's side. This new division of work, this new share of the work assumed by those on the management's side, is so great that you will, I think, be able to understand it better in a numerical way when I tell you that in a machine shop, which, for instance, is doing an intricate business—I do not refer to a manufacturing company, but, rather, to an engineering company; that is, a machine shop which builds a variety of machines and is not engaged in manufacturing them, but, rather, in constructing them—will have one man on the management's side to every three workmen; that is, this immense share of the work—one third [sic; one-fourth]—has been

deliberately taken out of the workman's hands and handed over to those on the management's side. And it is due to this actual sharing of the work between the two sides more than to any other one element that there has never (until this last summer) been a single strike under scientific management. In a machine shop, again, under this new type of management there is hardly a single act or piece of work done by any workman in the shop which is not preceded and followed by some act on the part of one of the men in the management. All day long every workman's acts are dovetailed in between corresponding acts of the management. First, the workman does something, and then a man on the management's side does something; then the man on the management's side does something, and then the workman does something. (Taylor, 1912: 44–45)

The need for management to displace workers as the group with the knowledge of and control over the work process was the essence of Taylor's vision, but he backed this central idea with an extensive analysis of the steps to use in implementing his program. These fall into three general categories: (1) an increasing division of labor, (2) a major speed-up, and (3) a number of technical changes.

The major change in the division of labor was the vast expansion of the management side, the removal of all brain work from the shop floor to the planning room. Taylor readily admitted that his system called for a great increase in the number of nonproducers (as he called them), but insisted that "no manager need feel alarmed when he sees the number of non-producers increasing in proportion to producers" since this system would ultimately result in lowering production costs (1903: 122). Similarly, Barth, a Taylor disciple in charge of installing scientific management at Watertown Arsenal, warned the officers in charge that "the Taylor system called for what was likely to strike the uninitiated as an astonishing number of 'non-producers'" (Aitken, 1960: 88). At that time, even Taylor found it incredible that only three-quarters of the employees would be production workers, and one-quarter would be engineers, clerks, and other management officials. There was no hiding the fact that basic to the Taylor system was a hitherto unheard of expansion in the size of bureaucracy.

At the same time, Taylor increased the division of labor on the shop floor. There were large costs involved in having all of the brain work done in the planning room, but the consequence was that workers had more specialized and less complex tasks, so that cheaper workers could be substituted for all-around mechanics.

> The adoption of standard tools, appliances, and methods throughout the shop, the planning done in the planning room and the detailed instructions sent them from this department, added to the direct help received from the four executive bosses, permit the use of comparatively cheap men even on complicated work. . . .
>
> The full possibilities of [scientific management] . . . will not have been realized until almost all of the machines in the shop are run by men who are of smaller calibre and attainments, and who are therefore cheaper than those required under the old system. (Taylor, 1903: 105)

Skilled workers no longer found their own tools and fixtures, no longer sharpened their own tools, and did not move the work from place to place. All of these things were to be done by unskilled workers, who would be paid commensurately less, making the work less interesting and more repetitive, but increasing profits for capitalists. Significantly, Taylor applied the same principle to the management side:

> "Functional management" consists in so dividing the work of management that each man from the assistant superintendent down shall have as few functions as possible to perform. If practicable the work of each man in the management should be confined to the performance of a single leading function. (Ibid.: 99)

In many ways the most visible and controversial aspect of Taylor's system was the fact that it called for a major speed-up. Taylor boasted that his system could double or quadruple output in exchange for a 30 to 100 percent increase in wages, primarily by eliminating the ability of workers to intentionally hold output below the level they knew to be physically possible. "The essence of [scientific] management lies in the fact that the control of the speed problem rests entirely with the management" (ibid.: 44). Taylor was fully aware, from bitter experience with the workers at Midvale Steel, that speed-up could not be achieved by simply ordering workers to produce more. His works recount at length the means he tried to force increased output:

I began, of course, by directing some one man to do more work than he had done before, and then I got on the lathe myself and showed him that it could be done. In spite of this, he went ahead and turned out exactly the same old output and refused to adopt better methods or to work quicker until finally I laid him off and got another man in his place. This new man—I could not blame him in the least under the circumstances—turned right around and joined the other fellows and refused to do any more work than the rest. After trying this policy for a while and failing to get any results I said distinctly to the fellows, "Now, I am a mechanic; I am a machinist. I do not want to take the next step, because it will be contrary to what you and I look upon as our interest as machinists, but I will take it if you fellows won't compromise with me and get more work off of those lathes, but I warn you if I have to take this step it will be a durned mean one." I took it.

I hunted up some especially intelligent laborers who were competent men, but who had not had the opportunity of learning a trade, and I deliberately taught these men how to run a lathe and how to work fast and right. Every one of these laborers promised me, "Now if you will teach me the machinist trade, when I learn to run a lathe I will do a fair day's work," and every solitary man, when I had taught them their trade, one after another turned right around and joined the rest of the fellows and refused to work one bit faster. (1912: 81–82)

This was only the beginning of Taylor's fight, and eventually he did prevail, but this struggle taught him that an entirely new management system was necessary in order to achieve a substantial increase in output.

The ordinary systems of management in use at the time made an open general demand for speed-up, an approach likely to provoke worker solidarity in resistance. The genius of Taylor's system was the concept of management as controlling the details of the work process rather than simply issuing general directives. His argument contains a clear awareness of scientific management as an instrument in the class struggle by capitalists against workers.

The mistake which is usually made in dealing with union men [Taylor said], lies in giving an order which affects a number of workmen at the same time and in laying stress upon the increase in the output which is demanded instead of emphasizing one by one the details which the workman is to carry out in order to attain the desired result. In the first case a clear issue is raised: say that the man must turn out fifty per cent more pieces than he has in the past, and therefore it will be assumed by most people that he must work fifty per cent harder. In this issue the union is more than likely to have the sympathy of the general public, and they can logically take it up and fight upon it. If, however, the workman is given a series of plain, simple, and reasonable orders, and is offered a premium for carrying them out, the union will have a much more difficult task in defending the man who disobeys them. (1903: 192–93)*

In this way, but in this way only, a 30 percent premium could be used to coerce workers into doubling output. Workers had to either disobey simple direct orders, or else double output in exchange for comparatively small wage increases. Taylor's own example of how his system worked is as follows: on one particular job, workers at Midvale had for years turned out four or five pieces a day, receiving 50¢ per piece. Taylor determined that they "should" be producing ten pieces per day, and set a rate of 25¢ per piece for nine pieces or fewer and 35¢ per piece for ten or more. A worker who produced nine pieces would therefore receive $2.25 a day, and a worker who produced ten pieces would receive $3.50 a day. Workers who continued to produce at the old rate would have their wages cut in half. This made it very difficult for workers to compromise with management, restricting output to, say, eight pieces a day. This differential piece-rate system (as Taylor called it) provided a strong incentive to workers to give in completely and produce at the rate determined by management. By setting the point at which the differential took effect management essentially determined the level of output, something which it had never before been able to do. Workers were almost forced to accept this determination, or else fight the system as a whole. Taylor demanded open war: one side or the other must emerge as victor.

It was not even possible for workers to appeal to custom and precedent, since the speed-up was accompanied by a complete reorganization of the work process—the establishment of a planning

---

*This statement emphasizes the way in which scientific management served to obscure the generation of surplus, as well as secure greater quantities of it (see Burawoy, 1979). It was not the mystification of scientific management which was crucial, however, but the new power position of management.

room, an increasing division of labor, and the addition of much-needed technical changes.

As I will demonstrate in detail in the next section, Taylor made a great point of introducing technical changes as part of the system, so that workers could not so easily reject it totally. Moreover, he made clear that these should be introduced first, as they would often be welcomed, and would accustom workers to management changes.

Thus, above all, Taylor stressed the need to introduce his entire system, and not simply one or another of the particular pieces (time and motion study, the stop watch, the piece-rate system, etc.) that are usually thought of as the essence of scientific management. In a letter to the officers of the Watertown Arsenal, Taylor

> emphasized strongly that it would be useless merely to install an incentive wage plan. The Taylor sytem had to be introduced complete if the desired results were to be achieved. "Anything short of this leaves such a large part of the game in the hands of the workmen that it becomes largely a matter of whim or caprice on their part as to whether they will allow you to have any real results or not." The goal was not simply the provision of incentives to which the workmen could respond or not as they chose; it was, ideally, control of the entire job situation. (Aitken, 1960: 77)

Management wanted to take control of the work process not for the abstract pleasure of knowing they were in control, but in order to shape the work process to better achieve capitalism's aims. Though Taylor liked to talk of the value-neutral benefits of the science of management, he accepted it as a given that "all employees should bear in mind that each shop exists, first, last, and all the time, for the purpose of paying dividends to its owners" (1903: 143).

Taylorism in Practice: Watertown Arsenal

The analysis Taylor presented agrees in large part with the argument I have been making. There can be no question that the broad changes Taylor called for have been generally adopted by American industry (although some of Taylor's specifics have of course been superseded by more sophisticated methods designed to achieve the same ends). Given this, and given Taylor's prominence and impact during the time that the changes were being made, it is highly probable that people in fact did what Taylor called for, and for the reasons Taylor suggested. Despite what seems to me a strong prima facie case for Taylor's importance, most academics have taken the position that Taylorism was primarily an ideology with little practical significance.* I have tried to meet this objection by listing some of the places Taylorism was used and some of the ways its influence spread. In addition, it is important to consider what Taylorism meant in practice.

For one thing, it needs to be clear that any assertions about Taylorism's widespread impact and importance certainly do not mean that in actual situations Taylorism operated in the way Taylor described it. Taylorism was (and is) important as a strategy by capital, it was (and is) a comparatively successful strategy, but this certainly does not mean that worker resistance ended or that capital acquired total control of the workplace. Capital is, after all, one of the two contending parties in the workplace.

Almost all historical studies of Taylorism rely exclusively on the records and writings of those on capital's side; thus the only conflict they see is within capital, that between the Taylor system experts and the old-line managers. The place to understand this historic class struggle is the U.S. government arsenal at Watertown, Massachusetts. A special House of Representatives committee which investigated the attempt to introduce the Taylor system at the arsenal took testimony from workers who protested it as well as managers. One useful study of Watertown already exists—Hugh Aitken's *Taylorism at Watertown Arsenal* (1960)—but incredibly, even Aitken makes almost no use of the testimony of the workers in the shops. Not surprisingly, this has produced a very distorted view of Taylorism, one which tends to focus on public relations, "science" claims of Taylor and his disciples, to the neglect of the more candid parts of Taylor's own work, and the exclusion of worker opposition to Taylor. Harry Braverman has already shown how much can be done simply

---

*They have done so without themselves offering counter evidence. The one systematic attempt to study whether Taylor's followers in practice introduced the changes Taylor called for concludes, or that "the results indicate that Taylor's colleagues were generally faithful to his teachings" (Nelson, 1974: 490).

by considering what Taylor actually said. Beyond this, it is useful to look at the conflicts which ensued when an attempt was made to introduce Taylor's system.

I have placed heavy stress on the labor and organizational aspects of Taylor's system, which I believe, and he believed, were the crucial element in improving a shop; an understanding of these problems, and a solution to them, is what made Taylor great. However, he and his disciples began as engineers, and they made many technical changes in the shops where they worked. For any given shop, these changes might be as important as the organizational changes, especially in the short run. I have neglected these changes because they were in no sense unusual, and they made no lasting changes in the nature of work: many other experts recommended or implemented very similar changes, and the management journals were filled with literature on the subject. Though Taylor contributed to this literature, and though he and his disciples were undoubtedly competent at bringing run-down shops up to the best prevailing standards, had Taylorism been nothing more than this, it would have had no enduring significance.

In practice, of course, these technical improvements were an important part of the Taylor system, as the changes at Watertown demonstrate. Taylor and his disciple Carl Barth visited the Watertown Arsenal in April 1909; Barth began work in June 1909, and it was almost two years later (May 8, 1911) before any time and motion study was introduced (Aitken, 1960). During these first two years, Barth brought the shops up to standard—reorganizing the storeroom and cost-accounting system, improving the belting, changing the toolroom procedure, buying new tool forging and grinding equipment, rehabilitating the machine tools, standardizing ancillary equipment, increasing the electric generating capacity, and many other such changes (ibid.: 87–115).

At the same time Barth began organizing his planning room—the department which was to be the nerve center of the whole organization. . . . Space for the planning room was found on the second floor of the machine shop, directly over the engine room. Desks, boards, files, and all the other paraphernalia were ordered to Barth's specifications, and blank forms of about twenty different types—job cards, route sheets, storehouse tags, routing tags, and so on—were printed. The electric time-recording clocks, which [Colonel] Wheeler had so recently congratulated himself for installing, were discarded on the grounds that they did not fit the job cards used by the Taylor system and that all recording of times would be done in the planning room. A new electric timing system, consisting of a master clock, four electric time stamps, four secondary clocks, batteries, and so on, was installed. By the end of January 1910, the planning room was completed and ready to begin functioning. (Ibid.: 96–97)

These changes were introduced gradually. For example, at first the planning room dealt in detail only with the machine shop, "leaving the pattern shop, the smith shop, and the foundry organized as in the past, except that they would receive their instructions on work required from the planning room instead of from the main office" (ibid.: 89).

It was normal Taylor procedure to make all of these changes before beginning the time study. The whole purpose of time and motion study was to make a "correct" determination of the time in which work could be done, and then to set a rate and output level which would not be changed. General Crozier argued at the hearings that the reason piece rates had been cut is that they had not been set correctly in the first place; if a "scientific" determination of the correct rate were once made, there would be no further reason to cut rates (U.S. House of Representatives, 1912: 833). If the machinery, belting, tools, and procedures had not been fixed, it would not be possible to set a rate and stick to it: each time one of these other elements changed, it would be necessary to change the piece rate as well. In all his writings Taylor emphasized the necessity of making these changes first, not only so that rates would never need to be changed, but also so that the workers would get used to the experts and their changes. This was especially important, since these early changes were not generally opposed to workers' interests, and were less likely to arouse opposition. As Taylor wrote to General Crozier: "I have told you time and again that . . . it is only after a year or two of continually harassing men and making them change their ways in minor matters that it is safe to begin on time study and those steps which lead to task work" (letter of September 21, 1911, quoted in Aitken, 1960: 162).

In fact, workers welcomed many of these technical changes. As one person explained, the shops needed modernizing regardless of the system used (U.S. House of Representatives, 1912: 327): the newest building was over fifty years old, and "about 40 per cent of the machine tools had been in service for fifteen years or more" (Aitken, 1960: 86). When a new trolley was installed one machinist pointed out that while the new trolley would be a help, he had been asking for it for three years (U.S. House of Representatives, 1912: 285, 290). One person testified: "We have a bolt and strap room recently installed, which is in itself of great assistance to the men in setting up. Whether put in by the Taylor system or any other system I must say it was a step in the right direction, a good thing" (ibid.: 318). The master mechanic, who had the confidence of the workers, testified that he had heard of no "objections on the part of the workmen to better facilities being furnished them for doing their work," and explained that "they like to have tools and good equipment to work with" (ibid.: 508). All of this is hardly surprising, but it appears necessary to stress the obvious in light of the way Taylorism is sometimes portrayed.

Mr. Chase, a shipyard worker, was one of the most militant and intransigent workers to testify. In concert with other workers at a shipyard, he refused to accept a job inside the Taylor-system planning room, and when asked, "Mr. Chase, is not that an act of conspiracy against the President, who is the Commander in Chief of the Army and Navy?" answered, "Well, if that be treason, make the most of it" (ibid.: 534–35). Clearly, Mr. Chase was not one to avoid a fight. Nonetheless, he went out of his way to stress that "the workingmen, as workingmen, don't object to the introduction of high-speed steel; we don't object to the taking the proper size of stock to turn out our work; and we don't object to the introduction of the modern systems" (ibid.: 528).

Workers and Technological Change

This is not to suggest that the workers welcomed all of the technological changes introduced by the Taylor system. Tools were a case in point. In his book *On The Art of Cutting Metals** Taylor had developed a set of standard tool sizes and shapes, to which all tools were to comply. Drawings of the form of tool to be used were sent to the shops, and "the men had to use those tools whether they wished to or not." Workers vehemently objected to the tools, insisting that the ones they were using, which they ground or had ground in the way that seemed best to them, were superior. These were not objections to change just because it was change, nor were they simply defenses of the freedom and flexibility afforded by the opportunity to select and grind their own tools. On at least two occasions, workers' tools were demonstrated to be superior to Taylor system tools. The first such proof was a scientifically conducted test:

> The test was made by Mr. Nelson [master mechanic, or superintendent, of the shop] and Mr. Barth [Taylor's hand-picked expert], I believe, at that time, of a turning tool, which is known as a roughing tool, for roughing out heavy shafting. As to the height of the tool, it was after the fashion of what was known as a half diamond point with a corner of it rounded off and standing exceedingly high, so high that the tool did not prove a success. It would bite under a heavy chip. Mr. Nelson made a demonstration with the tool we had in use and proved conclusively that it was a better tool.† It would stand longer in turning, and would make a better looking finish on the work than the tool adopted by the Taylor system. (Ibid.: 330)

The other demonstration of the inadequacy of the Taylor system tools was less scientific, but more costly:

> This was a case where a man had insisted on getting what is known in the trade as a gooseneck tool. The Taylor system did not provide a gooseneck tool with it and the result was that this tool post broke under the strain, on account of the advanced point in getting up into a corner, and knocked the man unconscious on the bed of his planer. After that, that particular phase of the Taylor tool was eliminated and the gooseneck tool provided for the men to use in operations of that kind. I just simply want to call that to the attention of the committee to verify the statements made that with this system came a kind of tool

---

*In his early work Taylor continually refers to "art," specifically including the "art" of management. Only later does he refer to his system as the "science of management," though once the term is coined Taylor insists on its use.

†Note that the plant superintendent was the person selected to conduct the test, in keeping with his position as the most highly skilled worker, the "master mechanic."

that was absolutely dangerous for the men to use, and they were compelled to use it, and that it was insisted upon by the officers in charge. (Ibid.: 331; see also 415)

The worker was struck in the head and had to have nine stitches—obviously the same tool could quite easily have cost his life. Incidents such as these helped confirm workers in their opposition to changes introduced by management, even when they were exhaustively and scientifically tested.* Workers' opposition, combined with such unquestionable evidence of the superiority of the workers' tools, did lead to some modifications in the tools used.

It was fundamental to Taylor's system, however, that workers not influence such changes: they could not suggest modifications or improvements even if they did so to be helpful. Cooperation for workers meant they were "to do what they are told to do promptly and without asking questions or making suggestions" (Taylor, quoted in Aitken, 1960: 46). Back when Taylor was still at Midvale, the statement of his which most often aroused the opposition of his workers was, in the words of one of his employees, "one he sometimes used when we opposed him or discussed a proposition with him. 'You are not supposed to think,' he would say. 'There are other people paid for thinking around here.' " Another of Taylor's workers from that time adds, "I never would admit to Mr. Taylor that I was not allowed to think" (quoted in Copley, 1923, I: 189). Today, of course, workers are socialized from an early point to know that they are not supposed to think, though since the point is so unequivocally established management is usually tactful enough to claim they welcome workers' thoughts. In the 1880s, however, it was almost idiosyncratic for Taylor to hold that workers were not supposed to think: if they did not, who would?

By 1910, Taylor's idiosyncratic position had become management's general position, as a direct result of Taylor's influence. This

---

*As an illustration of the problems and biases that are introduced by relying solely on Taylor, it is worth contrasting the above account with Taylor's analysis:

"It is far simpler to have all the tools in a standardized shop ground by one man to a few simple but rigidly maintained shapes than to have, as is usual in the old-style shop, each machinist spend a portion of each day at the grindstone, grinding his own tools with radically wrong curves and cutting angles, merely because bad shapes are easier to grind than good." (Quoted in Copley, 1923, I: 268)

did not, however, make workers any the more willing to accept it: they continually fought to be able to use their own knowledge and experience. It was not that they were unable to see the superiority of the "science" of management and stubbornly refused to concede that the old ways were inferior. They held as a consciously articulated policy the superiority of using skilled workers, who could think for themselves, directing and planning their own activity and the activity of the work group. For example, Mr. Chase, the shipyard worker, insisted:

> The men must have a scientific knowledge. That is, that a man should know, for example, if the guns were knocked out of parallel, and the shots would go a long way apart; to complete that work quickly it is absolutely essential, I believe, that men should understand that work, men who can determine how the change should be made in order to bring that convergence that is necessary, and if the guns converge one-sixteenth of an inch, for example, at how many yards those shells would crash. I believe those things are absolutely essential if the Navy is to be made practically useful. . . . I believe it is essential to have men there who know, for example, the difference between the travel of a gun, or the travel of the sight on the side, who can figure it out on a target and determine when it is correctly set. And if I understand the system, all that reckoning will be done in the planning department and it will not be necessary to have workmen who are capable of doing that. (U.S. House of Representatives, 1912: 534)

Mr. Nelson, the master mechanic of the Watertown Arsenal, but himself someone who had been a worker, had worked on piecework and had his prices cut, and in most ways had an "old-fashioned" approach to management, also felt that it was better to use skilled workers who could think for themselves and plan the work. The government, as part of the installation of the Taylor system, paid for Mr. Nelson to visit Bethlehem and Midvale Steel, two places where Taylor himself had introduced his system, and which were to be used as models of the benefits and efficiencies of Taylorism. Mr. Nelson, however, reached the opposite conclusion:

> In Bethlehem, so far as I could see, it seems to have a big number of low-grade mechanics in the shop, especially where the small naval mounts were assembled; there were about 300 men in that department. By the use of good mechanics I think the cost could be reduced. (Ibid.: 515)

By paying higher wages the company could attract more skilled workers, and thus make do with fewer workers who would produce more work at less cost, Mr. Nelson held. The workers at Watertown firmly held the same position: Mr. Cooney testified that he could do more work if he made the decisions and plans (ibid.: 254).

Under the Taylor system, there was no reason for workers to think. All they were supposed to do was follow the instructions issued by the planning room, which did not require any judgment, independence, or foresight.

> *Mr. Johnston.* May I ask whether, in your judgment, the carrying out of the Taylor system in its fullness . . . will tend to cause deterioration in the skillfulness, the independence, and the self-reliance of the mechanics?
>
> *Mr. Crawford.* I should think it would. (Ibid.: 414)

The workers' skill deteriorated because they had less need for it. They were no longer all-around workers who planned their own work and made decisions about the productive process, but instead followed detailed orders received from above. This helped create the narrow, repetitive, detail workers which characterize production today:

> *The Chairman.* If the instructions as to how the work should be done by the machinists are issued from the planning room, and he is required to follow these instructions, of what advantage is it to the machinist to have high skill or additional skill?
>
> *Mr. North* [a foreman]. It would be of no advantage that I see. . . .
>
> *The Chairman.* Then, if that is the case, of what value is it to a mechanic to have greater skill than some other mechanic, if he simply must follow automatically the instructions that are handed to him?
>
> *Mr. North.* Well, if a man does one thing over and over, the same thing all the time, he does not require the skill that he would if he were an all-round operator. He becomes a part of the machine. (Ibid.: 357)

The Taylor system went beyond simply making the workers' skill unnecessary: it was designed to make the production process incomprehensible to workers, to structure the situation so that workers not only did not need to understand the production process, they could not understand it. An example involved the new system of naming tools at the Watertown Arsenal.

Not only were tools standardized under the Taylor system, workers were given instruction cards issued by the planning room that specified which tools they were to use. The tools were then either brought directly to the machinist by an unskilled helper, or the machinist went to the toolroom clerk and requested them, whereas formerly workers went to get their own tools, kept those which were particularly useful to them, furnished many of their own,* and had more or less total control of the tools.

All of this devalued the workers' ability to make decisions. In addition, as one part of the Taylor system, a new set of symbols was devised, and all tools and machines were to be known only by their symbols. These involved a series of letters and numbers to replace the customary and commercial names. Many of the symbols were fairly easy to understand—for example, "7M H" meant "horizontal miller no. 7." Even in the best circumstances, however, the workers did not find the new symbols especially useful. As one foreman said, "Take the '7M H' as the Colonel spoke of it. It is just the same to me as if I should say, 'Horizontal miller No. 7.' . . . The only difference is in writing it. . . . It would be more convenient if you were writing it, because it would be quicker" (ibid.: 346–47). This of course was the point: management found these symbols convenient, because they were much easier to *write* down, and the Taylor system required them to do a great deal of writing (instruction cards, machine utilization records, job cards, etc.). It could be argued that the system was introduced simply for the convenience of management with no thought to how it would affect the workers, but this was not the case. As a matter of policy, workers were not allowed to see the symbols, so they could not learn the new names of the tools and machines. In practice, this meant that a worker was unable to challenge an instruction card until the very last moment, since until the tools were actually in his or her hand he could not tell for sure what he was supposed to do. Since at one time or another most workers successfully challenged the instructions they received from "the experts," this was more than an abstract handicap. During the hearings one

---

*When the molders went out on strike they had to return to fetch their tools.

machinist produced a copy of the symbols which had been passed to him by someone else, probably a toolroom or planning-room worker, though the machinist refused to say. He used the list to establish that the foreman testifying, who had said he no longer had trouble with the symbols, was unable to identify tools which any of the machinists could identify by their common names:

Mr. Cain. Mr. North, did I understand you to say that you were pretty familiar with symbols?

Mr. North. On the machines only.

Mr. Cain. Well, now let us suppose you were working in the machine shop, or boss in the machine shop where you formerly were, and a man wanted to use a certain article. I won't specify the article, but he says, "I want a ⅝ by 11 by 2¾ P. D. H. S. B.", would you understand what he meant? . . .

Mr. North. The only thing I could think of would be a parallel.

Mr. Cain. I will state, Mr. North, for your particular benefit and for the benefit of the machinists who are here and who work in the arsenal, that it is a little giant die; the commercial name of it. (Ibid.)

The inability of workers to understand the symbols led to a characteristic bureaucratic problem. Since those who support Taylor's system (and modern bureaucracy) always refer to the characteristic faults of the old methods of production, it seems only fair to point to a characteristic fault of the new system, one which is inherent in a system that intentionally keeps workers in ignorance and requires them to obey orders "without asking questions or making suggestions." The use of arbitrary and incomprehensible symbols meant that slight errors in transcription could cause machinery, tools, and equipment to be sent to wildly improbable places, places where they never would have been sent under the old system:

Mr. Fitzgerald. . . . You never knew of a base ring being on the top floor then? You never knew that to happen?

Mr. North. No; I never did.

Mr. Fitzgerald. Or found a gun lever in the west wing?

Mr. North. No. (Ibid.: 344)

In an extreme but not atypical case, some "move men" (unskilled workers whose job was to move tools, materials, and equipment to skilled machinists) obediently followed the instructions on their "move ticket" and "used a large amount of time and labor" trying to get a jig, a very large casting, to an upper floor. The jig was far too large to go up the stairs, so they tried to take it "up through a kind of hatch through the floor." The reason they had so much trouble getting the casting to the location called for on their move ticket was that the symbol for the location had been transcribed incorrectly, and the part was in completely the wrong place. The machines in that area were not equipped to handle such large castings, and therefore no adequate access routes existed for pieces of that size. As soon as the foreman and machinist saw the piece they told the move men that they were in the wrong wing of the building, the piece could not possibly fit on any machine up there.

> *The Chairman.* Under the former system could that mistake have occurred, or would the machinist or his helper, when he went for the piece, have found by seeing it that it was not suitable for his machine?

> *Mr. North.* Well, I don't think the foreman would have ever sent a piece to a machine where he could not machine it. . . . You would not attempt to put a piece of work on so large that you could not machine it on that particular machine, whereas the move man would not really know the difference in some cases. (Ibid.: 345)

At the time the Taylor system was introduced management was trying to learn what workers already knew: how to do the work. The new symbols, and their secrecy, were one of a number of steps that helped shift the balance of knowledge: suddenly management, in at least one respect, "knew" more about the tools and machines than workers did.

Interestingly enough, if Taylor made a significant technological contribution to capitalism, it was simply that he learned what workers already knew. This was no easy task, and it is something that other managers did not do. In fact, this is what the famous time and motion studies, the use of the stop watch, and so on, were all about.

Taylor's Time and Motion Studies

When Taylor first went to his boss, William Sellers, asking "for permission to spend some money for experiments designed to reveal what his men ought to be able to do with their machines, he was told that the thing had been tried before and could not be done." It was not just Taylor's boss who felt this way: "the best minds up to this time had all come to the conclusion that for the management to determine possible output was impossible" (Copley, 1923, I: 222). When Taylor presented his first full-scale paper before the American Society of Mechanical Engineers, it criticized the previous pay plans, and was based on the assumption that it was possible to determine maximum output, though Taylor did not yet feel sure enough of himself to reveal how he made this determination. In reply to Taylor's paper, Frederick Halsey, the originator of what until then was probably the most famous payment plan, commented:

> If Mr. Taylor can determine the maximum output of the miscellaneous pieces of work comprised in the everyday operation of the average machine shop, he has accomplished a great work, and the present paper should be followed at once by another giving the fullest possible details of his method. It is this universal difficulty of determining the possible output which is at the bottom of the difficulties besetting the piece-work plan, and it was its contemplation which led the writer's thoughts to the Premium Plan. With that plan, the attempt to determine the possible output is abandoned. Present output is taken as the basis. (Cited in ibid.: 404)

All pre-Taylor pay plans were based, in one way or another, on how much had been produced in the past. Taylor's "technological" innovation was to observe workers closely and try to determine how much they could produce if they did their maximum. At first Taylor did his timing of workers in secret, but this sort of timing could produce only the grossest and least satisfactory estimates of the time it should take to do a job. Taylor could tell if the time taken included a rest break away from a machine, but he could not observe the details of the work process (ibid.: 231). Taylor quickly decided that if time study was to determine the maximum possible output, it would have to be done with the knowledge—and if possible, with at least the tacit consent—of the worker. In its fully developed form, time and motion study involved a Taylor minion standing over a worker, using a notebook to list all the motions the worker made and a stop watch to time these motions. The time-study expert would question the worker about the work to decide which motions were "waste" or "superfluous," and these would not be counted in determining the time that it should take to do the job.

Taylor was very proud of time and motion study, claiming it was what gave his system a right to be called "scientific" management. It was scientific because it wrote down and classified knowledge. The same knowledge had previously existed in the heads of the workers, but this was not science because it was not classified and organized. Using his methods, Taylor claimed, it was possible to determine scientifically exactly how long a worker "should" take to do a job, and exactly how much work a worker "should" do in a day (or week or month). At last, it was possible to give scientific meaning to the expression "a fair day's work."*

Such claims were ludicrous, of course, for at least three reasons. First, there is absolutely no reason to assume that the maximum possible output is what a worker "should" do. Second, since Taylor's "scientific" summations of the "necessary" times invariably ended up being below the total time taken by the fastest worker (even if that worker proceeded in the approved manner), Taylor's system always added in extra time in determining the "scientific" time. Taylor could never adequately explain how he and his minions arrived at the amount of time to add, but he nonetheless insisted that this additional time was "scientific" and not arbitrary. Third, the determination of the "waste" motions was often arbitrary—for example, the strike at the Watertown Arsenal resulted from a stop watch time study being made

---

*Taylor and his followers held that a fair day's work was the maximum a worker could produce on a sustained basis, day after day, all year long. The question arises, if a fair day's work was all a worker could produce without destroying himself, why wasn't a "fair day's pay" the maximum wages which a company could pay without going bankrupt (i.e., allowing money for new investment, but nothing for stockholders)? Taylor explained that it would never do to pay the maximum an employer could afford:

> It is the writer's judgment . . . that for their own good it is as important that workmen should not be very much over-paid, as it is that they should not be under-paid. If over-paid, many will work irregularly and tend to become more or less shiftless, extravagant, and dissipated. It does not do for men to get rich too fast. (Taylor, 1903: 27)

on molders by a Taylor system "expert" who knew nothing about molding—and still disallowed many motions as "waste." The expert may have been right about some motions, but he certainly had no claim to scientific exactitude. As Hugh Aitken comments, "It is tempting, though it is only part of the truth, to define time study as a ritual whose function it was to validate, by reference to the apparently objective authority of the clock, a subjective estimate of the time a job should take" (1960: 26). Time study was more than a ritual, because it actually did allow management to make far more accurate determinations of the time which it should take to do a job. In many situations, workers could restrict output while still looking continuously busy if the management left them alone. These same workers would be unable to deceive a knowledgeable observer stationed at their elbow, timing them with a stop watch, all day long, day after day. Time study could be a powerful tool to end the restriction of output.

Taylor used time and motion study not only to determine the length of time which a piece of work should take, but also to determine the "one best way" of doing the work, stating that workers were too stupid to figure this out. He selected pig-iron handling as an illustration, because it "is the simplest kind of human effort. . . . A man simply stoops down and with his hands picks up a piece of iron, and then walks a short distance and drops it on the ground." Nonetheless, he added:

> I can say, without the slightest hesitation, that the science of handling pig iron is so great that the man who is fit to handle pig iron as his daily work cannot possibly understand that science . . . and this inability of the man who is fit to do the work to understand the science of doing his work becomes more and more evident as the work becomes more complicated, all the way up the scale. (1912: 48)

It is undoubtedly true that Taylor and his followers often found ways of doing the work which were better than the existing average, and perhaps in a few cases better than the practices of the very best workers. If nothing else, having the money, opportunity, time, and facilities to study the work process systematically was likely to lead to improvements.* However, in general Taylor and his followers

---

*Having explained that workers were too stupid to understand the science of pig-iron handling, at the exact same time Taylor said that workers could not develop the science because they did not have the time, money, and facilities.

have almost certainly received far too much credit for improvements in work methods. I know of no systematic (or even unsystematic) attempt to independently assess to what extent Taylor improved the methods of production: essentially all accounts of Taylor's changes in the work process begin by accepting his report of the facts, and usually even his general unsupported conclusions. This would be inexcusable in the best of circumstances, but the fact is that Taylor never conducted anything which remotely approximated a scientific experiment to test the possible output of workers with and without the benefit of his science of doing the work, so even if we accept Taylor's account in its entirety we still have no way of telling whether he improved the methods of doing the work. This fact has been obscured because later commentators have followed Taylor in focusing on the increase in output achieved by his methods, and simply attributing this increase to improved methods.* Taylor may have chosen to present his examples in this way, but he realized full well that the main reason for the increase in output was an increase in effort. The whole point of his system was to break up and destroy "systematic soldiering," as he emphasized in every piece he wrote. The fact that a pig-iron handler loaded twelve and a half tons before Taylor, and forty-seven tons following Taylor's instructions, tells us *nothing* about the worth of those instructions. Taylor's entire "science" of pig-iron handling consisted of having the worker rest periodically during the day, in specified amounts and times. Taylor wants us to believe that without this "science" of pig-iron handling Schmidt would have been unable to load forty-seven tons a day. However, Taylor never tried to test this idea, and even before he received any instruction from Taylor Schmidt specifically said he could load forty-seven tons a day.

Taylor wrote as if one of the keys to his success was his development of "the one best way" to do any given kind of work. He told the congressional committee that

> shoveling is a great science compared with pig iron handling. I dare say
> that most of you gentlemen know that a good many pig iron handlers
> can never learn to shovel right; the ordinary pig iron handler is not the

---

*For example, without the benefit of any expert advice workers acheived more than a 600 percent increase in output in producing McClellan saddles (see Chapter Five), a greater increase than in almost any of Taylor's examples.

type of man well suited to shoveling. He is too stupid; there is too much mental strain, too much knack required of a shoveler for the pig iron handler to take kindly to shoveling. (Taylor, 1912: 50)

The science of shoveling was so complex that even experienced shovelers had to be taught how to shovel. Not only that, but if they were not constantly watched they were likely to soon forget how to shovel, with the result that they would fail to meet their quotas. When this happened, a shoveling teacher would come to the workers, warn that they would be thrown off the gang if they did not improve, and then watch to see if they knew how to shovel right. Most probably, Taylor said, the teacher would find that the only problem was that the shoveler had forgotten how to shovel right (that is, the worker would not be under any physical strain and would not be restricting output). "And the teacher would stay by him two, three, four, or five days, if necessary, until he got the man back again into the habit of shoveling right" (ibid.: 61).

Workers and Time Study

If all of this "science" and "instruction" was necessary in order to teach shovelers how to shovel, imagine how much more must have been involved in teaching machinists how to do machine shop work, particularly since machinists were less capable of understanding the science of their work than shovelers were of understanding the science of theirs! It is interesting to consider, therefore, what happened in the machine shop at the Watertown Arsenal, for in this case we have the testimony of the workers who benefited from the "science" and "instruction" of the Taylor system experts. Before considering the comments and reactions of the workers, it is necessary to stress that the Watertown Arsenal received the benefits of a full installation of the Taylor system. Taylor himself was intimately involved in the entire case, visiting the arsenal at the beginning and submitting a report on what needed to be done, corresponding with the officers involved and advising what course to take at particular junctures, and so on. Most of all, Taylor—who by 1909 no longer worked himself—personally picked the disciple who was to install the system, overriding the person who had been the first choice of the Department of Ordnance. Taylor also picked the time-study person for the arsenal, writing to General Crozier: "By getting Merrick as a teacher you would save, I should think, a year at least in the rapidity of your time study and similar work. He is the best detail man for this work who is at all available" (letter of January 12, 1911, quoted in Aitken, 1960: 106).

Taylor continued to think well of Dwight Merrick, the time-study expert, after the arsenal work was completed, so there is no question of Taylor breaking with his own selection because Merrick did not do the job correctly. So the Watertown Arsenal case is a relatively full and fair test of Taylor's system (probably no case did everything exactly as Taylor would have wanted it); the only way it differs from others is in allowing us to see the workers' perceptions of the process as well as those of management.

Not surprisingly, the workers felt that they knew more than the Taylor system experts. One foreman summed up the workers' view when he said that no expert had "ever suggested any improved methods not already known" to him, but he had frequently had to correct the instructions given to him by the experts (U.S. House of Representatives, 1912: 349). Almost every worker who testified had examples to show that in at least some cases, the instructions given by the experts either would not work at all, or could be greatly improved on. Mr. Reagan, a machinist, reported that if he followed the expert's instructions he "could not do the work as it should be done" and he therefore got the approval of the foreman and the master mechanic to do the job "at a lower speed with more feed, and get better results" (ibid.: 432). When Merrick challenged the changes, the worker, foreman, master mechanic, and Merrick himself conducted a test of the two ways, and the worker's way was agreed to be better. The next job came with no instructions, but a time based on the assumption the worker would do it his own way, which took less time than the expert's way.

Another worker disregarded his instruction card and did the job his own way, seeking approval from his foreman after the fact. The foreman endorsed the change, commenting: "There was not anything else he could do. The tool would not stand the cut at the speed it was rated to go" (ibid.: 372).

A third machinist, Mr. Burns, reported that a time study was made of the time it took him to produce some gears or pinions. Merrick instructed him in the way to do the work, and timed the production of the first eleven of these gears (out of a total of thirty-three) in order to establish a "scientific" time and method. The worker did as he was instructed without comment, even though Merrick had him do one gear at a time and the worker knew perfectly well it was possible to cut two such gears at the same time with little additional complication. After Merrick left, and the worker was on his own, he continued to follow instructions, doing one gear at a time, since he knew that Merrick cut the time allowance whenever a worker developed an improved method. When Mr. Nelson, the master mechanic, spoke to him, the worker explained the situation, saying that there was no advantage for him in doubling up since Merrick would just cut the time allowance. The worker was obviously angling for the master mechanic's support, and he got it. As the worker explained, "Now, do you want the master mechanic's exact words when I said that—'Not by a damned sight, he won't change the time'" (ibid.: 286). Mr Nelson went to the office and spoke to the major to get a guarantee that the time would not be changed. With that assurance the worker used his own experience rather than the scientific way, and did the remaining gears two at a time.

In a fourth case, the instruction card specified speeds that were approximately correct but made no allowance for the differences in the hardness of the castings. Had the instructions been followed conscientiously and unthinkingly (as Taylor claimed to want) the tools would not have stood the cuts, but the machinist improved the method, and got his foreman's approval:

> *Mr. Barker* [a foreman]. Well, we have got a man on premium system who was working and had a hard casting on, and he could not run the machine at the rate it was going. The tool would not stand, and he came to me and said he could run slower and use a coarser feed and a deeper cut and still get the operation done in the required time, and, furthermore, he said he was using 10 amperes less power. I told him I did not think there would be any objection to that, as it was saving the coal pile. (Ibid.: 370)

In this case, the instructions did not make allowances for the ways in which the work could vary, and any one set of instructions would have been inadequate. They had to rely on the skill and judgment of the worker to vary speeds and procedures for the castings in this group. In other cases this same foreman had encountered, it was not a question of variation, but of mistakes by the planning room: one job had to be taken back to the planning room for new instructions because as soon as the machinist started to work on it he could see the instructions would not work (ibid.: 382–83). In another case the instructions did not call for certain work which could perfectly well have been done at the same time, with the same machine set-up. The foreman (with the master mechanic's approval) therefore went ahead and had the work done, in order to avoid having the work come back later and have to be set up all over again (ibid.: 382).

In another case a worker explained that his instructions were accurate, in that if he followed them he would do the job adequately. However, if he had been allowed to plan the work himself he could have gotten more work done with less effort (ibid.: 253–54).

It was not only that the experts were often wrong, or that they did not provide the extensive instruction and training of which Taylor boasted; when challenged the experts could seldom make practical or effective suggestions.

> *Mr. Burns.* . . . I thought from my previous experience that for these six the time first given, the minimum time, was lower than I could possibly do the work. I told Mr. Merrick that and we talked it over quite a bit. Now, I said to Mr. Merrick, "You have the machine time, you know that perfectly; you know approximately, or very near, perhaps, how long it will take me to make my changes." I said, "Now, if you can not tell me where I can eliminate some movements that I am making now how am I going to change my time; how am I going to gain on you?" . . .

> Well, Mr. Merrick said, "You will make your changes quicker." I says, "How am I going to do that if I have got to do the same amount of changing that I do now; if you can not tell me anything that I can eliminate, I have got to make all of these movements." I said "I think you are perfectly willing to say that I am an average active man." He was willing to admit that, and then I said, "The only way I can see that I can gain on your time is in walking around the machine, and instead of walking, run." (Ibid.: 280)

These workers were not at all impressed with the scientific and technical expertise of Taylor and his minions. (It is probable that if we had the testimony of Schmidt the pig-iron handler, or any of Tayor's shovelers, they would be equally contemptuous.) They felt, and they had plenty of evidence to back them up, that they knew more about the work than did the experts. Essentially every worker who testified managed to bring up one or more such incidents, and probably this only scratches the surface, since no one else at the hearings was interested in evidence on this point.*

Taylorism and Technology

Taylor's contribution is often portrayed as primarily technological. He is supposed to have devised better and more efficient ways of doing work, finding the "one best way" to perform operations which had hitherto been done in various inadequate ways. Taylor made a number of technical innovations, including high-speed tool steel, which Aitken calls "probably the most revolutionary change in machine-shop practice within the memory of anyone living at the time" (Aitken, 1960: 102).† Aitken argues that in order to get the full benefits of the new steel—which could be operated at far higher speeds and temperatures than any previous steel without melting or losing its edge—it was necessary for management to completely reorganize the shop, and dictate the desired speeds and feeds: "this major innovation . . . made necessary a whole series of minor innovations. . . . The Taylor system of management . . . was essentially a means of adjusting the arsenal to the impact of high-speed steel." Since "few of the machinists and foremen who had grown up in the carbon steel era had any conception of what the new steels could do," and since it goes without saying that—being bound to custom and the old ways—they were unable to figure this out, "hence the necessity for Barth's slide rules and the prescribing *by management* of

---

*Over and over workers tried to make this an issue in the hearings. Everyone else dismissed it as irrelevant but at the same time sought out evidence indicating the superiority of scientific management expertise.

†This claim is the more remarkable since this was the period when electricity was being introduced to machine shops.

speeds and feeds which, to men of the older generation, were literally fantastic" (ibid.: 103; emphasis in original).

Aitken's position is a variant of technological determinism: bureaucracy itself is said to follow from the nature of the technological changes. On the other hand, Harry Braverman cites approvingly Peter F. Drucker's statement that Taylorism "was not concerned with technology. Indeed, it took tools and techniques largely as given" (1974: 86).* As I argued in Chapter Two, I think both these positions are inadequate: they overlook or deny the dialectical interplay of technological and organizational factors in producing capitalist control of the labor process.

While high-speed tool steel was in fact one of the most important technological innovations of the period, Aitken and others who take this position have exactly reversed the causal order. It was not that the technology of high-speed steel required the management reorganization of the Taylor system: on the contrary, it can easily be shown that Taylor began by trying to increase the output of his workers, and tried to develop a management system that would allow him to do so. He himself insisted that time study was the beginning of scientific management (Copley, 1923, I: 224), and his standard biography reports, quite correctly, that his experiments in cutting metal were inspired by his time-study experiments. Taylor knew perfectly well that it was the speed-up of scientific management that led to high-speed tool steel, and not high-speed tool steel that required him to develop scientific management. As Taylor said: "The moment that scientific management was introduced in a

---

*While Taylor was not always a technological pioneer—he opposed the use of the first traveling electric crane (Copley, 1923, I: 199)—he did make some genuine technological contributions to the industry of his time. In addition to high-speed steel, he patented a number of designs (not all of them as inconsequential as the spoon-handled tennis racquet he used to win the U.S. doubles championship in 1881, in partnership with the son of the owner of Midvale Steel), including a steam hammer with enough flexibility that it did not batter itself to pieces—all previous steam hammers had relied on great mass and rigidity. This was plainly an important technological experiment—the steam hammer cost $200,000 in the 1880s, a fabulous sum—and Taylor deserves the credit for its success (ibid.: 198). Braverman is right, however, in that by themselves Taylor's technological contributions would merit at most a paragraph in a history of the technology of the period, and his name would be forgotten by all but a few technological historians. Taylor made the kind of incremental improvements which made industry work better, but which were not in themselves particularly significant or revolutionary.

machine shop, that moment it became certain that the art or science of cutting metals was sure to come" (Taylor, 1912: 234; also cited by Aitken, 1960: 30).

However, it is also important to note, contra Peter F. Drucker and Harry Braverman, that Taylor was very concerned with technology. He went to incredible trouble and expense to find and develop a tool steel which would operate successfully at high speeds. Before Taylor began his experiments, there were no tool steels available which could be used at the speeds at which Taylor wanted machinists to work. When Taylor succeeded in speeding up his machinists, he ran into a technological limitation—all of the available tool steels melted after short periods of work at the speeds which Taylor insisted his machinists use. This did not cause Taylor to give up and decide that scientific management was impossible. On the contrary, at incredible expense and disruption of the shop where he was boss, Taylor conducted 40,000 experiments in order to find and develop better materials and methods for cutting metal, specifically a steel which not only could stand the heats and temperatures generated by speed-up, but which worked better under these conditions (Copley, 1923, I: 246). Some idea of the expense and disruption this involved can be gained from Taylor's own admission that

> in order to regulate the exact cutting speed of the tool, it was necessary to slow down the speed of the engine that drove all the shafting in the shop. . . . For over two years the whole shop was inconvenienced in this way, by having the speed of its main line of shafting greatly varied, not only from day to day, but from hour to hour. (Ibid.: 239)

Moreover, it must not be supposed that this was allowed to continue because of the great results it was producing: six months of such constant experimenting produced only negative results. Technology, Taylor was well aware, was one of a number of weapons which could be used against workers. Taylor did not at all, as Drucker and Braverman would have it, take "tools and techniques largely as given" (Braverman, 1974: 86); rather, he did his best to develop a technology which would serve the same purposes as his management reorganization.

The Dictatorship of the Bourgeoisie

From its inception, a key part of Taylorism was struggle, an unyielding battle until one side or the other won an unequivocal victory, as this chapter has tried to show. The foundation of Taylor's approach was the realization that under a capitalist system workers and owners could not share authority and the direction of the work. As long as workers controlled most of the technical details of the work process, they would also maintain social control in the shop, enforcing their own standards on the speed of production, the level of quality, and the methods of procedure.

> In any executive work which involves the cooperation of two different men or parties, where both parties have anything like equal power or voice in its direction, there is almost sure to be a certain amount of bickering, quarreling, and vacillation, and the success of the enterprise suffers accordingly. If, however, either one of the parties has the entire direction, the enterprise will progress consistently and probably harmoniously, even although the wrong one of the two parties may be in control.

> Broadly speaking, in the field of management there are two parties—the superintendents, etc., on one side and the men on the other, and the main questions at issue are the speed and accuracy with which the work shall be done. Up to the time that task management was introduced in the Midvale Steel Works, it can be fairly said that under the old systems of management the men and the management had about equal weight in deciding how fast the work should be done. . . . The essence of task [scientific] management lies in the fact that the control of the speed problem rests entirely with the management. (Taylor, 1903: 43–44)

Under the 1880 practices, workers and managers (or owners) shared the power to determine the speed of production and a host of other details. Taylor's aim was to have control of speed rest entirely with management, but neither he nor other capitalists, then or now, succeeded in crushing all opposition by workers. Lenin made much the same point, but in a less static, less all-or-nothing way, in 1919, when he argued:

> In capitalist society, whenever there is any serious aggravation of the class struggle intrinsic to that society, there can be no alternative but

the dictatorship of the bourgeoisie or the dictatorship of the proletariat. Dreams of some third way are reactionary petty-bourgeois
lamentations. (1964: 103)

What Taylor introduced into the industry of his day, and what
continues to prevail in the factories of today, is a dictatorship.* This
is usually more-or-less disguised—in Taylor's case, by the claim that
value neutral "science" determined a fair day's pay and a fair day's
work, in modern industry, by the sham of collective bargaining,
grievance procedures, and human relations. To say there is a dictatorship is not by any means to imply that capital successfully controls all
aspects of the situation—many dictatorships are highly ineffective in
imposing their will. Inside the workplace today, the dictatorship of
capital prevails. In quite a literal way, there is no better characterization of the internal political structure of American work organizations (see Spencer, 1977; Pfeffer, 1979). This is not to imply that
workers have ceased to struggle, or that their resistance is bound to
fail; dictatorships can be overthrown in the workplace as in the state.
I believe, however, that under capitalism attempts at reform and the
introduction of "workplace democracy"—necessary though they
are—are bound to be shortlived and unsuccessful unless they are
part of a continuing dynamic pushing on to socialism and communism.

---

*Taylor recounts one incident where he took a vote. He was working to "systema-
tize" the management of the largest bicycle ball factory in the country. The workers,
all women, minutely inspected small steel balls for defects, work which "required the
closest attention and concentration." Taylor decided to shorten the work hours,
requiring the same output per day and paying the same wages. The foreman talked to
the workers and reported that all of the women approved of the change. With this
assurance, Taylor decided to take a vote, confident it would approve his intended
course of action:

> The writer had not been especially noted for his tact so he decided that it would
> be wise for him to display a little more of this quality by having the girls vote on
> the new proposition. This decision was hardly justified, however, for when the
> vote was taken the girls were unanimous that $10\frac{1}{2}$ hours was good enough for
> them and they wanted no innovation of any kind.

> This settled the matter for the time being. A few months later tact was thrown
> to the winds and the working hours were arbitrarily shortened in successive
> steps to 10 hours, $9\frac{1}{2}$, 9, $8\frac{1}{2}$ (the pay per day remaining the same); and with
> each shortening of the working day the output increased instead of diminish-
> ing. (1911: 88)

The similarities to capital's recent attempts to "humanize the workplace" and introduce "worker participation" are not accidental.

The view of bureaucracy as a control mechanism—a view implicit in Frederick Taylor's proposals and Harry Braverman's analysis—sees its origins in the realization by capital that so long as capital relied on general rules and directives too much control was left in workers' hands. Capitalist factories had long had rules and regulations, a division of labor, and hierarchy, and formally they had always been dictatorships. Bureaucracy was created as a way of moving beyond such general directives to specific detailed control of the work process. Such a view of bureaucracy is in stark contrast to the main American sociological view, derived from Weber, which characterizes bureaucracy in terms of its remote and impersonal qualities. The latter view, surprisingly, also emerges in Richard Edwards' *Contested Terrain:*

> Bureaucratic control establishes the impersonal force of "company rules" or "company policy" as the basis for control. . . . Capitalists were to retain overall control of the enterprise's operations through their power to establish the rules and procedures. But once the goals and structure were set, the management process was to proceed without need of, and (except in exceptional circumstances) without benefit of, the conscious intervention of the personal power of foremen, supervisors, or capitalists. (1979: 131)

Taylor, on the other hand, specifically emphasized that what was new in his system was detailed control. Moreover this control did not simply rest on impersonal rules, but required the conscious intervention and *force* of managers. As Taylor wrote to the dean of Harvard's Graduate School of Business Administration:

> The great trouble with the men who have been too many years getting an academic education is . . . they almost invariably attempt to get other men to do what they ought to do by reasoning, persuasion, and talk, and by giving them orders and directing them what to do. And this way of dealing with men, as I have said many times, is productive of very small results. I have found it necessary almost invariably to talk but little to men, but to go right ahead and MAKE them do what I wanted them to do. (Cited in Copley, 1923, II: 320; emphasis in original)*

---

*As this quote makes clear, Taylor's own view of bureaucracy and his system is directly at odds with modern analyses which focus on information flow and communication processes, a view found even on the left, as in Edwards' account of Taylorism:

> The newly defined tasks needed to be communicated to the workers who were

This is why the bureaucratic apparatus must involve large numbers of people (one-fourth or more of the workforce, Taylor said), not simply a few people promulgating general rules.

My claim that Taylorism is the dictatorship of the bourgeoisie should not be taken to imply that it ended workers' struggles. The workers at Watertown Arsenal certainly resisted the system. In his general statements Taylor always minimized workers' opposition, but his writings are filled with evidence that he was well aware that workers resorted to sabotage in an attempt to combat him. In his first job, when Taylor introduced a planning board to route the work, the board had to be encased in glass to prevent workers from ripping off the tags (Copley, 1923, I: 272). Taylor discussed a special notebook concealing stop watches which could be operated by pressing on the cover. Though in general he favored open timing, he realized that in many cases open timing "would only result in a row" (Taylor, 1903: 153). In public Taylor professed to fear management, but in discussing the implementation of his system it is worker opposition which concerns him:

> In making this decision, as in taking each subsequent step, the most important consideration, which should always be first in the mind of the reformer, is "what effect will this step have upon the workmen?" Through some means (it would almost appear some especial sense) the workman seems to scent the approach of a reformer even before his arrival in town. Their suspicions are thoroughly aroused, and they are on the alert. (Ibid.: 136)

Taylor realized that the united opposition of many workers could defeat him, so he insisted on the necessity of changing only one worker at a time.* "At no time during the introduction of the system should any broad, sweeping changes be made which seriously affect a large number of workmen. . . . Throughout the early stages of organization each change made should affect one workman only" (ibid.: 134).

---

to carry them out, and this involved specifying to workers exactly what they were expected to accomplish each day. Taylor recommended that each worker receive an instruction card at the beginning of each workday, giving explicit written form to this communication process. In other words, direction of work tasks was to emerge from orderly processes of information discovery, organization, and communication. (1979: 100)

†Just as Towne argued that piecework rates should be changed for one worker at a time (see above, Chapter Five).

In my opinion, the main reason managers and capitalists were reluctant to introduce Taylorism was that it provoked worker opposition and demanded an all-out fight. An article in *Engineering Magazine* noted that Taylor's differential piece rate could produce much better results than ordinary piecework, but warned, "It is evidently unsatisfactory and dangerous in a weakly organized works with an inexperienced 'piece-work' staff" (Darlington, 1899a: 449). Every manager wanted to run a shop where the fight had been waged and won, but many people quailed at the prospect of undertaking such a costly and dangerous fight.*

Efficiency and Class

While Taylor saw the introduction of scientific management and a bureaucratic organization of production as a part of the class struggle, it could be objected that this is beside the point: whatever reason Taylor may have had for proposing his system, it would not have been widely adopted were it not more efficient than the craft system it replaced. This is true only if the term "efficiency" is given a very special class-biased meaning. One method is usually said to be more efficient than another if it achieves greater output with the same inputs, or the same output with fewer inputs. Thus from the point of view of an individual company it would be possible to argue that the company became more efficient simply by cutting wages of its workers (less input of labor from the company's point of view), but this is plainly a class-biased assessment. It is more reasonable to say that the company maintained the same efficiency, since it continued to use the same physical inputs, but became more profitable because its power position enabled it to cut workers' wages. Similarly, if

---

*Obviously there were other reasons why capitalists and managers opposed Taylorism. Taylor spent money freely (Copley, 1923, I: 198), some of the specifics of his system did not work (significantly, Taylor himself stopped using functional foremanship and the differential piece rate, even though he continued to advocate them—ibid.: 309), some managers were reluctant to take on the extra duties involved, and as is true with any revolutionary innovation, it both condemned the old ways (not something all managers were eager to hear) and offered a comparatively untested proposal.

Taylor were able to make workers do more work without equivalent increases in pay, this could make his system appear more efficient from a capitalist's point of view, even though what was really involved was a greater input of labor as a result of workers giving up their rest periods and comfortable work pace. The use of force was necessary precisely because workers were being reasonable in resisting Taylorism.

Theoretically it should be possible to determine whether Taylor's system was more "efficient" in some abstract and value neutral sense than the craft system it replaced, but in practice the difficulties seem insuperable. For example, at the Watertown Arsenal, for which we have the best data, all of the bookkeeping and accounting procedures were changed coincident with the introduction of the Taylor system. One intended affect of these changes was to make it impossible to determine the overhead and planning costs in the manufacture of any item. It is not only that the examples offered by the officers were plainly not representative of the experience of the shop as a whole, more important, every example was basically inadequate or misleading as evidence of Taylorism's efficiency. I have already pointed out that even if we accept Taylor's own examples they only show increased output, and this is more likely to be the result of extra effort than of extra efficiency (especially given that someone was standing over the worker all day). The officers' favorite examples were even worse: they simply presented cases in which workers had earned large premiums, but this does not indicate any cost savings unless the premium rates were accurately set to begin with. A number of workers testified that they had been offered substantial premiums for producing at the old rate. On one job Mr. Lawson told his foreman:

> "They have set the time wrong. I never took as much time on any of them that I have made, unless I have had to spend lots of time fixing the flash." "Well," he says, "if you have any objections, do it in writing and send it to the commanding officer." "Well," I says, "it looks good on the face of it, to give me six hours extra pay where I have completed the job in 24 hours before." I said, "That's pulling me right into the halter," I says. I said, "That is just giving me money for nothing, and I have been fighting here two years for a quarter. But you can't shove it down my throat that's going to last." (U.S. House of Representatives, 1912: 206)

Any premium that Mr. Lawson earned would have been used by the officers as proof of the economy of the system, when in fact it shows just the opposite. Workers tried to present evidence to indicate that costs had increased and that bookkeeping methods had been changed expressly to conceal this fact, but the congressional committee not only refused to follow these leads, but prevented the workers from making their case (ibid.: 470).

Of course the question of whether the Taylor system increased efficiency and productivity was of little interest to capitalists. If the Taylor system could cut costs, from a capitalist's point of view it did not matter whether the cost reduction came from a technically superior organization or from making people work harder without equivalent increases in pay. The Watertown Arsenal and other cases seem to indicate that the introduction of Taylor's system did not lead to any dramatic reductions in over-all costs,* yet it could still be worthwhile for a capitalist to introduce it. It could be costly to make the transition from the old system of workers controlling the details of production to the new system of management giving specific orders and keeping careful control over the production process, and after the transition the cost of production might be the same, or roughly the same, as before. Nonetheless, once the transition was accomplished, management was in a far better position to combat worker resistance. This meant that future changes in the production process—whether technical, organizational, or social—would benefit owners much more than workers. Instead of having their wishes and actions frustrated at every point, capitalists and managers would be able to do more nearly as they wished. In a given industry, if Company A made the transition to Taylorism, and Company B did not, there might be little difference in profitability for the period of the transition, and even for a couple of years after that. In the ensuing years, however, Company A would probably begin to pull ahead of Company B, since it had made a qualitative leap into a new organizational form which allowed it to force workers to do what the management wanted, far more than could be done at Company B.

As Aitken says of Watertown Arsenal, Taylor and Barth "were

---

*Taylor of course insisted that his system cut costs, but he also admitted that there was no "apparent relation between good shop management [i.e., the use of his system] and the payment of dividends" (1903: 17).

disrupting an established social system and trying to build a new one. Nothing they did was, in this respect, neutral; nothing was merely technological or administrative" (1960: 135). This was why Taylor was so vehement in his insistence that his entire system must be introduced, not simply some one part. Only by radically uprooting the old ways of doing things, and substituting in their place new methods, was it possible to solve the basic problem: workers controlled production. Craft production and Taylorism are opposed systems for organizing the production process. Craft production is based on the worker's skill and training, training which is received (for the most part) on the shop floor from other workers, who teach not simply technical skills but also a view of the workplace and a consciousness of class interests. Craft production can succeed only in so far as the worker uses his or her initiative; the people who do the work must also plan it and introduce improvements. Taylorism is based on the skill and training of a group of workers who are separate from production workers, who today are socialized primarily in schools and colleges and not on the shop floor. These people do not themselves produce the goods, but they organize work in such a way that production workers have as little need as possible to use their skill and initiative. The work which used to be united in one group is now split into two, but it is important to understand that both parts—the bureaucratic apparatus and the routinized de-skilled production work—are aspects of one unity. The bureaucracy is not simply an addition, a purely repressive apparatus which has been artificially added to production, and which, were it simply abolished, would leave us with socialism. The bureaucracy does a great deal of work which is necessary for production—planning, development, coordination, and so on. Socialism will involve a transformation of work for everyone—what production workers do will be totally transformed, and not simply by the abolition of hierarchy and control, but far more so because they will take over activities which are now forbidden them.

7
Conclusion:
Socialism or Barbarism?

As capitalism has developed, the dynamic within the labor process has been toward more control by capital and less control by labor. Before factories, people worked in their own households, took breaks when they wanted to, and decided for themselves how many hours to work. Working without outside supervision, they were able to make their own decisions about the intensity of labor, the methods and quality of production, and socialization while at work.* Capitalists increased their control dramatically by successfully imposing a factory system that allowed them to determine many of these aspects of the labor process—where work was done, the total number of hours of work, the patterning of work.

Factories, however, did not give capitalists total control. Capitalists may have claimed a right to make all the major decisions about the labor process (although even this is dubious), but workers continued to have considerable practical control over many aspects of work. The factory setting obviously changed the possible limits of variation, but within these fairly wide limits workers continued to predominate in the determination of work rhythms, the intensity of labor, the selection and organization of the work group, socialization at work, the quality of production, and the planning and execution of work. Workers were able to control these elements of the labor process only to the extent that they actively struggled to do so. In their constant effort to increase the rate of surplus value, capitalists needed increasing control over the workplace. Because of worker resistance, their early initiatives were only partially successful. Over

*We should avoid romanticizing this situation: male heads of household may have autocratically and oppressively controlled their families, work may have been isolated and monotonous, and the material conditions may have been harsh and unpleasant.

and over, workers were able to absorb or resist capitalist changes and still maintain a considerable degree of control over the shop. Thus while early capitalists managed to control certain work groups and practices, they were unable to replace the general system that allowed workers to maintain a large measure of social and technical control over the workplace. The institution of piecework is a good example: in some places it pitted workers against each other and led to a great speed-up, but in others it actually strengthened workers' power and provided a justification for ignoring capitalist orders (on the argument that employers only paid for actual production, so it cost them nothing if workers took a break).

Frederick Taylor's genius was twofold: the recognition that a system of divided control existed and would have to be abolished if capital was to dominate, and, even more remarkable, the creation and introduction of a system that provided a basis for such domination.* The key to Taylor's system was removing control over the work process and the planning of work from shop-floor workers. A new group, "management," amounting to perhaps one-third of the workforce, was to plan and control the work. Taylor introduced bureaucratic management specifically to increase control by capital, to allow capitalists full control of production.

The bureaucratic reorganization of the labor process developed, then, not through some technological imperative, but through a historically specific process of class struggle which was understood and articulated as such by the contending parties. The consciousness and activity of the contending classes have been, and continue to be, crucial factors in determining the nature of this development. Classes take shape only in relation to this process of struggle; neither class consciousness nor the material forces of production can be understood except in relation to this historical process. Within this struggle, nothing is inevitable.

---

*I have focused on Taylor because I believe he was important in making the quantum leap from one system to another, but very similar changes probably would have been made in a piecemeal fashion had he never existed. What is crucial is that this quantum change did take place, the key changes were made in the late nineteenth and early twentieth centuries, and the changes were made for approximately the reasons Taylor articulated. Whereas the question of Taylor's importance is of interest only to academic historians, the issues of the existence, timing, importance of, and motivation for these changes are relevant both historically and politically.

This certainly does not imply that anything is possible and all outcomes are equally likely. Capitalists have no choice but to accumulate capital or be wiped out by other capitalists, and this virtually compels them to attempt to degrade labor and take ever more control of the labor process. This is the fundamental law of capitalist development, the culmination of Marx's analysis in Volume I of *Capital,* the "general law of capitalist accumulation":

> Within the capitalist system all methods for raising the social productiveness of labour are brought about at the cost of the individual labourer; all means for the development of production transform themselves into means of domination over, and exploitation of, the producers; they mutilate the labourer into a fragment of a man, degrade him to the level of an appendage of a machine, destroy every remnant of charm in his work and turn it into a hated toil; they estrange from him the intellectual potentialities of the labour-process in the same proportion as science is incorporated in it as an independent power; they distort the conditions under which he works, subject him during the labour-process to a despotism the more hateful for its meanness; they transform his life-time into working-time, and drag his wife and child beneath the wheels of the Juggernaut of capital. But all methods for the production of surplus-value are at the same time methods of accumulation; and every extension of accumulation becomes again a means for the development of those methods. *It follows therefore that in proportion as capital accumulates, the lot of the labourer, be his payment high or low, must grow worse.* . . . Accumulation of wealth at one pole is, therefore, at the same time accumulation of misery, agony of toil, slavery, ignorance, brutality, mental degradation, at the opposite pole, i.e., on the side of the class that produces its own product in the form of capital. (1867: 604)

I quote this at length because it so exactly describes the history analyzed here, the process involved in the creation of workplace bureaucracy.* What I have called the craft system of produc-

---

*As Marx notes, for every law of capitalist production there are counteracting tendencies. In this case, perhaps the most important such tendency derives from the fact that maximum accumulation of capital requires constantly revolutionizing the means of production—reorganizing processes, introducing new machinery, and so on.

When this happens, when new machinery and methods are introduced, the success of the new system usually depends on the creativity and initiative of workers. Capitalists and their servants (engineers, etc.) are simply unable to systematize or plan the work and break it into routine tasks until workers have ironed out the bugs. Right

tion, which dominated much of nineteenth-century U.S. industry, relied for its success on the initiative, skill, technical understanding and organizational abilities, creativity, and planning of production workers—primarily skilled workers to be sure, but workers nonetheless. The craft system both demands and develops the creativity and capacity of the workers; it can succeed only insofar as they use these qualities.

From the capitalist's point of view, the problem with this system was not that workers were unable to mass produce goods or engage in, and even improve, technically sophisticated processes, but rather that they used their position of centrality to attempt to shape the work process for their own ends. Workers wanted to do "a fair day's work for a fair day's pay," but to them this meant not only that they produced the goods, but also that they had varied and interesting activity, the opportunity to use their skill and creativity, a chance to produce quality goods in which they could take pride, an opportunity to socialize, and a comfortable work pace which would not leave them exhausted at the end of the day. To maximize the accumulation of capital, capitalists were forced (by the comparative failure of earlier initiatives) to introduce Taylorism: to replace all-around craft workers by "semiskilled" workers who were mutilated into fragments of persons; to destroy every remnant of charm in the work and turn it into a hated toil of repeatedly performing a mindless operation; to subject workers to the mean despotism of the stop watch; to estrange from workers the intellectual potentialities of the labor process by removing all possible "brain work" from the shop floor to the planning room, thereby developing the "science of management."

In place of the craft worker able to both plan and execute the work, Taylorism introduced a fundamental split in the work process. On the one hand, production workers were to repeatedly perform simple specified operations, mindlessly obeying detailed orders.

---

after a new method or machine is introduced, therefore, workers are often allowed considerable freedom and autonomy, since without their assistance the new way cannot succeed. However, once workers solve the basic problems, capital acts to reassert control. (For concrete examples of this see Greenbaum, 1976; Spencer, 1977: 155–66.)

> The work of every workman is fully planned out by the management at least one day in advance, and each man receives in most cases complete written instructions, describing in detail the task which he is to accomplish, as well as the means to be used in doing the work. . . . This task specifies not only what is to be done but how it is to be done and the exact time allowed for doing it. (Taylor, 1911: 39)

The use of such detailed orders made it possible to use workers "who are of smaller calibre and attainments, and who are therefore cheaper than those required under the old system" (Taylor, 1903: 105). On the other hand, the size of bureaucracy or management was to increase considerably, since it was to take over and perform all of the brain work that had previously been spread throughout the workforce. Most of the planning and conceptualizing that is now done by management and the bureaucracy is activity that was once done by production workers and which has been expropriated from them. The purpose of management is to plan and control all aspects of the work process without itself doing any of the work.

This split is a fundamental factor determining the class structure of modern Western society (see for example Ehrenreich and Ehrenreich, 1979). By definition, capitalists rely on employees to do the work for them. By dividing the workforce in this way, however, capital was better able to control it, both technically and politically. Once a mindless task is defined for a production worker, there are almost no acceptable excuses for failing to achieve a set quota, since all variation and need to solve problems have been assigned elsewhere. The workers who do the planning no longer perform the physical work. Their workplace and educational socialization leads them to adopt capital's goals and demands. Capital makes every effort to keep these workers separated from manual workers, and even if they have sympathy for workers it is likely to be abstract and ineffectual.

Historically, then, there was nothing inevitable or necessary about the development of management and Taylorism. Certainly it was not required by a technical imperative. As I argued in Chapter Two, Marx's analysis of the creation of the factory system demonstrated that the *social* and not the technological change was primary. *First* there was a change in the organization of the labor process: the collection of large groups of workers into central locations under the control of a capitalist. *Only after this, and on the basis of conditions created by this social change, was the technical innovation of machinery introduced.* At the same time, however, it is crucial that machinery, the new technical foundation, was necessary for capitalists to establish secure control.

An analogous process took place at the beginning of the twentieth century. Taylorism and the creation of management were social changes, introduced to increase capitalist control, not the result of technological innovation. This social change was primary and causative; immediately, however, technology appropriate to these new social relations began to develop. Taylor himself, for example, made a significant contribution: earlier tool steels had tended to melt or lose their edge at the speeds Taylor wanted used; the high-speed tool steel he developed made it not only possible but even desirable to use very high speeds. Far more important was Henry Ford's creation of the assembly line, the fitting technological embodiment of Frederick Taylor's principles on the organization of work. Taylor and the management movement did much to prepare the way for Ford by habituating workers to these relations of production, by developing techniques necessary to impose such a system, by perfecting the bureaucratic kinds of control needed, by showing how to analyze work into minute elements, finding ways to separate out repetitive tasks, collecting detailed stop watch time analyses. But while Taylorism requires a management which must play an active, continuing, and personal role in forcing workers to obey instructions, the assembly line is a technological system in which force and supervision inhere in the process itself. This is the key advance that Ford developed: a technological system that forced workers to work without thinking or questioning, forced workers to follow the work pace dictated by capital, and unequivocally separated the brain work and planning from the execution. It is important to realize that this was not an independent technological change which sprang spontaneously from Henry Ford's chance tinkering. Rather, U.S. capital had, over a period of thirty years, been attempting to devise a system of production that would remove planning and control from workers. For capitalists an assembly-line technology is obviously a much better, more secure, and cheaper way to ensure control than an elaborate management apparatus, but assembly lines are inflexible, suited only to the most routinized mass production, and find limited (though important) application.

Rosa Luxemburg perceived that while socialism was not inevitable, the modern world had reached a point where we must either have socialism or barbarism (Luxemburg, 1971: 334). Barbarism in this connection does not mean primitive or precivilized, nor does it simply refer to the ruins of civilization—Hiroshima, Auschwitz, Vietnam, or the destruction of the environment to achieve a higher rate of profit. The organization of work we have today can reasonably be called barbaric: it degrades workers (and the labor process) so as to guarantee the control of capital and the maximum rate of profit. This process is a vicious circle, for a reason articulated by Marx:

> The [labor] process demands that, during the whole operation, the workman's will be steadily in consonance with his purpose. This means close attention. The less he is attracted by the nature of the work, and the mode in which it is carried on, and the less, therefore, he enjoys it as something which gives play to his bodily and mental powers, the more close his attention is forced to be. (1867: 174)*

In modern capitalism, most workers are not attracted by their work, do not enjoy it, find little opportunity to give play to their bodily and mental powers. Therefore, in order to keep them to their work, capitalists must have an immense and costly bureaucratic apparatus. From any sensible point of view this is incredibly wasteful, inefficient, and irrational. Freely associated workers who cooperated with each other and coordinated the work among themselves, who enjoyed their work because it allowed them to think and create, to develop their capacities and abilities, to become fully rounded individuals—such workers would not only find their work far more fulfilling, they could be much more productive.†

This reorganization of the labor process, so that it becomes the most important arena for people to freely develop their human capacities rather than an area where people are mutilated and degraded, is perhaps the most central characteristic of a socialist or

---

*The importance of this statement is emphasized by the fact that it is the conclusion to Marx's famous section on the uniquely human quality of labor, the consciousness which distinguishes the worst architect from the best of bees, the explanation that by acting on the world and changing it people at the same time change their own nature.

†And of course the abolition of the repressive and unproductive aspect of the bureaucratic apparatus would enlarge the number of potential producers, thus allowing either a decrease in work time or an increase in material goods.

communist society. Volume I of *Capital* gives only brief glimpses of the future society Marx envisioned, but these glimpses usually focus on precisely this change in work:

> Modern industry . . . through its catastrophes imposes the necessity of recognising as a fundamental law of production variation of work, consequently fitness of the labourer for varied work, consequently the greatest possible development of his varied aptitudes. . . . Modern Industry, indeed, compels society, under penalty of death, to replace the detail-worker of to-day, crippled by life-long repetition of one and the same trivial operation, and thus reduced to the mere fragment of a man, by the fully developed individual, fit for a variety of labours, ready to face any change of production, and to whom the different social functions he performs are but so many modes of giving free scope to his own natural and acquired powers. (1867: 458)

Moreover, this is desirable "not only as one of the methods of adding to the efficiency of production, but as the only method of producing fully developed human beings" (ibid.: 454).

This vision of socialism or communism as a society where one would be able "to hunt in the morning, fish in the afternoon, rear cattle in the evening, criticize after dinner, just as I have a mind, without ever becoming hunter, fisherman, shepherd, or critic" (Marx, 1846: 22), is in sharp contrast with the views which are usually dominant today. All too often the vision of socialism (or communism) is of a society in which there is state planning, in which the economy has been rationalized, in which there is an equitable distribution of material goods. This is simply an image of capitalism with some blemishes removed: it is a far cry from socialism.

Socialist or communist society can more reasonably be characterized by the nature of social relations on the shop (or office, or kitchen) floor than it can by reference to the over-all coordinating mechanisms in the economy (markets, planning, etc.). Obviously, such a characterization is still partial and unsatisfactory. Any future socialist society will have to involve large elements of workers' control of somewhat the kind that existed in segments of nineteenth-century U.S industry. It is crucial to emphasize, however, that what I have called the craft system of the nineteenth century is not at all socialism or workers' control, and cannot serve as a model for the future society we envisage. At best, it provided a very partial sort of workers' control for a group of overwhelmingly white, male, American-born skilled workers. The system was unquestionably sexist and racist; even within the white, male, American-born work-force it was very far from involving equality or democratic decision making. Even if all this could be neglected, the system was grossly distorted by having to function within capitalism. This meant, for example, that nineteenth-century workers often had good reason to fight against machinery and technological innovations since these might cost workers their jobs or make the work more oppressive. In a socialist society machinery would be developed to make work lighter and more enjoyable;* its introduction would threaten no one since everyone would be guaranteed both material goods and a chance to work.

Taken within the context of the struggle for socialism, workers' control is not an attempt to recreate something which existed in the past, but is a demand for what we hope to create in the future. Moreover, by itself workers' control means little: it is a means of guaranteeing that work will be fundamentally transformed, that new technologies will be developed (and old ones abandoned), that work processes will be oriented toward encouraging sociability and making use of people's full human potential. Achieving anything like this would obviously be a long process. However, several transitional steps could be introduced immediately: everyone to engage in socially necessary labor, everyone to perform a variety of tasks that would be oriented toward breaking down the old divisions of manual and mental, pleasant and unpleasant, skilled and unskilled, "men's" and "women's." In a fully communist society this would happen without need for conscious plan; in building socialism, however, it would probably be necessary to consciously coordinate activity to achieve these results, results which at the same time would serve as necessary preconditions for beginning the long process of transforming the nature of work processes.

Socialist society is not a utopia created out of nothing. "Com-

---

*One of the ways of guaranteeing this would be that technological innovations would not be made by engineers or other privileged specialists; the people who did the ordinary production would also be the ones who developed the machinery. (Such people can not really be called "workers" in the way we use the term today, since they might equally well be "engineers," "managers," or "intellectuals.")

munism is for us not a stable state which is to be established, an ideal to which reality will have to adjust itself. We call communism the real movement which abolishes the present state of things. The conditions of this movement result from the premises now in exist-ence" (ibid.: 26). Only on the basis of a process of struggle is it possible to build communism. Marxists have tended to focus on machinery and technology (the so-called forces of production) as providing the base for socialist society. The level of material wealth made possible by machines is undoubtedly important, although existing machinery embodies capitalist relations and will therefore need to be transformed. Assembly lines, for example, would probably be abolished, although the individual machines of the line might be used after modifications. In any case, machinery and technology are probably less important than the social relations and unity that are achieved in the process of struggle. For example, workers' response to piecework, as described in Chapter Five, gives us a concrete insight into the way in which specifically anticapitalist and incipiently socialist values and social relations are created in the struggle against capital. The relative failure of piecework as a capitalist strategy in the effort to control the labor process should not make us forget the potential power of the attack. Workers' ability to resist production speed-up via piecework—and occasionally to go beyond this and turn it to their advantage—depended on the creation and enforce-ment of output quotas determined by workers and enforced without the use of a separate repressive apparatus. In doing this workers subordinated their individual self-interest to the collective good of the workforce as a whole. In many cases *every* worker adhered to the production norms, an amazing example of solidarity, of self-sacrifice for a higher (and collectively agreed upon) goal. This does not mean that this unity was achieved through an aggregate of individual spon-taneous decisions. The absence of a separate repressive apparatus in communist society does not mean that everyone will be allowed to go their own way and do whatever they choose (the ideal of bour-geois individualism). People who engage in antisocial activity (and under capitalism rate busting unquestionably is such) will quite rightly be subject to various social pressures.

The issues considered in this book and the struggle which it analyzes are very much with us today. One frequent response to

Harry Braverman's work has been to say: Braverman shows that while workers once engaged in important struggles, they are no longer capable of changing capitalism because of what Taylorism did to the workplace. Put another way, Braverman demonstrates that factors internal to the workplace (rather than external factors such as education, racism, sexism, advertising, etc.) atomise workers and prevent the emergence of class-conscious solidarity. *Labor and Monopoly Capital* is thus seen as yet another confirmation of the view that workers and the workplace are not of special importance to Marxists. This is an interpretation which I never would have expected; fear of such a (mis)interpretation of my analysis makes it necessary that I briefly discuss the current situation and the political implications of this book.

Very simply, I believe that the same sorts of processes that shaped the late nineteenth and early twentieth century also shape today's world. Some technologies are developed and others are neglected not because of their technical merits or promise but because of what they will or will not do for capital. The most obvious and widely discussed example of this today is the question of energy: nuclear energy and synthetic fuels require great amounts of capital and will be produced by oligopolistic firms. As technologies they are centralized and easily controlled by the power structure. Alternative technologies—passive solar, active solar, wood heat—are inherently decentralized and difficult (though not impossible) for the ruling class to control. The result is that huge quantities of capital, both government and private, have gone into the development of nuclear power and synthetic fuels, with comparatively trifling sums spent on alternative energy (and even the "alternative energy" money is controlled, to a significant degree, by the big oil–pro-nuclear energy establishment). Other environmental examples abound: the rate of profit for detergent manufacture is about twice that for soaps, with the result that "soap" companies have pushed detergents despite their harmful impact on the environment; similar arguments apply to steel and aluminum, returnable and nonreturnable bottles, natural and artificial fertilizers, or natural and synthetic fibers (see Commoner, 1971; 1976; 1979). The technological choices on environmental questions are widely known, but the same choices must be made within the less visible workplace. David Noble has shown how numerical control machine tools were developed, and record play-back machine tools ignored, because record playback worked equally well for small shops and relied on the machinists' skill, while numeri-cal control favored large firms and promised to replace skilled machinists with computer synthesized analyses (1979: 18–50).*

Factories today are dominated by Taylorism, applied in a more thoroughgoing way than when Taylor first formulated his principles and techniques. What for Taylor was clearly a conscious process, and at one important level remains a conscious process, is now at the same time unconscious in that it is accepted without question (by both management and workers) as the self-evident way to organize work processes and is seen as "natural," "inevitable," or simply "most efficient."

The success of capitalism both in applying Taylorism and in having its principles accepted as reasonable does not, however, mean that Taylorism has definitively triumphed. Taylor's ideal was to have workers unthinkingly and unquestioningly obey detailed written orders, "without asking questions or making suggestions." If Taylorism in this sense were a reality, if the majority of the work-force really had been reduced to unthinking automatons, then Marxism as a method of class analysis would be irrelevant if not meaningless and we would be left with nothing but utopian hopes. Taylorism in this sense never has been and never will be a reality. The testimony of the workers at the Watertown Arsenal showed the continuing necessity for workers to exercise skill and judgment. This continues to be true today, in both "skilled" and "unskilled" work. It is for precisely this reason that human labor is used. Jan Houbolt and Ken Kusterer (1977) correctly emphasize the vital importance of workers' know-how and initiative if even the simplest jobs are to be done successfully. The unskilled workers studied by Barbara Garson (1975) continued to be involved in their work, continued to want to do a good job, even though the work was repetitive and uninteresting. Bill Watson's classic article "Counter

---

*Significantly, in the end even numerical control had to rely on skilled machinists because the machines are expensive and need care and because they cannot be counted on to produce good finished parts otherwise: while "many manufacturers initially tried to put unskilled people on the new equipment, they rather quickly saw their error and upgraded the classification" (Noble, 1979: 41–42).

Planning on the Shop Floor" (1971) shows that for modern auto workers (working in perhaps the most completely Taylorized work settings) capital's insistence on producing shoddy goods, its refusal to allow workers to improve the product into something they can be proud of, remains a radicalizing experience which is built into the process of capitalist production. In one instance workers on an assembly line had a number of suggestions on how to improve a new motor they had just started to produce, one that ran rough with a very sloppy cam. Management's refusal to improve the engine led to so much worker sabotage that the company eventually was forced to shift production of that motor to a different part of the building.

As this example suggests, workers do more than "resist": they do not just mulishly dig in their heels to preserve the old ways, or try to ward off the blows and assaults of capital. Workers actively struggle in a thousand creative ways to try to take control of one or another aspect of the labor process. Instead of the dominant left view, which tends to see capitalists as the only historically active class, with workers reacting to capital's offensives, it is more reasonable to see workers as an equally active force: capitalists have to work hard to find ways to stay on top. Much of the management literature of the late nineteenth century (or of the last quarter of the twentieth) has an air of incredulity, occasionally of near hysteria: "How can they do such a thing? No matter how much you give them they always try to take more."

Obviously, to apply this argument to the world of today with any hope of convincing the unconvinced would require at least another book, but two facts are significant. First, each year in this country unionized workers file some 300,000 grievances (nonunion workers struggle over the same complaints, but they leave no equivalently obvious record). These grievances cover every aspect of work: the rate of production as a whole, the amount and type of work each person is to do, health and safety conditions, hiring, firing, layoffs and recalls of workers, the building of new plants, the transfer of work from plant to plant.

> If we examine these "local grievances" as a totality, both in the range of subjects with which they are concerned and the consistency with which they are put forward whenever the opportunity presents itself, only one conclusion is possible. . . . Workers are striving to substitute

their authority and control for the authority and control of management in the process of production. (Glaberman, 1964: 20; see also Spencer, 1977)

Moreover, grievances are only the tip of the iceberg: far more significant are day-to-day shop struggles where workers establish practices that they know have no chance of being codified in a contract.

Second, wildcat strikes are a continuing and significant part of workers' activities in the United States. These are strikes which take place outside of an official union framework, and often in conscious opposition to the union. Workers on wildcat have no institutional sanction for what they are doing, and face union as well as company penalties. And yet workers very frequently go out on wildcats, a *collective activity* that corresponds to the more individualized and passive filing of a grievance; very often wildcats focus on "workers' control" issues (see Fantasia, 1980).

At the same time, workers' struggles in the United States today are far from achieving socialism. One of the most important limiting factors is that workers today, like those in the late nineteenth and early twentieth centuries, do not hold, espouse, and self-consciously struggle for, socialist goals of controlling the workplace. In one sense the revolution does steal in, as Marx put it, "like a thief in the night"; at the same time, unless we have articulated and struggled for our ultimate goals (not just for higher wages), we can hardly expect to create socialism or communism. This book is an attempt to articulate and clarify some of the issues which seem to me to have been basic to workers' struggles but ignored or neglected in Marxist theory. But socialism is not established in the realm of theory: there must be a mass-based struggle, springing from the experiences of ordinary people and changing their day-to-day lives, or we will never achieve a future classless society.

Bibliography

Adams, Robert McC. 1966. *The Evolution of Urban Society.* Chicago: Aldine.

Aitken, Hugh G. J. 1960. *Taylorism at Watertown Arsenal: Scientific Management in Action 1908–1915.* Cambridge, Mass.: Harvard University Press.

Albrow, Martin. 1970. *Bureaucracy.* London: Macmillan.

Aminzade, Ronald R. 1977. "Breaking the Chains of Dependency: From Patronage to Class Politics, Toulouse France 1830–1872." *Journal of Urban History,* March.

Anderson, Perry. 1966. *Passages from Antiquity to Feudalism.* London: New Left Books.

Arnold, Horace L. 1896. "Modern Machine Shop Economics." *Engineering Magazine* 11: 59–66, 263–98, 464–77, 673–95, 883–904, 1089–96.

Ashton, T. S. 1964. *The Industrial Revolution 1760–1830.* New York: Oxford University Press.

Ashworth, John H. 1915. *The Helper and American Trade Unions.* Baltimore: Johns Hopkins University Press.

Avineri, Shlomo. 1968. *The Social and Political Thought of Karl Marx.* London: Cambridge University Press.

Bendix, Reinhard. 1956. *Work and Authority in Industry.* Reprint. Berkeley: University of California Press, 1974.

Bensman, David. 1979. "Hatmakers and the Culture of Work." Paper presented at Smith College Conference on Labor History, March 5. Photocopied.

Bettelheim, Charles. 1974. *Cultural Revolution and Industrial Organization in China.* New York: Monthly Review Press.

———. 1976. *Class Struggles in the U.S.S.R. First Period: 1917–1923.* New York: Monthly Review Press.

———. 1978. *Class Struggles in the U.S.S.R. Second Period: 1923–1930.* New York: Monthly Review Press.

Bingham, E. A. 1903. "The Labor Situation at the Baldwin Works." *Iron Trade Review,* February 12, pp. 40–41.

Bishop, J. Leander. 1864. *A History of American Manufacturing.* 3 vols. Reprint. New York: A. M. Kelley, 1966.

Blau, Peter M. 1955. *The Dynamics of Bureaucracy.* Chicago: University of Chicago Press.

————. 1956. *Bureaucracy in Modern Society.* New York: Random House.

Bliven, Bruce J. 1954. *The Wonderful Writing Machine.* New York: Random House.

Bloch, Marc. 1961. *Feudal Society.* Chicago: University of Chicago Press.

Blumberg, Paul. 1973. *Industrial Democracy: The Sociology of Participation.* New York: Schocken Books.

Braverman, Harry. 1974. *Labor and Monopoly Capital.* New York: Monthly Review Press.

Brecher, Jeremy. 1972. *Strike!* San Francisco: Straight Arrow Books.

Brecher, Jeremy, and Costello, Tim. 1976. *Common Sense for Hard Times.* New York: Two Continents/Institute for Policy Studies.

Brody, David. 1960. *Steelworkers in America: The Nonunion Era.* New York: Harper & Row.

Brooks, John Graham. 1899. "Strength and Weakness of the Trust Idea." *Engineering Magazine* 18: 351–60.

Browne, Sir Benjamin C. 1899. "Standardising in Engineering/Construction." *Engineering Magazine* 18: 33–40, 169–76, 403–9.

Buhle, Paul. 1978. "The Knights of Labor in Rhode Island." *Radical History Review* 17 (Spring): 39–74.

Burawoy, Michael. 1979. "Toward a Marxist Theory of the Labor Process: Braverman and Beyond." *Politics and Society* 8, nos. 3–4: 247–312.

Buttrick, John. 1952. "The Inside Contract System." *The Journal of Economic History* 12, no. 3: 205–21.

Bythell, Duncan. 1969. *The Handloom Weavers.* Cambridge: Cambridge University Press.

Carey, Alex. 1967. "The Hawthorne Studies: A Radical Criticism." *American Sociological Review* 32: 403–16.

Chapman, Stanley D. 1967. *The Early Factory Masters.* Newton Abbot, Eng.: David & Charles.

Clawson, Dan. 1978. "Class Struggle and the Rise of Bureaucracy." Ph.D. dissertation, State University of New York, Stony Brook.

Clawson, Mary Ann. 1980. "Fraternal Orders." Ph.D. dissertation, State University of New York, Stony Brook.

Clawson, Patrick. 1975a. "The Bolsheviks and the Theory of Productive Forces." Unpublished manuscript.

————. 1975b. "The New Chinese Bosses Consolidate Their Power." Unpublished manuscript.

Commoner, Barry. 1971. *The Closing Circle.* New York: Alfred A. Knopf.

————. 1976. *The Poverty of Power.* New York: Alfred A. Knopf.

————. 1979. *The Politics of Energy.* New York: Alfred A. Knopf.

Converse, John W. 1903. "Progressive Non-Union Labour: Some Features of the System of Management at the Baldwin Locomotive Works." *Cassier's Magazine* 23 (March).

Copley, Frank B. 1923. *Frederick W. Taylor: Father of Scientific Management.* 2 vols. New York: Harper and Brothers.

Dalton, Melville. 1959. *Men Who Manage.* New York: John Wiley.

Darlington, P. J. 1899a. "Methods of Remunerating Labour." *Engineering Magazine* 17: 444–54.

————. 1899b. "Systems for the Remuneration of Labor." *Engineering Magazine* 17: 925–36.

Davis, James J. 1922. *The Iron Puddler: My Life in the Rolling Mills and What Came of It.* Indianapolis: Bobbs Merrill.

Dawley, Alan. 1976. *Class and Community: The Industrial Revolution in Lynn.* Cambridge, Mass.: Harvard University Press.

Deyrup, Felicia. 1948. *Arms Makers of the Connecticut Valley: A Regional Study of the Small Arms Industry 1798–1870.* Vol. 33. Smith College Studies in History. Northampton, Mass. Printed by George Banta Publishing, Menasha, Wis.

Diemer, Hugo. 1899. "The Functions and Organisation of the Purchasing Department." *Engineering Magazine* 18: 833–36.

Duncan, John C. 1911. *The Principles of Industrial Management.* New York: D. Appleton.

Edwards, Richard. 1978. "Social Relations of Production at the Point of Production." *Insurgent Sociologist* 8, nos. 2–3: 109–25.

————. 1979. *Contested Terrain.* New York: Basic Books.

Ehrenreich, Barbara, and Ehrenreich, John. 1976. "Work and Consciousness." *Monthly Review* 28, no. 3 (July-August): 10–18.

————. 1979. "The Professional-Managerial Class." In *Between Labor and Capital,* edited by Pat Walker. Boston: South End Press.

Fantasia, Richard. 1980. "Wildcat Strikes and Workers' Consciousness." Unpublished manuscript.

Ferguson, Eugene S. 1967. "Metallurgical and Machine Tool Developments." In *Technology in Western Civilization,* edited by Melvin Kranzberg and Carroll W. Pursell, Jr. Vol. 1. New York: Oxford University Press, pp. 264–83.

Fitch, Charles. 1883. "Report on the Manufacture of Interchangeable Mechanism." *Manufactures of the United States.* 10th Census. Washington, D.C.: Government Printing Office.

Fitch, John A. 1911. *The Steel Workers*. Reprint. New York: Arno Press, 1969.

Fitton, R. S., and Wadsworth, A. P. 1958. *The Strutts and the Arkwrights, 1758–1830*. Manchester: Manchester University Press.

Fogel, Robert, and Engerman, Stanley. 1974. *Time on the Cross*. Boston: Little, Brown.

Foster, John. 1974. *Class Struggle and the Industrial Revolution*. New York: St. Martin's Press.

Freuchen, Peter. 1961. *Book of the Eskimos*. New York: World Publishing.

Garson, Barbara. 1975. *All the Livelong Day: The Meaning and Demeaning of Routine Work*. New York: Doubleday.

Genovese, Eugene. 1965. *The Political Economy of Slavery*. New York: Pantheon.

———. 1974. *Roll Jordan Roll: The World the Slaves Made*. New York: Pantheon.

Gibb, George S. 1943. *The Whitesmiths of Taunton: A History of Reed & Barton 1824–1943*. Cambridge, Mass.: Harvard University Press.

———. 1950. *The Saco-Lowell Shops*. Cambridge, Mass.: Harvard University Press.

Gitelman, Howard. 1974. *Workingmen of Waltham: Mobility in American Urban Industrial Development 1850–1880*. Baltimore: Johns Hopkins University Press.

Glaberman, Martin. 1964. "Marxism, the Working Class, and the Trade Unions." *Studies on the Left* 4, no. 3 (Summer): 65–70.

Greenbaum, Joan. 1976. "Division of Labor in the Computer Field." *Monthly Review* 28, no. 3 (July-August): 40–55.

Gutman, Herbert. 1976a. *The Black Family in Slavery and Freedom 1750–1925*. New York: Pantheon.

———. 1976b. *Work, Culture, and Society in Industrializing America*. New York: Alfred A. Knopf.

Hall, Richard H. 1972. *Organizations: Structure and Process*. Englewood Cliffs, N.J.: Prentice-Hall.

Halsey, Frederick A. 1891. "A Premium Plan of Paying for Labor." *Transactions* of the American Society of Mechanical Engineers 12.

Hill, Christopher. 1964. "Discussion" (of Keith Thomas, "Work and Leisure in Pre-Industrial Society"). *Past and Present* 29: 63.

———. 1967. *Society and Puritanism*. New York: Schocken Books.

Hobsbawm, Eric H. 1964. *Labouring Men*. New York: Basic Books.

———. 1969. *Industry and Empire*. London: Penguin.

Houbolt, Jan, and Kusterer, Ken. 1977. "Taylorism is Dead; Workers Are Not." Unpublished manuscript.

Hoxie, Robert Franklin. 1915. *Scientific Management and Labor*. New York: D. Appleton.

Hunnius, Gerry, Garson, G. David, and Case, John, eds. 1973. *Workers' Control: A Reader on Labor and Social Change.* New York: Vintage Books.

Jacoby, Henry. 1973. *The Bureaucratization of the World.* Berkeley: University of California Press.

Kakar, Sudhir. 1970. *Frederick Taylor: A Study in Personality and Innovation.* Cambridge, Mass.: Harvard University Press.

Katz, Michael. 1975. *The People of Hamilton, Canada West.* Cambridge, Mass.: Harvard University Press.

Kolker, Kenneth. 1948. "The Changing Status of the Foreman." *Business History Review* 22: 84–105.

Lampard, Eric. 1967. "The Social Impact of the Industrial Revolution." In *Technology in Western Civilization,* edited by Melvin Kranzberg and Carroll W. Pursell, Jr. Vol. 1. New York: Oxford University Press.

Landes, David S. 1969. *The Unbound Prometheus.* Cambridge: Cambridge University Press.

Lazonick, William. 1974. "Karl Marx and Enclosures in England." *Review of Radical Political Economics* 6, no. 2 (Summer): 1–32.

Lee, Richard B. 1968. "What Hunters Do for a Living." In *Man the Hunter,* edited by Richard B. Lee and Irven DeVore. Chicago: Aldine, pp. 30–48.

Lenin, V. I. 1919. "Theses and Report on Bourgeois Democracy and the Dictatorship of the Proletariat." First Congress of the Communist International, March 2–6. In *Selected Works.* 3 vols. Moscow: Progress Publishers, 1964.

Lenski, Gerhard. 1966. *Power and Privilege.* New York: McGraw-Hill.

Levey, David. 1973. "The Restoration of Capitalism in the Soviet Union." Unpublished manuscript.

Lewis, J. Slater. 1899. "Works Management for the Maximum of Production." *Engineering Magazine* 18: 59–63, 201–8, 361–68.

Linebaugh, Peter. 1975. "Eighteenth-Century English Shipbuilding." Talk given at the Marxist History Conference, New School chapter of the Union for Radical Political Economics.

Lipset, Seymour Martin. 1959. "Political Sociology." In *Sociology Today,* edited by Robert Merton, Leonard Broom, and Leonard Cottrell, Jr. New York: Basic Books, pp. 81–114.

Litterer, Joseph A. 1959. "The Emergence of Systematic Management as Shown by the Literature of Management from 1870–1900." Ph.D. dissertation, University of Illinois, Urbana.

————. 1961. "Systematic Management: The Search for Order and Integration." *Business History Review* 35: 461–76.

————. 1963. "Systematic Management: Design for Organizational Recoupling in American Manufacturing Firms." *Business History Review* 37: 363–91.

Luxemburg, Rosa, 1971. *Selected Political Writings*. Ed. Dick Howard. New York: Monthly Review Press.

Marburg, Theodore. 1948. "Aspects of Labor Administration in the Nineteenth Century." *Business History Review* 22.

Mantoux, Paul. 1928. *The Industrial Revolution in the Eighteenth Century*. Reprint. New York: Harper & Row, 1962.

Marcuse, Herbert. 1960. *Reason and Revolution*. Boston: Beacon Press.

Marglin, Stephen A. 1974. "What Do Bosses Do?" *Review of Radical Political Economics* 6, no. 2: 33–60.

Marx, Karl. 1846. *The German Ideology*. Reprint. New York: International Publishers, 1969.

―――. 1852. *The Eighteenth Brumaire of Louis Bonaparte*. New York: International Publishers.

―――. 1867. *Capital*. Vol. I. Reprint. Moscow: Progress Publishers, 1971.

―――. 1894. *Capital*. Vol. III. Reprint. Moscow: Progress Publishers, 1971.

Modell, John, and Hareven, Tamara. 1973. "Urbanization and the Malleable Household: An Examination of Boarding and Lodging in American Families." *Journal of Marriage and the Family*, pp. 467–78.

Monds, Jean. 1976. "Workers' Control and the Historians: A New Economism." *New Left Review* 97: 81–100.

Montgomery, David. 1972. *Beyond Equality: Labor and the Radical Republicans 1862–1872*. New York: Vintage Books.

―――. 1974. "The New Unionism and the Transformation of Workers' Consciousness in America 1909–1922." *Journal of Social History* 7, no. 4: 509–22.

―――. 1976. "Workers' Control of Machine Production in the Nineteenth Century." *Labor History* 17, no. 4: 485–509.

Moore, Charles W. 1945. *Timing a Century: History of the Waltham Watch Company*. Cambridge: Harvard University Press.

Myrdal, Jan. 1965. *Report from a Chinese Village*. New York: Pantheon.

Navin, Thomas R. 1950. *The Whitin Machine Works Since 1831*. Cambridge, Mass.: Harvard University Press.

―――. 1970. "The 500 Largest American Industrials in 1917." *Business History Review* 49: 360–86.

Nelli, Humbert S. 1970. *The Italians in Chicago 1880–1930*. New York: Oxford University Press.

Nelson, Daniel. 1974a. "Scientific Management, Systematic Management, and Labor 1880–1915." *Business History Review* 48: 479–500.

————. 1974b. "The New Factory System and the Unions: The National Cash Register Dispute of 1901." *Labor History* 15, no. 2: 163–78.

————. 1975. *Managers and Workers: Origins of the New Factory System in the United States 1880–1920.* Madison: University of Wisconsin Press.

Nelson, Daniel, and Campbell, Stuart. 1972. "Taylorism Versus Welfare Work in American Industry: H. L. Gantt and the Bancrofts." *Business History Review* 46: 1–16.

Nettl, J. P. 1965. "The German Social Democratic Party 1890–1914 as a Political Model." *Past and Present* 30: 65–95.

————. 1966. *Rosa Luxemburg.* London: Oxford University Press.

Nevins, Allan, and Hill, Frank. 1954. *Ford: The Times, the Man, the Company.* New York: Scribner's.

Noble, David F. 1977. *America by Design: Science, Technology, and the Rise of Corporate Capitalism.* New York: Alfred A. Knopf.

————. 1978. "Before the Fact: Social Choice in Machine Design. The Case of Automatically Controlled Machine Tools." Paper presented at the Organization of American Historians Convention, April. Revised version in *Case Studies in the Labor Process,* edited by Andrew Zimbalist. New York: Monthly Review Press, 1979.

Norris, H. M. 1898a. "A Simple and Effective Form of Shop Cost Keeping." *Engineering Magazine* 16: 384–96.

————. 1898b. "The Depreciation of Plant, and Its Relation to General Expense." *Engineering Magazine* 16: 812–20.

————. 1899. "Actual Experience with the Premium Plan." *Engineering Magazine* 18: 572–84, 689–96.

Norton, Nancy. 1952. "Labor in the Early New England Carpet Industry." *Business History Review* 26: 19–26.

Oliver, John W. 1956. *History of American Technology.* New York: Ronald Press.

Orcutt, H. F. L. 1899. "Machine Shop Management in Europe and America." *Engineering Magazine* 16: 549–54, 703–10, 921–31; 17: 15–22, 268–76, 384–98, 594–601, 743–49.

Outerbridge, A. E., Jr. 1895. "The Prevailing Scarcity of Skilled Labor." *Engineering Magazine* 10: 227–35.

————. 1896. "Labor Saving Machinery the Secret of Cheap Production." *Engineering Magazine* 12: 650–56.

————. 1897. "The Advantages of Mechanical Stoking." *Engineering Magazine* 12: 807–14.

————. 1899. "The Policy of Secretiveness in Industrial Works." *Engineering Magazine* 18: 861–68.

Ozanne, Robert. 1967. *A Century of Labor-Management Relations at McCormick and International Harvester.* Madison: University of Wisconsin Press.

Perlman, Mark. 1961. *The Machinists: A New Study in American Trade Unionism.* Cambridge, Mass.: Harvard University Press.

Perrow, Charles. 1972. *Complex Organizations: A Critical Essay.* Glenview, Ill.: Scott, Foresman.

Pfeffer, Richard M. 1979. *Working for Capitalism.* New York: Columbia University Press.

Pollard, Sidney. 1963. "Factory Discipline in the Industrial Revolution." *Economic History Review* 16, no. 2: 254–71.

————. 1965. *The Genesis of Modern Management.* London: Edward Arnold.

Roe, Joseph W. 1916. *English and American Tool Builders.* New Haven: Yale University Press.

Roland, Henry. 1896–1897. "Six Examples of Successful Shop Management." *Engineering Magazine* 12: 69–85, 270–85, 395–412, 831–37, 994–1000; 13: 10–14.

————. 1897–1898. "Cost Keeping Methods in Machine Shop and Foundry." *Engineering Magazine* 14: 56–63, 225–38, 464–72; 15: 77–86, 241–48, 395–400, 610–20, 749–58, 1000–16; 16: 37–48, 207–14.

————. 1899. "The Revolution in Machine Shop Practice." *Engineering Magazine* 18: 41–58, 177–200, 729–46, 903–6.

Rosenberg, Nathan, ed. 1969. *The American System of Manufactures.* Edinburgh: Edinburgh University Press.

Rothschild, Emma. 1973. *Paradise Lost. The Decline of the Auto-Industrial Age.* New York: Vintage Books.

Sahlins, Marshall. 1968. "Notes on the Original Affluent Society." In *Man the Hunter,* edited by Richard P. Lee and Irven DeVore. Chicago: Aldine, pp. 85–89.

Schwartz, Michael. 1976. *Radical Protest and Social Structure: The Southern Farmers' Alliance and Cotton Tenancy 1880–1890.* New York: Academic Press.

Service, Elman R. 1966. *The Hunters.* Englewood Cliffs, N.J.: Prentice-Hall.

Singer Sewing Machine Company. 1880. *Genius Rewarded.* No city or publisher listed.

Smelser, Neil J. 1959. *Social Change in the Industrial Revolution.* Chicago: University of Chicago Press.

Smith, Oberlin. 1885. "System in Machine Shops." *American Machinist* 8, no. 44 (October 31).

Spencer, Charles. 1977. *Blue Collar: An Internal Examination of the Workplace.* Chicago: Lakeside Charter Books.

Stinchcombe, Arthur L. 1959. "Bureaucratic and Craft Administration of Production." *Administrative Science Quarterly* 4, no. 2: 168–87.

Stone, Katherine. 1974. "The Origins of Job Structures in the Steel Industry." *Review of Radical Political Economics* 6, no. 2: 61–97.

Sweezy, Paul M. 1974. "The Nature of Soviet Society." *Monthly Review* 26, no. 6 (November): 1–16.

————. 1975. "The Nature of Soviet Society." *Monthly Review* 26, no. 8 (January): 1–15.

————. 1976. "More on the Nature of Soviet Society." *Monthly Review* 27, no. 10 (March): 15–24.

Szymanski, Al. 1978. "Braverman as a Neo-Luddite?" *Insurgent Sociologist* 8, no. 1 (winter): 45–50.

Taylor, Frederick Winslow. 1885. "Comment." *Transactions* of the American Society of Mechanical Engineers 7: 475 ff.

————. 1895. "A Piece Rate System." *Transactions* of the American Society of Mechanical Engineers 17. Reprinted in *Engineering Magazine* 10 (January 1896).

————. 1903. *Shop Management.* Reprinted in Frederick Winslow Taylor, *Scientific Management.* New York: Harper and Brothers, 1947.

————. 1911. *The Principles of Scientific Management.* Reprinted in Frederick Winslow Taylor, *Scientific Management.* New York: Harper and Brothers, 1947.

————. 1912. *Testimony Before the Special House Committee to Investigate the Taylor and Other Systems of Management.* Reprinted in Frederick Winslow Taylor, *Scientific Management.* New York: Harper and Brothers, 1947.

Thomas, Elizabeth M. 1959. *The Harmless People.* New York: Vintage Books.

Thomas, Keith. 1964. "Work and Leisure in Pre-Industrial Society." *Past and Present* 29: 50–66.

Thompson, Edward P. 1963. *The Making of the English Working Class.* New York: Pantheon.

————. 1967. "Time, Work Discipline, and Industrial Capitalism." *Past and Present* 38: 56–97.

————. 1979. *The Poverty of Theory.* New York: Monthly Review Press.

Towne, Henry R. 1886. "The Engineer as Economist." *Transactions* of the American Society of Mechanical Engineers 7: 428–32.

————. 1889. "Gain-Sharing." *Transactions* of the American Society of Mechanical Engineers 10.

Udy, Stanley H. 1970. *Work in Traditional and Modern Society.* Englewood Cliffs, N.J.: Prentice-Hall.

United States Bureau of Census. 1880. *Report on Manufactures.* 10th Census. Washington, D.C.: Government Printing Office.

United States Commissioner of Labor. 1905. *Regulation and Restriction of*

Output. U.S. Bureau of Labor. Eleventh Special Report. Washington, D.C.: Government Printing Office.

United States House of Representatives. 1912. *Hearings Before the Special Committee of the House of Representatives to Investigate the Taylor and Other Systems of Shop Management.* 3 vols. 62nd Cong., 2nd sess. Washington, D.C.: Government Printing Office.

United States Senate, Committee on Education and Labor. 1885. *Report upon Relations Between Labor and Capital.* 48th Cong., 1st sess. Washington, D.C.: Government Printing Office.

Ure, Andrew. 1835. *The Philosophy of Manufactures.* Reprint. New York: A. M. Kelley, 1967.

Walker, Charles R. 1922. *Steel: The Diary of a Furnace Worker.* Boston: Atlantic Monthly Press.

Walker, Charles, and Guest, Robert. 1952. *The Man on the Assembly Line.* Cambridge, Mass.: Harvard University Press.

Walkowitz, Daniel J. 1974. "Statistics and the Writing of Working Class Culture: A Statistical Portrait of the Iron Workers in Troy, New York, 1860–1880." *Labor History* 15, no. 3 (June): 416–60.

Waltham Watch Company. n.d. Original company records. Harvard University, School of Business Administration, Baker Library, Department of Archives and Manuscripts.

Watson, Bill. 1971. "Counter Planning on the Shop Floor." *Radical America* 5, no. 3: 1–10.

Weber, Max. 1958. "Bureaucracy." In *From Max Weber,* edited by Hans Gerth and C. Wright Mills. New York: Oxford University Press, pp. 196–244.

Whitin Machine Works. n.d. Original company records. Harvard University, School of Business Administration, Baker Library, Department of Archives and Manuscripts.

Williams, Albert. 1895. "Racial Traits in Machine Designing." *Engineering Magazine* 10: 92–98.

Williams, Raymond. 1977. *Marxism and Literature.* Oxford: Oxford University Press.

Williamson, Harold F. 1952. *Winchester: The Gun that Won the West.* New York: A. S. Barnes.

Wood, Norman J. 1960. "Industrial Relations Policies of American Management 1900–1933." *Business History Review* 34: 403–20.

Woodbury, Robert S. 1960. "The Legend of Eli Whitney and Interchangeable Parts." *Technology and Culture* 1, no. 3: 235–53.

Wright, Erik Olin. 1978. *Class, Crisis and the State.* London: New Left Books.

Index